BETRAYED

by

Askold S. Lozynskyj

MCG

McGilligan Publishing

3707 Cypress Creek Pkwy Ste 310 #505

Houston, TX 77068

www.mcgilliganpublishing.com

ISBN

Hardcover: 978-1-969733-39-0

Paperback: 978-1-969733-38-3

Dedication

Dedicated to the resilient and courageous people of Ukraine

About The Author

Askold Lozynskyi was born on February 8, 1952, in New York City to Ukrainian parents who fled Western Ukraine during World War II. His father survived imprisonment in Auschwitz and other concentration camps, and his parents met in a resettlement camp in Bavaria before immigrating to the United States in 1951.

Askold studied at St. George's Ukrainian Catholic School, Regis High School, and Fordham University, earning a degree in classical languages and a Juris Doctor. He was admitted to the New York State Bar in 1977 and practiced law for over three decades, representing Ukrainian interests in prominent cases and supporting Ukrainian American institutions.

From his student years, Askold was active in the Ukrainian student movement, advocating for dissidents and leading organizations such as the Society of Ukrainian Student Youth (TUSM). He edited publications including Torch, Ray of Freedom, and The Thaw. In the 1980s, he headed the Ukrainian American Youth Association (SUM-A) and served on the Board of Directors of CARE.

Askold later became a prominent leader in the global Ukrainian community. He served as President of the Ukrainian Congress Committee of America (1992–2000) and of the Ukrainian World Congress (1998–2008), representing the organization at the United Nations. Since 2013, he has chaired the Ukrainian Free University Foundation and continues to serve in multiple Ukrainian institutions.

A prolific journalist and author, Askold has published nearly one thousand articles and seventeen books in Ukrainian and English and has initiated historical film projects with the Dovzhenko Film Studio in Kyiv. He has received numerous awards and honorary doctorates for his lifelong service to Ukraine.

Askold resides permanently in the United States with his wife, Roksolana Stojko, and their two children, Maksym and Kyra.

Table of Contents

He was Always an Enigma – Now He is an Existential Threat – I Speak of the Holy Father

Pope Francis, the Holy Father and current leader of the Catholic Church, was an enigma during his Argentinian days. Still, Catholic Cardinals worldwide believed that with the help of the Holy Spirit, who hovered over the College of Cardinals somehow, they got it right when they voted him in as the Primate of the Universal Catholic Church. Unfortunately, the Cardinals missed this time. It has happened in the past.

After the election, eventually a new period saw renewed puzzlement when Pope Francis chose to entertain criminals at the Vatican in the persons of Putin and Kirill. His alleged political mantra to unite Christians worldwide exposed his lack of humanity for the long-suffering people of Ukraine, particularly at a time of great peril for them, and a bizarre affection for Russian history and its criminal leaders was very disturbing. It also posed a question: how politically involved should a Pope become? There is a reason why religion and politics should not mix and why the Lord Jesus said to render unto Caesar and to God, etc. Pope Francis appears to have forgotten that part of Christian teaching. As a Jesuit, he cannot be excused, although he can be forgiven if he mends his ways.

Perhaps, now his support for an agency of the Kremlin's criminal regime is not surprising. The Catholic Church, using its own terminology, appears to have been taken over by the Devil. Perhaps this is a Biblical realization. The ramifications may have been forecast, but nevertheless, to the average believer, the Apocalypse is now, and there cannot be anything more frightening. Given his age, biologically, the situation with the Pope will only get worse. Physically, he will become frailer, and mentally, he will be even more cognitively challenged.

The Russian or Ukrainian (as it now calls itself in Ukraine) Orthodox Churches belonging to the Moscow Patriarchate are "de iure" and "de facto" creations of one of the most heinous killers in history, Josef Stalin. It is not a religious institution but an agency of the Kremlin's special services. The Moscow Church, in fact, was installed in Ukraine to create a false impression and an alternative to the liquidated Ukrainian Christian churches. Even after Ukraine proclaimed renewed independence, the Moscow Church in Ukraine never registered as a foreign agent. That in and of itself was sufficient to have it banned in Ukraine, and its leadership brought before the courts. That did not happen because of Ukrainian religious tolerance.

That church's predecessor was not a religious institution either, but an agency of the czarist regime. The criminality has extended for some four centuries and includes the establishment of the Moscow Patriarchy in the late 17th century, contrived through criminal kidnapping and holding hostage of the Ecumenical Patriarch. Every significant leader of the Church had to be a member of the Muscovite secret service.

Is Pope Francis familiar with history? Frankly, it's not relevant. He does have advisers. His behavior, while bizarre, is the product of his unhinged mind. There may be more to it than that, unfortunately.

August 25, 2024

The Vatican News Provided:

"In his words following the Sunday Angelus, Pope Francis expresses his fears over Kyiv's decision to ban the Orthodox Church linked to the Moscow Patriarchate. He appeals 'Let no Christian Church be abolished directly or indirectly.'"

Perhaps the problem is with the Catholic concept of Papal infallibility. It is often misplaced and, too often, extended to areas where the Pope's mind cannot reach because of frankly limited exposure to fields of education. No human being is even astute, much less infallible, on every issue. Even more so when the possessor of this trait, bestowed upon him gratuitously, is reaching his nineties and is not educated in the first place, especially on matters other than theology, such as history and politics. We are all with a great many flaws, so we should learn to forgive. However, the biography of this Pope is so abysmal that there is no room for forgiveness or even Christian consideration.

This is perhaps both funny and sad. Naturally, the Vatican News report concludes with "Your contribution for a great mission. Support us in bringing the Pope's words into every home".

The words of the Pope came a day after Ukraine's Parliament had enacted legislation later signed by the President to forbid the Moscow Patriarchate Orthodox Church in Ukraine. The legislation was a result of at least a year-long active discussion by the Parliament and Ukrainian society as to the propriety and even Constitutionality of such legislation. During the course of the war, many criminal cases had been brought against the hierarchy of the Church for treason, among other crimes. The patience and tolerance of both the Ukrainian authorities and society had been exemplary, bordering on the ridiculously excessive. Two of the three holiest places of Ukrainian Christianity have belonged to the Moscow Church.

As the discussion ensued, the Moscow Patriarchate Church in Ukraine reached out to the Ecumenical Orthodox Patriarch in

Istanbul to lend its legitimacy to the Church. Only several days before the legislation, representatives of the legitimate Orthodox Church of Ukraine under Metropolitan Theophany met with the Ecumenical Patriarch, who stated unequivocally that he would not be lending legitimacy to the Moscow Church in Ukraine.

Both the decision of the Ecumenical Patriarch and Ukraine's Parliament and President sparked outrage in the Kremlin, surprisingly. But there is no moral component in the Kremlin or within the Moscow Church. The Kremlin has not commented on the condemnation by the Pope as of now. Because the two are in accord.

As a Catholic, I suspect that once again, the role of the Catholic Church and Pope Francis in particular cannot get any more disgraceful than this. It would appear that the Universal Catholic Church now carries the same mantra as the Kremlin and the "Representative of Jesus Christ on Earth" Pope Francis, and the war criminal under a warrant by the International Criminal Court for kidnapping children, Vladimir Putin, speak with one voice. How bizarre!

Perhaps nothing can be done because the Pope's tenure is a life term, and he appears to be deaf to the entreaties of his own flock. Yet not only Catholics but Christians and believers need to speak out. This may not affect the behavior of Pope Francis, but we need to remember at all times that evil prospers when good people remain silent. Do not allow evil to prosper!

August 26, 2024

MISERANDO ATQUE ELIGENDO

A Long and Glorious History, Often Tragic

I am in Kyiv, the capital of Ukraine. It has been said that the Apostle Andrew visited the hills of Kyiv and blessed them for Christ, planting a wooden cross. The City of Kyiv was actually founded in the late 5th century. It flourished as a commercial center since it was located on a major waterway running from what is now the middle of Belarus to the Black Sea, the Dnipro River. From the Black Sea, you could travel and trade almost anywhere.

By the middle of the 9th century, Kyiv had grown into a state with adjacent lands and rulers, initially two brothers Askold and Dyr, who during one of their forays to Constantinople took on Christianity and spared the City, protected by the Holy Mother. The State of Kyiv and its people did not officially become Christian until the reign of Prince Volodymyr the Great in 988, who himself was baptized in Crimea. The Kyiv empire stretched as far south as parts of Crimea.

Whenever I am in Kyiv, I observe Sunday service at a Ukrainian Orthodox Cathedral named after Prince Volodymyr, who is recognized as a saint by all the Ukrainian Christian denominations. The prelate of the Church is Patriarch Filaret, not of the Orthodox Church of Ukraine, blessed by the Ecumenical Patriarch Bartholomew. Kyiv, like the rest of Ukraine, is panoramic and diverse in its religions, including a variety of Christians, Jews, and Muslims. The people are very religious and managed to endure communist atheism, retaining their belief in God. It has been said that in Ukraine during Soviet times, the Communist Party of the Soviet Union was unable to deal effectively with this opiate, as Lenin referred to religion, so his successor, Stalin, created his own Church, the Russian Orthodox Church, Moscow Patriarchate. That institution has been an agency of the Russian government ever since.

This Sunday, September 15, 2024, was no different. The service was long by my Catholic standards, but notwithstanding the duration, Patriarch Filaret, 95 years old, con-celebrated throughout. The Church was packed. There were many children and soldiers on leave. The choir, as usual in Ukrainian culture, was very moving. There was much audience participation. Unfortunately, of course, there were no women priests, only elderly women commanding the front rows.

Several days earlier, I witnessed the unveiling of a sculpture honoring Ukraine's preeminent film screenwriter and director, of global acclaim, on the 130th anniversary of his birth. Oleksandr Dovzhenko's best works were "Zvenyhora," "Arsenal," and "Zemlya" (Earth). The film "Zemlya" is considered one of the best silent films of all time in the entire world. The Dovzhenko film studio, where the sculpture sits, is located one mile up the hill from the St. Volodymyr Cathedral. Such cinematic gems as "Shadows of Forgotten Ancestors" and "Famine 33" were produced by that Studio.

These two venues and events serve as magnificent reminders of the length and breadth of Ukrainian culture and, unfortunately, serve as tragic motivation for Russian aggression, war crimes, and ongoing genocide. "Ukrainians have to be wiped off the face of the earth", said one Russian religious leader.

It is that history which Russian strongman Vladimir Putin referred to in his perverse account of Russian and Ukrainian history in July 2021. There is so much more, but in microcosm, the Kyivan Prince Saint Volodymyr and the much persecuted by the Soviets Ukrainian film genius Oleksandr Dovzhenko manifest the long and glorious, albeit tragic history of the Ukrainian nation, which is at the heart of Russian hatred and evil. Muscovy, as a village in the swamps, dates to the 12th century, and the Russian empire came into existence only in the 18th century. That will never change, and Ukrainian history and culture will go on.

September 15, 2024

A Potemkin Summit

A brainchild of the Western financial services industry more than twenty years ago has grown like a cancer to become an opportunity for Russia's current rehabilitation. This is at a time when Russia is increasing its atrocities in Ukraine, even utilizing the resources of a global pariah, North Korea, and Kim Jong Un, whom even Russia had sanctioned in the past. Ironic? Certainly. An aberration? Hardly! The West has, unwittingly, mostly done much to enhance its greatest perils over the last century. And so the West will suffer the consequences. Unfortunately, so will the rest of the world.

The original BRIC (now BRICS+) was the brainchild of an American investment banker from Goldman Sachs to spur investments in emerging economies. The time was 2001, and Vladimir Putin was just getting started as Russia's president. By the time the idea began taking root in 2006 at the United Nations, Putin was serving his second term as Russian President. He was beginning to flex his muscles, but mostly with threats and also clandestinely, where he excelled. Brazil, Russia, India, and China, which were emerging economies and democracies, mostly in name only, formed the original union. Putin was an unknown, but he should not have been. After all, he had been a KGB operative with the rank of colonel for a long time before Yeltsin brought him in as his successor. During the formative years after 2006, Putin really flexed invading Georgia in 2008 and Ukraine in 2014. For some reason, this did not deter the members or new applicants.

The recent BRICS Summit in Kazan, Tatarstan, Russia, was a Potemkin display expertly choreographed and directed by Russia and Putin. True, ultimately, Russia did not achieve all it wanted since there were few tangible results and its aggression in Ukraine was not manifestly approved or condoned by the participants. The Western press only tangentially attempted to embarrass Russia and only because of its North Korean connection and the presence of some three to eleven thousand North Korean soldiers on Russian territory, preparing to aid Russia in the war in Ukraine.

Frankly, such illicit cooperation between Russia and North Korea brazenly contravenes United Nations' resolutions and sanctions, but UN Secretary-General Antonio Guterres disregarded that little matter. He was at the Summit. What was he thinking? I submit that there will be no consequences for Guterres at the UN. That is certainly part of the problem. International institutions and the rule of law cannot succeed when such international leaders disregard them. In an everyday world, Guterres should be dismissed.

New members joined BRICS, including Egypt, a military dictatorship, and nonetheless a major recipient of United States aid on an annual basis. Turkey, a NATO member, has applied for BRICS membership as it currently slaughters its Kurdish minority, a US ally during the war in Syria. Some thirty nations participated in the round table in Kazan. Apparently, about forty nations wish to join BRICS.

UN Secretary General Guterres was greeted formally by Russian dignitaries and a welcoming committee of attractive Tatar women dressed in their traditional attire. It appeared that the Tatar population within the Russian Federation was flourishing, once again proving that the RF is a home of diverse ethnic groups. Nothing could be further from the truth. Putin is known as a strongman, a criminal, a thug, in particular when he deals with the captive nations within the Russian Federation. Here he played the role of a global leader, a public relations maven.

In 2001, a Goldman Sachs banker envisioned Russia as an emerging market suitable for good-faith economic alliances and opportunities for investors. Goldman Sachs was delusional. Today, perhaps the idea would not have included Russia. But Brazil, whose second largest trade partner is the United States, Turkey, which is a NATO member, and Egypt, which is a consistent annual recipient of American aid, all essentially enabled and did so willingly, Russia's and Putin's criminality. They attended his Summit in Russia because Putin is under a criminal arrest warrant from the United Nations' International Criminal Court and cannot travel worldwide, which is aiding and abetting criminal activity. Once again, poor Guterres should explain why he visited Putin in Russia when the UNICC has an arrest warrant against Putin.

Unfortunately, I must admit that Vladimir Putin played his hand extremely well. It was a three-day rehabilitation of Putin by many of the West's allies. Or, is it that the West and the United States played theirs very poorly? In any event, it was a display of gross incongruity and even betrayal that has marred international relations for at least seventy-five years, or at least since the founding of the United Nations.

There is a Ukrainian concern here because all of the Summit participants betrayed Ukraine.

October 25, 2024

Russia will arm the Houthis

"The New York Times" reported that Russia has been providing small arms to the Houthis. American officials, including Secretary Austin during his recent visit to Ukraine, indicated that, according to American military intelligence, Russia is considering providing the Houthis with missiles should the West escalate the war in Ukraine. Apparently, the recently released in a prisoner exchange with the West, Russian arms dealer Viktor Bout is negotiating the sale of advanced missiles. This information was given to the Ukrainians to justify Western reluctance to allow Ukraine's use of Western weapons deeper into Russia.

I suppose that any excuse is as good as another, but this one is so far-fetched that the Ukrainian side cannot possibly accept this alleged justification.

Suffice it to say that American Intelligence has been duplicitous throughout the war in Ukraine, and frankly, long before. CIA director William Burns has been sharing information with Ukrainian military intelligence throughout. At the same time, he and his people have been meeting with Russia's foreign minister, Sergei Lavrov, and his people. What is not known is the extent or purpose of the CIA's meetings with the Russians. The CIA is not the agency for diplomatic negotiations, so the purpose must be something else. From the outside, it looks like the United States is playing both sides, helping Ukraine not to lose, but not assisting sufficiently so that Russia retains its influence in that part of the world.

According to "The Moscow Times:"

"Russian President Vladimir Putin said Sunday (October 27, 2024- AL) he hoped the West 'heard' his warning about the danger of a direct war with NATO if it allowed Ukraine to use long-range weapons against Russia.

Putin made the initial threat in September after Britain and the United States mulled letting Kyiv use long-range arms against Russian targets, warning this would put NATO 'at war' with Moscow.

'They didn't tell me anything about it, but I hope they heard,' Putin said in remarks to a state TV reporter when asked if the West had listened to his warning.

'Ukrainian troops cannot use these weapons on their own. Only specialists from NATO countries can do it, because they need space intelligence, which Ukraine naturally does not have,' he said.

Ukrainian President Volodymyr Zelensky had for months been pressing his Western allies for permission to use long-range missiles against targets deep inside Russian territory, arguing the move would 'motivate' Moscow to seek peace.

Western officials signaled last month that a decision on the matter was imminent, but British Prime Minister Keir Starmer and US President Joe Biden later put it off amid Moscow's dire threats.

Biden played down Putin's warning, with US officials saying the missiles would likely make a limited difference to Ukraine's campaign."

And now for the truth. The Houthis not only possess hypersonic ballistic missiles but have actually used them against Saudi Arabia and Israel. America is very much aware of that because American destroyers in the Red Sea have shot down sophisticated Houthi missiles. Thus, American arguments are specious and once again point to the fact that the US is appeasing yet another Russian red line. These Russian red lines are drawn flippantly and often. The West apparently deliberates for so long that its response no longer aids Ukraine. Even more ridiculous is that the West often then proceeds to tell Ukraine what Ukraine needs instead of what it says it needs.

What are some, if any, of NATO's and America's red lines? Certainly, war crimes and attempted genocide are not. Killing babies and mothers about to give birth has not been considered a red line. Inviting soldiers of a country that is an international pariah, sanctioned by the United Nations, appears also not to be a red line.

I suppose that a long-range missile aimed at Brussels, London, or Washington would be deemed a red line. But by then, it may be too late, and the only possible result will be Armageddon.

October 27, 2024

The American Elections

And so the elections are upon us. Some twenty million have already voted in early voting and mail-in ballots. The deciding vote will take place on Tuesday, November 5, 2024. Polls indicate that the vote will be close.

Several facts are indisputable. Candidate Donald J. Trump has made fascist, racist, and authoritarian remarks. Many of his statements have proven to be lies. This has not been surprising as his educational level is a bachelor's degree in real estate, and he admits that he does not read anything of substance. His character is that of a narcissist with no regard for the truth. His mentor Roy Cohn, a notorious lawyer-liar who was disbarred, taught him to deny and attack. That is his modus operandi.

There is a disorganized Ukrainian American contingent supporting Trump that has two identifying characteristics. They are lifelong Republicans, and they do not participate at any serious level within the Ukrainian American diaspora. There are some local pirogi makers.

Before his presidency in 2017, Trump had developed a relationship with Russia and its strongman, Vladimir Putin. Trump wanted to build a Trump Tower in Moscow and to become Putin's close friend. In the course of this quest, Trump was often placed in compromising positions. This long-sought quest for friendship with Putin was on full display during his embarrassing press conference with Putin in July 2018 in Helsinki. Trump sided with Putin rather than America's intelligence services.

Trump had no relationship with Ukraine and most likely very little knowledge until his 2016 election. He did, however, praise Putin for being smart in the manner in which he occupied and annexed Crimea. His initial encounter with Ukraine occurred when, through the advice of his sycophantic adviser Rudy Giuliani, Trump attempted to enlist Ukrainian assistance to disparage his potential opponent in the upcoming presidential election (2020). He tried to blackmail the Ukrainian president by withholding aid to Ukraine, which had been approved by Congress.

Trump lost the 2020 election. In the course of the next four years, he made at least seven telephone calls to Putin, even following Russia's full-scale aggression against Ukraine in February 2022. The extent and subject of those communications and whether they violated American law have yet to be determined.

Throughout the current campaign, Trump has made many disparaging remarks about Ukraine. On the war in Ukraine, he has insisted that the war would never have started on his watch and that he would end the war within 24 hours of being elected. His formula for settlement is Ukraine's unconditional surrender, meaning accepting current borders and agreeing not to seek NATO membership. Interestingly, the war, albeit not full-scale, began in 2014, and from 2016 to 2020, President Donald Trump did nothing about the war. His lack of leadership, in fact, weakened NATO severely. He explicitly stated that he would not defend NATO countries that do not meet their defense spending targets and let Putin take over. Trump has also said that he would lift the sanctions against Russia.

He chose a running mate, J.D. Vance, who has stated explicitly that he would end US military assistance to Ukraine. Trump himself has ridiculed Ukraine's President Zelensky for coming to the United States and seeking money and has painted Ukraine as a country in ruins outside its capital, Kyiv, short on soldiers and losing population to war deaths and neighboring countries. He questioned whether the country has any bargaining chips left to negotiate an end to the war.

He said that the Democrats will not be satisfied until they send American kids to Ukraine. He insisted that America is not going to have its soldiers die across the ocean. After meeting with President Zelensky in New York in September 2024, Trump boasted of his friendship with President Putin, thereby demeaning his role as an honest broker. In the future, should he, heaven forbid, become president?

If you are a Ukrainian American or even if you are simply an American with a deep commitment to democracy, human rights and global security and concerned with the war crimes perpetrated by the Russians in Ukraine involving women and children, these words are fairly definitive and frightening, even if you allow for the fact that they come from a man who is a notorious liar and blowhard.

October 28, 2024

A Final Plea

This plea is to all Americans, regardless of party affiliation. It is addressed to people who care about other human beings, not only their immediate neighbors but people anywhere who are suffering because of human cruelty and aggression, even more so now, since their future is in greater peril each day.

For almost three years, the people of Ukraine have been fighting fiercely against a brutal aggressor committing war crimes, abducting children, targeting maternity wards, and indiscriminately executing civilians. In fact, the war has lasted more than ten years, but the situation has been most drastic over the past three years.

The people in the regions of Russian immediate aggression and occupation are the most affected, but young and old are very much involved in the defense and in assisting their Ukrainian brethren. Children are being slaughtered in the western regions of Ukraine. The villages, towns, and cities of Ukraine are strewn with new burial mounds as far west as the Ukrainian border with Poland.

There is a deep depression in Ukraine because of the uncertainty of the American presidential election. It is palpable among the civilian population and also within the leadership and the military. As a result, Russia has made advances in the Donbas region so that it now controls 20% of Ukraine. Russia has also recovered some of its lost territory, where North Korean troops have taken on Russian uniforms.

Several days ago, I had an interview with Ukrainian television in Ukraine. My two interlocutors were very professional but visibly very much upset and looking to me for comfort. The entire subject was the American presidential elections. Their main question was quite pointed: Is there a chance that Trump will prevail? This was not a journalistic or even a political issue. Their faces said that they were concerned about survival. I was not able to provide any comfort.

I responded as best I could that the election was very close. I tried to encourage them by pointing out that early voting was very strong, which is generally good for the Democratic ticket. I tried to explain the complex American electoral system and that seven states essentially held the balance of power. I also noted that I appreciated their concern, as I had been in Ukraine only a month earlier, and many asked me the same questions.

I did not want to offend or concern them even more by telling them that there were a few Ukrainian Americans who were supporting Trump. That would have been very unsettling. The people in Ukraine would never understand, as I find it very difficult to accept. In any event, the focus of my response was that Ukraine will always exist because of its people and that the people of America will continue supporting Ukraine. Clearly, I was withholding bad information, but I simply could not face their despair.

And so I am using this final opportunity to turn to my fellow Americans with a plea – do not forsake Ukraine. The Harris-Walz ticket is the only guarantee of Ukraine's survival. Trump-Vance would not only be a victory for Russia but the end of Ukraine and perhaps a free and democratic world in Eastern Europe. Most recently, Trump stated in Michigan that had he been president in February 2022, he would never have gotten involved in Ukraine.

Ukraine and Ukrainians need us, America and Americans. The world we live in requires reciprocal assistance. That is why we have formed international structures, but so far, they are evolving at a very slow pace. Ukraine is not in a position to save itself and Eastern Europe from the Russian scourge.

Russia's strongman, Vladimir Putin, has on many occasions threatened World War 3 and the use of nuclear arms. That has to be a wake-up, not a red line. Ukraine is the battleground today. If Ukraine is lost, the battleground will be the North Atlantic, which will invariably involve NATO and the United States. There are at least two very sound reasons for helping Ukraine. The first and perhaps the most important reason is that it is the right thing to do.

The second is a political strategy to prevent Russian aggression from spreading.

How many times do Trump and Vance have to repeat their message that they simply will step aside and let Russia and Putin do what they want? Vice President Kamala Harris and her running mate have been very clear that they support the people of Ukraine.

I have been to Ukraine some ten times during this recent full-scale war. I have been the recipient of words of gratitude from the people for the support of the American people. Most recently, I have been on the receiving end of not only gratitude but tears and pleas. Every person in Ukraine who has approached me is very much afraid of a Trump presidency. How do I know? No, I am not guessing. The people have expressed their fear in no uncertain terms.

Please listen to their pleas. Stop Russia! Help Ukraine! Stop Trump! Elect Kamala Harris President of the United States, Ukraine's best friend!

November 2, 2024

A Disservice to Ukraine

Two respected Ukrainian English-language communication networks have done a great disservice to Ukraine, wittingly or not. On the eve of the US presidential election, which will formally take place in a day, they posted a weak but shameful article by Ukrainian-American Roman Golash from Chicago to support the candidacy of the dreaded Donald Trump. The disservice comes not so much from the article itself, but because of its timing (almost on the last day), the outlined qualifications of the author, and the absence of transparency.

Roman Golash is not a special figure, except for Ukrainian-American voters who have not yet voted. That's why he can be special. He is a Ukrainian American. Both his parents served in the Ukrainian Insurgent Army (UPA). He was raised by them and by the Ukrainian American Youth Association in Chicago, and then served many years honourably, apparently in the American armed forces, gaining the rank of colonel. This is a good biography. These qualifications are partially separately listed in both publications. For a Ukrainian-American voter who was undecided until the last minute, this seems like a person who might render sound advice.

The first network that initiated this unnecessary intrigue is the well-known publication "The Ukrainian Weekly." It is owned by the highly respected Ukrainian National Association, the first and most prominent Ukrainian American fraternal organization. "The Ukrainian Weekly" is probably the most widely read Ukrainian English-language publication, both in print and digitally in America and Canada. It is also known outside the North American continent, as this troublesome article found its way into the "Kyiv Post" in Ukraine. I do not know whether it was a conspiracy of the editors-in-chief, although both editors-in-chief told me several times in the past that the exclusivity of an article was important to them. Well, this is not how it turned out, ironically, under very important circumstances.

There is no great criticism here, but rather possibly great harm to Ukraine and Ukrainians in the war. I could be exaggerating, but I simply cannot foresee the consequences. Roman Golash is not strictly what has been written about him in both publications. He is also a right-wing extremist. I have known him for over 50 years. I knew his parents. I know not only what was written about him in the two publications, but also, simply as one example, that he was fired from his job after his military service because, in the course of his work, he proselytized other employees and customers with his extreme opinions, including severe criticism of "Black Lives Matter". He took his employer to court, where he claimed that he was fired "because of his race and gender". These assertions, particularly of white discrimination, were not the first time. He lost the lawsuit. Naturally, this information was omitted in the two publications.

In the last issue of "The Ukrainian Weekly", where Roman Golash's article appeared, there appeared two articles in favor of the candidacy of Kamala Harris. One was written by former Congresswoman Jane Harman from California, and the other by former ambassador to Moscow Michael McFaul. It would appear that there was a balance after a congresswoman and an ambassador balanced out a Ukrainian American colonel.

However, for the average Ukrainian reader, none of those persons bear serious qualifications or influence, and, certainly, they do not compare to an American Ukrainian from a great family who completed a military career with the rank of colonel. Frankly, Harman and McFaul may be of note, but only in California, which is not a relevant state today. Additionally, I have not seen a serious article by a Ukrainian-American author in favor of Kamala Harris in recent issues of "The Ukrainian Weekly". I may have overlooked it.

On the most recent pages of the "Kyiv Post," there are two articles also on the American presidential election. The editor points out that the Golash article is being reprinted from "The Ukrainian

Weekly" for the sake of balance. However, those articles are one by the head of an organization that plans to go to the planet Mars (the author writes that Trump will not help with this) and an article by the former military adviser of the White House under President Trump, Alexander Vindman, who is a Jewish American who came from Ukraine and encourages people to vote for Harris based on his experience with Trump in the White House. For the Ukrainian-American electorate, the piece by Roman Golash is certainly much more of an attraction and influence. Even more so, since there is no mention that the author is a right-wing extremist who spreads ideas about the white race

For me, it is indisputable that this article by Roman Golash on the pages of these important networks can have an impact on the votes of Ukrainian Americans, particularly in Arizona, Wisconsin, Michigan, North Carolina, Georgia, and especially in Pennsylvania, where there are many Ukrainians. That is why it is disturbing, because Ukraine, its people, its armed forces, and its president do not want the same American presidential election result that Roman Golash encourages.

November 4, 2024

A Request and Challenge to President-Elect Trump

According to "Politico," there are seven NATO member countries opposed or reluctant to extend an invitation to Ukraine to join NATO. Citing four anonymous US and NATO officials and diplomats, "Politico" named the seven countries: the United States of America, Germany, Spain, Belgium, Slovenia, Hungary, and Slovakia.

While some countries are more important than others in the case of an invitation to NATO, the operative rule is consensus rather than a vote, majority, or otherwise. So each country has to be addressed individually, regardless of size or military value, because NATO is an alliance of equals. Granted, their contributions, but also their influence, vary widely. The USA contributes and influences more than any other member.

Hungary, because of its reputation and history dating back to the world wars, and its current populist autocratic leader, is perhaps the worst member in terms of loyalty, but maybe the easiest to persuade. Viktor Orban is a buffoon, recognized as such by all of Europe, if not the world, and even in Hungary. He has been in power for fourteen years, much longer than any democratically elected ruler, which is a sign of a problematic society. He is currently serving a six-month term as President of the Council of the European Union, which has proven to be a great embarrassment to Europe. This is a symbolic role, but Orban has been anything but symbolic. He has no ideological or moral underpinning. His country is under sanctions by the European Union, and in the past, his waiver at least could be purchased with only a moderate release of some money withheld, the balance remaining to influence his behavior in the future.

Robert Fico in Slovakia is similar yet less egregious. Fico is a recent problem, not the outrageous caricature like Orban, and a very corrupt functionary, so amenable at the right price. His affinity for Russia and Putin is not very strong. Frankly, Slovakia should not even be in NATO as it offers very little military might. Its Soviet past as a satellite country but united with the dominant Czechs is a matter of some interest. Fear of Russia based on proximity is a factor common to countries within the former USSR, such as Moldova and Georgia, that are desperately trying to be independent but are fearful. Slovakia is close enough to Russia that any pro-Russian rhetoric has to be balanced with that proximity in mind.

Tiny Slovenia, with a population of 2 million people, shares an apparently troublesome border with Hungary. As a NATO member, it deployed from 60 to 90 troops in Afghanistan and several IFVs (Infantry fighting vehicles) and armored transport vehicles. Given its size, it is difficult to fault Slovenia on its contribution. "Politico" fails to provide any information on why Slovenia would oppose Ukrainian NATO membership. There is no history between Slovenia and Ukraine, and the only influence or concern may be its proximity to the border with Viktor Orban's Hungary.

Belgium contributed a C-130 Hercules and four F-16 aircraft and no forces to the Afghanistan effort. Belgium is a quandary. No one benefits more from its NATO association since Brussels is the hub of NATO and the European Union. Yet Belgium gives nothing back, and in addition, despite sanctions against Russia, it profits from its continued trade with Russia. Explaining its opposition to Ukraine's NATO membership is easy because of its continued trade with Russia, but at the same time, its position on Ukraine can be ignored because it relies on being the center of NATO and the EU. Frankly, while the move may be costly in terms of new infrastructure, Brussels can be very easily replaced with a more reliable hub.

In view of the above, these four obstructionists are a very temporary problem, easily disposed of with a modicum of, let's call it, persuasion. In the case of Hungary and Slovakia, President-elect Trump certainly holds much influence.

Spain, Germany, and the United States are a curious group of naysayers. They are also the biggest contributors to Ukraine's war effort.

Researching the issue of Spanish opposition, my conclusion is that Spain is cowering behind the United States. Similarly, so is Germany. So the only question that remains is why the United States, which has supplied under President Biden the most military assistance to Ukraine, is also Ukraine's biggest opponent to NATO membership. Can it be the same reason as the specious justification for limiting the range of American missiles in Russia?

Spheres of influence, balance of power, and appeasing the enemy are all as antiquated concepts as the Monroe Doctrine. The Democrats under President Biden represented a very old guard, anti-Russian, but let's call it circumspect to the point of appeasement.

The Democrats under Presidents Barack Obama and Joe Biden have been shortsighted and feckless. President Obama was a disaster in foreign policy, particularly on Ukraine. President Biden has been much more experienced but much too slow (call it deliberative) and too appeasing in his actions. As a result, the free world has been misled, and Ukraine has suffered. Spain and Germany, as well as the four minor players, can be led by the United States if America decides to lead and not simply deliberate and appease.

If President Trump is inclined to lead the world and NATO, at the same time, help Ukraine with little expense, enhance NATO with Ukraine's experience, and not continue the policies of his predecessor, he should invite Ukraine to join NATO.

November 6, 2024

A Democratic Election Jeopardizes Democracy in America

Ukraine has to defer to reality and make President Trump the advocate for Ukraine's peace plan. At first glance, that is a ridiculous proposal, yet since politics is the art of the possible, Ukraine must defer to the powers that be.

Whether we like it or not, and skepticism aside, the reality is that President-elect Donald J. Trump will control all three branches of the American government. The people of America have spoken and done so resoundingly. The idea of complete control is not suitable for any democracy, but it is a reality in America. The closest election took place in the House, but the result was not that close.

The perspective here is what this reality will do to American democracy and what effect it will have on the war in Ukraine. The first question is very difficult to assess. America is a strong, long-standing, but somewhat anachronistic democracy based on the protection of states' rights. Does that make any sense today? Probably yes, because otherwise, campaigning would be limited to large cities. This election proved that even the vote of the six largest cities was diverse. New York, Los Angeles, Chicago, Houston, Phoenix, and Philadelphia are not homogeneous. In any event, the electoral system is a very complex, even revolutionary topic.

On the Ukrainian issue, only several months ago, seemingly the simplest, yet most shortsighted response would have been for Ukraine to turn to Europe. But, with Germany's political situation so broken today, that is no longer an available option. France and the United Kingdom remain staunch allies, but lack the financial wherewithal of Germany, which is the third-largest world economy.

So, in terms of American-Ukrainian relations, all avenues must remain available, pride must be swallowed, and even language must be toned down to become more deferential, as aside from the bravery and talents of the people of Ukraine, America remains Ukraine's best hope.

I recall some ten years ago when Trump, the businessman and potential but unlikely politician, voiced to interviewer Bill O'Reilly the likelihood that he might run for president. O'Reilly essentially told Trump that that is not very realistic since American society generally does not take Trump seriously. Trump turned furious. In any event, Trump does not deal with criticism or insults well. That leaves flattery and diplomacy.

Narcissism is a Trump flaw that should be addressed as both a negative and an avenue of approach to Trump. Putin is Trump's friend, according to Trump, but only insofar as both are of similar undemocratic persuasion and because long ago, Trump was excited about the prospect of building a Trump Tower in downtown Moscow. Trump's friendship generally terminates where his ego begins. The United States cannot negotiate a settlement of the war. It can only serve as a conduit. In order to continue American support for Ukraine and perhaps even more because the Biden-Harris support was inconclusive, President Trump must be led to believe that he is in control. That is very problematic because he can never be in control.

The United States of America has contributed heavily to Ukraine's military support. Only Europe, in the aggregate, contributed more. The problems were delays, restrictions on types of weapons, and their range of use. Clearly, the American position on refusing Ukraine NATO membership was a huge diminishing of any negotiating position that Ukraine may have possessed. In fact, this item is probably Ukraine's greatest need.

Some Trump strategists have suggested a twenty-year ceasefire, with a buffer under the control of Europe, perhaps through the United Nations, and Russia holding on to the roughly 20% of Ukraine which it currently controls, and Ukraine's forbearance from NATO membership during those twenty years, with America continuing to supply arms to Ukraine. I am not sure what the last part actually means since there would be a ceasefire monitored by the UN. That formula would be an essential surrender by Ukraine, which the Ukrainian side could never accept.

Trump is not a chess player. He certainly does not think long-term. However, it is important to include him in the negotiating game if only for his instant gratification and to preclude bad behavior. Otherwise, he will simply choose the side that to him appears most beneficial personally, meaning financially. That could be Putin. Trump should be invited to Ukraine, but he probably will not come. Nevertheless, the invitation will feed his ego.

There was a large contingent of Ukrainian Americans who supported Trump. They were made up predominantly of bigots, racists, white supremacists, misogynists, and so-called religious zealots. So-called because that zealotry is mostly contrived. Trump understood that by making such outrageous comments, he was saved from assassination by God because he is a vessel for God. I expected lightning, but there was none. Unfortunately, even after victory, in terms of devising a strategy on how to reach Trump on Ukraine, these Ukrainian Americans have been and will probably continue to he useless. Most are very primitive politically, and many look out only for themselves, not caring much for Ukrainian issues. One Ukrainian American Trump supporter stated that higher education is a waste of time and money. Another stressed that if you talk about higher education, how do you expect plumbers and electricians to work for you?

Anecdotally, the situation in Ukraine is dire, and people are distraught. In Europe, Putin's and Trump's friend Viktor Orban of Hungary is walking with a swagger and just hosted European leaders in Budapest. Although his position in the European Council is ephemeral and symbolic only, he is flexing his muscles. That is what bullies do.

The will of the American people was expressed quite resolutely with overwhelming results, even in the popular vote, which a Republican had not won since Ronald Reagan. That's probably the only similarity between Reagan and Trump. However, was this an example of democracy in action? Trump was elected essentially by a white, non-college-educated electorate.

There were at least two prejudicial factors against Vice President Harris. Her skin color and gender were not helpful, even though they should have been. Democracy is greatly diminished when it is exercised by a poorly educated, race and gender biased electorate. There were so many uneducated Trump advocates hosting right-wing podcasts. This is a phenomenon that can only be called the numbing or dumbing of America. Most countries strive to provide better education for their citizens. Trump's America goes the other way. Even books are an inherent evil. Many have been banned from libraries in red states.

The reality of a democratic society is that it is very imperfect, but better than anything else, as Winston Churchill once said more eloquently. This is predicated on the evolution of the electorate to become better informed. That is irrelevant in MAGA circles. The Republican Guru, Karl Rove, does not have a college degree. Frankly, most MAGA leaders possess degrees of questionable worth or none at all.

Within two days following the election, both the losing candidate and the sitting president from a party other than that of the victor conceded and promised a smooth transition. These overtures were not lost on those who understand and appreciate democracy. I am not sure that President Trump's supporters or even the President-elect himself saw the irony between the 2020 and 2024 democratic transition processes. It simply went over their heads. To date, Trump has not conceded the 2020 election, and there was no transition from one President to the other in 2020. Trump did not attend the Biden inauguration. To date and until the next election, Trump and his people will believe that they did nothing wrong in 2000. People died, the Capitol was severely damaged, but so what? It was for some cause.

"American exceptionalism" and "this is not who we are" are hollow phrases. If any election proved that fact, this one certainly did. America is not only not exceptional, as Americans like to consider themselves, but it has a long way to go, starting with the President-elect. Americans are what the last election results show. There is a term in sports – you are what your record is.

So, America elected a twice impeached former president, a felon waiting to be sentenced, three times married, known for and adjudicated by a court of law for groping women, a notorious liar, charged with additional criminal counts, which may go away only because he was elected. Marital infidelity with affairs with a pornographic actress and a Playboy centerfold, and so much more, are only the tip of the iceberg.

Still, he was not prevented from running for the presidency, and even facilitated in this quest by judges that he himself had appointed, who refused to recuse themselves. And all of this not in ancient or medieval but modern times, when there is an expectation of the rule of law and that no person, even a president, is above the law. In many democracies, Donald J. Trump would today be prisoner number so and so. In America, he is the president.

Still, the strength of democracy lies in its perseverance, and so the system will, in all likelihood, outlive Trump, his vice president, his Supreme, District, and Circuit courts appointments, as well as his sycophant in Congress. Speaking of which, Senator Ted Cruz prevailed once again. But that is Texas, and we might as well be speaking of another country. Still in one place in Texas, which is more than 90% Hispanic, Trump prevailed. And this was after his surrogate called Puerto Rico a garbage island. What a country and what forgiving, essentially good, people!

In all fairness, such aberrations occur in many democracies. Populism has a long existence, and it is still on the rise. Europe struggles with it today as well. The essential problem is education. America is the richest country in the world, but only 51st in terms of literacy.

In the interim, life goes on. And wars go on. For undaunted Ukraine, which is seriously concerned about the election of Donald Trump, President Zelensky, perhaps better than anyone, understands what approach needs to be taken. Ukraine cannot prevail without the United States. The elections in America, even before the results, seemed to give Russia a green light for more aggressive behavior. During election week, Russia sent an onslaught of drones and missiles on Kherson, Zaporizhzhia, Kharkiv, Odesa, and Kyiv. Finally, President Biden sent American mechanics to deal with Ukraine's defense systems. As a lame duck, he could have done so much more, including lifting restrictions on American weapons and even inviting Ukraine to NATO, because President Joe Biden is the problem. America still leads even if the president is lame. In his waning days, Biden can initiate a solution- make Ukraine a NATO member.

Ukraine cannot accept the peace plan drawn up by President Trump and his advisers. It's tantamount to a surrender. Frankly, it is very similar to the Putin plan. Russia is greatly rewarded for its bad behavior. Ukrainian refugees cannot return home because their homes are occupied by the Russians. Furthermore, there is no long-term security guarantee, such as NATO membership.

Ukraine has to draw up an acceptable peace plan that includes immediate NATO membership, sell it to President Trump, and then negotiate with Russia through President Trump. Ukraine's NATO membership should suit President Trump, as Ukraine would immediately become the second or third strongest NATO member, and Ukraine would certainly pay well more than 2% of its GDP annually because it has been most affected by Russian aggression. There are so many other matters that have to be addressed, such as Russian war crimes, reparations, etc.

Ukraine cannot prevail on its own. Success is not inevitable even with the support of the President of the United States. What is likely is that Ukraine's deference to President Trump as its mediator will make him an ally. And that's pretty good, considering the alternative.

For President Trump, he has to be in control even when he is not. As long as he represents American and Ukrainian interests, it is compelling to convince him that American and Ukrainian interests are mutually compatible.

Recognizing reality is what politics is all about. Donald J. Trump is the President of the United States. He will be so for the next four years. Ukraine cannot survive for the next year and, certainly, not four without American support. Ukraine, its people, and Ukrainian Americans need to reach out to President Donald J. Trump, no matter the personal aversion. There is no other option. Hopefully, life goes on, even under the worst of circumstances. After all, politics is an art, but only of what is possible. Today, the possibility lies with America under Donald Trump.

November 8, 2024

An American Ukrainian Farewell and Last To Do List for President Biden

Joe Biden has always been a friend of the American Ukrainian community and Ukraine. He has always said the right things, even when he didn't express himself well. His friendship with John McCain went a long way in this regard and was sincere. Joe Biden, as a Senator, Vice President, and President, displayed an affection for a moral component. That was the essence of support for Ukraine. He would never side with thugs or autocrats.

There were many reasons for his positions, most importantly, his values. The John McCain connection helped as well. Joe Biden will be remembered because he was a good man who genuinely believed what he said when confronting evil within his own country: "This is not who we are!" And also, around the world.

Two factors were very important in his late decline. While his physical abilities did decline, particularly in the area of mobility, that was reasonably expected in a person of advanced age. His cognitive skills were commensurate with a younger individual. He was always deliberative in a positive sense, but not so much resolute.

I recall a meeting with him as part of a Ukrainian Congress Committee of America delegation in the White House in 2014 on the subject of Russia's initial foray onto Ukrainian territory, at that time surreptitiously and not, since Russia tried to present that incursion as an internal separatist action. That concept, as most Russian lies, was quickly dispelled when Russia annexed Crimea two weeks later.

Vice President Joe Biden was most sympathetic to the Ukrainian cause, recognizing internally that his President was a neophyte in matters dealing with Russia. Earlier, President Barack Obama had embarrassed himself in an open mike conversation with Russian president Dmitri Medvedev, telling him to relay to the real President

Vladimir Putin that he would be more open to discourse following the election. In the meeting, VP Joe Biden was sympathetic, but it was notable that he was weak or somehow constrained.

Senator John McCain was the foreign policy guru for Joe Biden. But John McCain passed away. President Barack Obama was a diversion. And so Joe Biden came up against Donald Trump in 2016. He had never encountered anyone like Trump. Washington rarely had. Without disparaging Trump any more than I have over the years, and as exhibited most recently by Trump's purported Cabinet nominations, Trump was not only a man not to be trusted, but the very essence of what is wrong in American democracy.

So Joe Biden prevailed, and he became President. Mostly, he was helpful to Ukraine. Often, his rhetoric stopped short. He was deliberative but not resolute. To summarize, perhaps why Ukraine has been able to hold off the Russians is because of America under President Joe Biden. But also, why Ukraine could not prevail through Western support and is currently somewhat on its heels is because of America and President Joe Biden.

American military aid has been substantial, but not exactly what Ukraine has asked for, and delivered often much too late, to the point that the current delivery promised frankly by October 2024 is at 10%. That means that 90% has not been delivered, and we are in November. Further and unreasonably. Joe Biden has restricted the use of even the arms that have been approved and delivered.

There is another factor that is little reported or analyzed. Russia's GDP is growing despite US sanctions. Russian weapons contain American components. There are American sanctions on Russia, but they are so poorly monitored that today, Russian weapons with American components are killing Ukrainian soldiers and civilians.

Finally, there are 32 member countries of NATO, and the preeminent one is the United States. Ukraine has been shut off because of President Biden's decision. Please excuse me, but little contributors like NATO members, Slovenia, Belgium, Slovakia, and

Hungary have followed the American directive, conveniently. President Biden has played directly into Putin's game by taking this reticent position and justifying it by his personal fear of a third world war, which is a bluff.

The bottom line is that President Biden has two months to get it right and rewrite his biography and legacy:

Monitor the implementation of sanctions, deliver the approved military aid, release the restrictions, and immediately invite Ukraine to accelerated NATO membership. Please do all this before you leave. You are a good man. A suffering Ukraine needs your resolute action.

November 14, 2024

The Fecklessness of the Global Community

Most recent Putin rants, including a revised threshold for the use of nuclear weapons by Russia, as well as the total elimination of Ukraine as a country, and in tandem, the use of ICBMs on Ukrainian territory, should be alarming for the global community. The world cannot simply stand by and do little or nothing. Clearly, the message here is that negotiations with Putin are not an option. One way or another, Putin has to be taken out before any negotiations can begin.

Three recent events have been highly instrumental in emboldening the Russian strongman. The BRICS summit in Kazan, Russia, was bad enough, with the participation of more than thirty countries and an expansion of membership. The worst part was that the United Nations' Secretary General, Antonio Gutierrez, attended. He spoke with no mention that the Summit's host was under a UN criminal arrest warrant and failed to condemn Russian aggression in Ukraine, which has been the subject of several UN General Assembly resolutions since the aggression on February 24, 2022. Gutierrez has to account for this "diplomatic mishap". Suppose the UN's highest functionary does not respect a UN ICC arrest warrant and UNGA resolutions. Where are we with the international rule of law or respect for any international bodies? Gutierres has not been asked to account for his behavior, even by Ukraine's Foreign Ministry, its Permanent Mission to the UN. He certainly will not do so on his own.

German Chancellor Olaf Scholz recently reached out to Putin by telephone, thus breaching a Western consensus to isolate the Russian dictator. The subject and tone of the official communication are not relevant. Perhaps the German Chancellor felt that he was doing nothing wrong because former American president Donald J. Trump, during his presidential hiatus, reached out to Putin seven times. Following the example of Donald Trump is not justification, firstly because Trump has no moral compass, is a political primitive, and was not the president of the United States at the time. Chancellor Scholz was publicly reprimanded by Ukraine's President, but not by any other world leader.

Finally, the Russia-North Korea alliance with some 11,000 or so North Korean soldiers on Russian soil fighting the Ukrainians and about to be deployed onto Ukrainian territory has been reprimanded by the global community tangentially. The alliance is a blatant affront to the international community. Russia should be stripped of its membership in the UN (Russia is not really a member of the UN), the G20, the WTO, and other international institutions, but nothing of substance has transpired in this regard. Aside from the President of Ukraine, Ukraine's Foreign Ministry and its UN Mission, and elsewhere, have been asleep. The only alleged exception to this typical practice of rhetoric with no substance was President Biden. The American president used this as misplaced motivation to permit Ukraine's use of ATACMs deep into Russian territory. This was merely an opportunity for Biden to correct his dilatory behavior, as Ukraine has begged for this license for a long time. Biden has certainly sullied his legacy by being dilatory and feckless on aid to Ukraine.

Ukraine fatigue is a term employed by insensitive primitives who fail to understand that Ukraine fatigue is really freedom fatigue and international rule of law fatigue. International law and its institutions, such as the UN, the European Court on Human Rights, the International Court of Justice, and the ICC, have not evolved because of the lack of resolve on the part of global leaders.

On the subject of Russia's recent use of an ICBM on Ukrainian territory and some of the other Russian transgressions, Peter Stano, a spokesman for the European Union, recently stated:

"We are, of course, following reports that Russia has used an intercontinental ballistic missile against a target or targets in Ukraine... It's obvious that such an attack or attacks could mark another clear escalation from the side of Putin. He [Putin] is playing yet again a nuclear gamble with the recently updated nuclear doctrine of Russia. He enlisted North Korean soldiers to come to European soil. So these are all clear signs of the will to escalate, not the will to find paths to peace. So, indeed, if they [the Russians] used an intercontinental missile, that would be yet another quantitative and qualitative change in this approach and a clear mark of escalation."

This was yet another example of rhetoric with no substance.

November 22, 2024

PS It was later determined that the missile involved was an Intermediate Range Ballistic Missile (IRBM) with nuclear warhead capability, still an overkill for an attack on the Ukrainian city of Dnipro, but catching the attention of European countries.

Annual Holodomor St. Patrick's Requiem Brings Back Memory of a Special Ukrainian Catholic Prelate

The observance on Saturday, November 23, of this year, was, at least in my mind, a magnificent tribute to the victims of the events of 1932-33 in Ukraine, but a celebration of the life of the recently deceased Ukrainian Catholic Prelate Bishop Basil Losten. The annual commemoration at St. Patrick's Cathedral in New York City is one of the preeminent observances of the Holodomor in the Ukrainian diaspora.

Preparing for the observances of the 60th anniversary of the Holodomor in 1993, Bishop Losten came to me with an idea to hold a Requiem observance of the Holodomor in November at a prominent religious venue in New York City. I was then the president of the Ukrainian Congress Committee of America, and Bishop was not only a spiritual guide but a dear and longtime friend.

The Bishop stressed that it was important to include both the Catholic and Orthodox communities. We agreed that Catholic and non-Catholic venues should be considered. The Bishop suggested St. Patrick's Cathedral at 5th Avenue and 51st Street, and we agreed to explore St. John the Divine. I traveled to the Episcopal Cathedral of St. John at Amsterdam Avenue and 110th Street, and while I was very impressed by the structure, I was disappointed by the location, primarily because of the safety factor and remoteness from the East Village.

We agreed that St. Patrick's would be more suitable because of its location, which is the center of Manhattan, and because of the throngs of people walking along Fifth Avenue who very often step into the Cathedral simply to view one of the great sights of New

York. We then reached out to the Consistory of the Ukrainian Orthodox Church of America (specifically Bishop Antony) and quickly reached an agreement of joint celebration and sponsorship. Bishop Losten's friend Bishop Vsevolod Maidanski of the Ecumenical Ukrainian Orthodox Church also participated in the discussions. Bishop Losten reached out to the Archdiocese of New York. Cardinal John O'Connor was most accommodating, and an unwritten agreement was entered into, lasting into perpetuity.

And so, since 1993, Ukrainian Americans, simply Americans, and tourists from other states and countries have gathered to commemorate and honor the victims of the Ukrainian Holodomor at St. Patrick's Cathedral. The Requiem service at all times has been concelebrated by Ukrainian Catholic and Orthodox metropolitans, archbishops, bishops, and priests, accompanied by the excellent Ukrainian Chorus "Dumka" of New York under various conductors, most recently over more than a decade by the brilliant Vasyl Hrechynsky. The program has included kind words of sympathy by representatives from the United States government, federal, state, and city, and Ukrainian diplomats and representatives of the Ukrainian American community, spearheaded by the Ukrainian Congress Committee of America.

Bishop Basil Losten has been foremost among the celebrants during most of this time, even after his retirement, and over the last few years, he has participated from the front pew near the altar. This year, he was not there because he had passed away at the age of 94 in September.

I would like to take this opportunity at a time of special Thanksgiving to acknowledge this tremendous contribution of Basil Losten, the People's Bishop, to this remarkable and historical event. We thank Almighty God that He chose to bless the entire Ukrainian American community with this remarkable religious and civic leader and gave him a long life during which he was responsible for so much good. Every year, many of us will recall Bishop Basil Losten as we commemorate and honor the 7-10 million Ukrainian victims of the Holodomor at St. Patrick's Cathedral in New York City. May his memory live in our hearts and minds, and may his good deeds serve as an example for each of us to follow.

November 28, 2024,

The Russian Orthodox Church

Russian strongman Vladimir Putin has made much of Russian Orthodoxy as a moral paragon, while intentionally omitting from his alternative history that Christianity came to Russia from Kyiv and that the Muscovy Patriarchate was established at gunpoint after the Muscovites kidnapped the Ecumenical Patriarch.

An interesting question for the uninformed is whether the Russian Orthodox Church in the Russian Federation or abroad is, in essence, a religious institution or simply a tool of Russian imperialism. In the United States, this matter is quite vague as the Russian Orthodox Church has never registered as a foreign agent with no repercussions from the United States Departments of State or Justice.

Similarly, the accommodation or treatment of the Moscow Church by the Catholic Church in Rome and Pope Francis in particular has been bizarre at the very least. The Pope has not accorded any such special treatment to other religions, but he has met with both Russian strongman Vladimir Putin and his surrogate Patriarch Kirill. He has also voiced his concern about the banning of that institution in Ukraine.

For much of the Cold War, American intelligence services served as a vehicle for Russian anti-Communist disinformation, insisting that Russians were a captive nation within the Union of Soviet Socialist Republics. In fact, the Central Intelligence Agency worked tirelessly without much success to establish a level of cooperation between the nations comprising those listed in the Captive Nations' Week Resolution and the Russian Anti-Communists. I am not sure whether the Ukrainians in the United States collaborated with the CIA in this regard because they were duped or simply went along for the money. Probably both.

In any event, the Russian Orthodox Church was an integral part of this conspiracy. The Russia Publishing Co., based on Canal Street in New York City, published a monthly magazine RUSSIA. Its December 1952 issue carried a continuation of an article by Archpriest Peter G. Kohanik entitled THE BIGGEST LIE OF THE CENTURY "THE UKRAINE". This purported religious leader wrote:

"We must openly state that no American should participate in meddling in the internal affairs of other countries. Of course, we dislike the abhorrent Bolshevism (sic)and its sinful work in Russia and all over the world, but this does not mean that we should also hate Russia and her people. In trying to destroy bolshevism (sic), we have no right whatever to undermine the former Great Russian Empire by striving as the 'Ukrainian' Separatists do (assisted by good and honest, but misled Americans) to detach from her the 'Little Russians' (known at present as 'The Ukraine') only because some arrogant Galician aggressors, instigated by Polish and Austro-German enemies, deliberately changed 'Little Russia' into 'Ukraine!'"

Fast forward to March 27, 2024. A Cathedral Congress was held in the Hall of Church Cathedrals of The Cathedral of Christ the Savior in Moscow under the Chairmanship of the head of the Supreme Council of His Holiness Patriarch Kirill of Moscow and All Russia. The following Order was issued:

"The special military operation is a new stage of the national liberation struggle of the Russian people against the criminal Kiev regime and the collective West behind it, which has been conducted on the lands of South-western Russia since 2014. During the SVO (sic), the Russian people defend their lives, freedom, statehood, civilizational (sic), religious, national, and cultural identity, as well as the right to live on their own land within the borders of a single Russian state. From a spiritual and moral point of view, a special military operation is a Holy War, in which Russia and its people, defending the single spiritual space of Holy Russia, fulfill the mission of "Holding", protecting the world from the onslaught of globalism and the victory of the West that has fallen into Satanism."

The more things change, the more they remain the same. Seventy years have passed. The archpriest was an anti-communist. The patriarch was a communist and a KGB agent. With the dissolution of the USSR, he changed his affiliation from the KGB to Putin and the FSB, and from a Bishop, he became a Patriarch. The Russian Orthodox Church is not a religious institution. It never was, and it never will be. It is an agency of the Russian Empire, irrespective of the Empire's form or name. There is no spirituality to it. There is no God in it as well. It is simply another policing mechanism and propaganda tool of the empire. Is it effective? Just ask the Pope! Don't ask American intelligence agencies because they have no clue, and in any case, they usually play both sides.

December 10, 2024

Dear Editor

The study of history is a deeply flawed subject because it is very often written by the victorious side and thus unfair to the victim. World War II was very complicated in this regard. We Americans should understand this very well since we were both victors over one brutal regime and collaborators with another even more grotesque. Hitler was evil incarnate, but our ally Stalin was ultimately responsible for more brutality in terms of sheer numbers. Suffice it to say that Josef Stalin and Romanian dictator Nicolae Ceaușescu murdered more Romanians, including gypsies, than the Nazis.

One thing is certain. Malicious disregard for the truth is never justified.

I certainly do not know Romanian history sufficiently to cast aspersions against Romanian anti-communist freedom fighters, even if they were accused of war crimes during World War 2, because the accusers were the Soviets, who were among the victors. Naming streets after them is an internal matter for the Romanian people.

Americans frankly sold out Central and Eastern Europe to Joseph Stalin at the Yalta Conference in February 1945. I certainly did not, nor will I ever examine the evidence against these anti-communists. I am certain that neither did Mr. Andrew Wiggins, who wrote the piece "Romanian Fascist and Communist Past Colors its Politics."

I do know that people who fought the communists were brought up on specious charges very often by the Soviets.

It is one thing to report on controversial contemporary matters and quite another to gratuitously and maliciously malign heroes of other nations without a scintilla of evidence. I do not know the motivation or rationale, but Mr. Wiggins does exactly that. He writes:

"Many countries in Central and Eastern Europe, where fascist terror before and during World War II gave way to communist tyranny after 1945, have rallied to defend war criminals as patriots because they opposed communism. Ukraine honors Stepan Bandera, a nationalist responsible for the slaughter of Jews and Poles."

Who was Stepan Bandera? These are undisputed facts. He was a leader of one faction of the Organization of Ukrainian Nationalists (OUN). He left the territory of Ukraine before 1939, before the Soviets invaded Western Ukraine pursuant to the Molotov-Ribbentrop pact. He did write to Hitler prior to the German invasion of Western Ukraine, warning Hitler that the OUN would be proclaiming an independent Ukraine. He stressed that if the Germans stand in their way, Ukrainians will be Germany's worst enemy.

On June 30,1941, the Bandera OUN faction proclaimed an independent Ukraine. The Germans insisted that the proclamation be withdrawn. Ukrainians refused. Thereafter, the Nazis began to arrest the Ukrainian nationalists. Among them, they arrested my father. They also arrested two of Bandera's brothers. They were taken to the notorious German concentration camp at Auschwitz, where both of Bandera's brothers were murdered by Polish capos. My father survived, weighing 90 pounds.

Bandera himself was interned in the Sachsenhausen concentration camp, where he remained until the end of the war. After the war, he remained in Germany as a migrant. On October 15, 1959, Bandera was assassinated by a Soviet agent in Munich, ostensibly because the legend of Bandera became the incentive for the Ukrainian dissident movement. The name actually became synonymous with Ukrainian patriot. That euphemism remains to this day.

Bandera was never brought up on charges at Nuremberg or anywhere else for war crimes. Mr. Higgins' quote is taken directly from Soviet and Russian disinformation.

Unfortunately, this is not new for The New York Times. In 1932-33, 7-10 million Ukrainians were starved to death by Josef Stalin and his henchmen. This was one of the largest genocides perpetrated in the modern era. Walter Duranty was a journalist working for The New York Times in the USSR. He sided with Josef Stalin in a cover-up of this atrocity. The New York Times carried his disinformation and has never apologized.

December 12, 2024

Rehabilitation and Personal Ruminations

Friends of the newly elected US President Trump have decided to use his populism, evidenced by his recent election, as proof that Donald Trump rose from the ashes like a phoenix, and history will be sympathetic to him. Who knows! Populist elections do not always affect history. After all, Hitler was also popularly elected. This does not change his history. Today's Vice President-elect Senator Vance called Trump the American Hitler back in 2015. The opprobrium has not been forgotten, no matter Vance's remorse.

I previously wrote against my moral convictions that we must accept that Trump will be the President of America in January 2025 for four years, or his deputy, who is even worse. Therefore, we must deal with that as well. Do not dream the impossible dream, but find ways to help Ukraine. Do not seek favors on a human or even politically strategic level, but convince Trump and his people that helping Ukraine and its victory serve his interests as well. Well, one may add the interests of America, but, in my opinion, this is not key for Trump. For him, the good of America is simply a slogan for populism.

It is undeniable that history will not be silent on his sex scandals, or his double impeachment, and worst of all, his betrayal of the American Constitution, on January 6, 2021, by attacking the symbol of American democracy. There is no way except by appeal to a higher court to change the 34-count criminal verdict against him by a New York court. This is all history. How can history be kind?

We must realize that in the history of America, there have been many blemished presidents, although taking into account the context of the period in which they worked. There were war criminals, racists, and slave owners. President Trump mostly respects President Andrew Jackson, a man far more educated than

Trump, but a slave owner, a racist, and also a brutal war criminal against indigenous people on American soil. President Andrew Jackson was very popular, but this was in the first half of the 19th century. Hasn't American society evolved enough to be tolerant of a similar individual two hundred years later?

The evolution of American society is very slow. I previously suggested that we should accept the reality that Trump is the elected president and that we need to approach him. But Trump's first steps in selecting his so-called cabinet are just overwhelming. At the same time, we should ask ourselves who is more corrupt: Ukraine, which has only 33 years of democracy, or America, which boasts 250 years. For the record, Ukraine has a constitution from 1710 that can compare with any.

For a balanced analysis, we should start with the current President Biden, who, after repeated assurances, decided to pardon his own son for crimes not before a court but already established by a court.

Trump began his political appointments by offering the State Department position to the senator from Florida, in order to transfer his position as a senator to his daughter-in-law, who does not have the slightest political experience. There is no need to even mention the appointment of ambassadors, because there is a whole range of family appointments here. Let's look for other manifestations of corruption. He appointed his friends without the slightest qualifications as Secretary of Defense, an alleged neophyte to be responsible for eighteen American intelligence agencies, who was a former Democrat and one whom Hillary Clinton called an agent of Moscow, and who once praised the now-ousted dictator Assad of Syria. It does not get more ridiculous.

True, the candidate for the head of the Department of Justice has already stepped down. However, the renegade of the Federal Bureau of Investigation is still parading around and forcing the current FBI director to step down from the position to which Trump once appointed him. America has not seen such an appointment of unqualified lackeys since the time of Andrew Jackson.

But all this is tangential. Trump came to Paris recently at the invitation of President Macron. President Zelensky also came there at the invitation of President Macron. A meeting took place regarding Ukraine. President Zelensky, an actor and diplomat, said that the meeting was useful. Trump came completely unprepared. By the way, he doesn't read anything or listen to intelligence reports. Trump said that Ukraine is a matter for Europe, but America is against Ukraine joining NATO. He did not specify why because he does not know.

There can be two disparate views here. One is that Ukraine has nothing to expect from America. The second is much better, as Trump will not interfere with America's moral duty and role of global leadership. He is not only not interested, but also not informed. Let Ukraine, Europe, and the US Congress, in which the majority are Republicans but also many friends of Ukraine, take on this matter. I would ask the new President Trump just one thing: do not interfere. This is a unique approach for any President of the United States. But we have to go back 200 years in American history to understand Andrew Jackson in the XXI century.

December 15, 2024

Merry Christmas and a Happy New Year!

At this time of Christmas and the New Year, we send greetings to all on the birth of God's Son, because He is our Savior and Hope. We thank God the Father for giving us His beloved only Son. We celebrate this great Holy day, traditionally with the first star we sit down to our traditional Ukrainian family Holy Supper, we remember those close and far who, for various reasons and mainly because of the completely unjust aggression by the Russian enemy, cannot sit down to the Holy Supper, we sing carols, and then take stock of and express our wishes and prayers for the coming year.

First of all, we thank our heroic defenders on various fronts - Donetsk, Kherson, Zaporizhia, Kharkiv, Sumy and Kursk, the President of Ukraine for his devotion and tirelessness, as well as his extraordinary ability to be the voice of Ukraine at international fora and express our heartfelt gratitude to the international community that provided and continues to provide myriad assistance, especially air defense and other military systems. We thank Mother Mary, who gave birth to the Son of God and holds our defenders in her care.

Most of all, we thank the people of Ukraine for their extraordinary resilience, dedication, and sacrifice. As the Ukrainian poet Ivan Franko wrote, everyone believes that millions of people are depending on him/her and that he must answer for the fate of millions. Therefore, almost everyone in Ukraine has dedicated themselves to the best of their ability to repel the terrible aggressor - the Russian and preserve every corner of Ukrainian land, helping our defenders who are experiencing very difficult circumstances because of the enemy's far greater forces in numbers and armaments.

Nonetheless, we are filled with hope for the best. Hopefully, this coming year, we will achieve a victory over the enemy, the establishment of peace and tranquility, and the securing of the future, so that our young state can flourish and be a benevolent mother to all its children. We are aware that much effort and sacrifice are still needed to complete this picture.

We again turn to the international community with a pure heart and with an outstretched hand of our Ukrainian Kolyada. Help us save both you and us from the most brutal aggressor - the Russian, who wants to grab with his dirty paws the entire democratic and civilized world. Understand at the same time, dear Europeans - English, French, Germans, Poles, Lithuanians, Latvians, Estonians, Finns, and others, as well as Americans, Canadians, Australians, that we Ukrainians protect all of you from Satan himself, that Moscow is the embodiment of the antithesis to the Lord God and His beloved son Jesus and the Holy Spirit.

This year's Christmas, as in the last two years, is actually an inspiration and a new kind of salvation for those who fight evil every day. The personification of this evil is Moscow, but salvation from this evil is visible at the end of the long road for many and palpable even today by current events because of the birth of Our Lord.

We also welcome our brothers and sisters of other nationalities who still suffer in the Evil Empire, Kazan Tatars, Ingush, Chechens, Erzya, Bashkirs, Kalmyks, Sakha, and others. We thank them for joining our struggle and call for an uprising internally against our common enemy. Our task is to join efforts in one common front to overthrow this evil empire and to introduce a new democratic life for the enslaved peoples in the empire, where their human and national rights will be ensured and respected.

The forces of good will overcome the aggression of evil. The only question is how much time and sacrifice it will take. In unity lies the strength of our effort and the assurance of our victory. This will be the victory not only of Kyiv against Moscow, but also the victory of the newborn baby Jesus over evil incarnate. This should be the essence of our Christmas celebration and the anticipation of the New Year with renewed hope and conviction of victory. May the Lord God and baby Jesus bless us on this holy path.

December 20, 2024

An Assessment

Well, Christmas has passed, and so has goodwill to all men. I gave it a try, but now with the New Year, it's time to not only make an assessment of the past but to plan for the future. Ukraine has many enemies. They sit in the Kremlin but also in the upcoming White House and often celebrate Mas in St. Petr's Basilica. This is a difficult pill to swallow as Ukraine continues its observance of Christian holidays.

I was particularly moved by the words of the President of Ukraine on the eve of the recent Usyk-Fury bout. The President suggested to the Ukrainian boxer that he take it easy on Fury because of the United Kingdom's support of Ukraine in the Russian aggression.

Let me consider the obvious. The first is not a revelation, but rather a confirmation of our worst expectations. Donald Trump was and is not a friend of Ukraine. There was hope. I, for one, still hoped that I would be wrong. So many Ukrainian Americans supported Trump. Why?

Trump's appointee for special envoy on the Russia-Ukraine conflict, Clark Kellogg, reacted to Ukraine's assassination of a Russian General who introduced chemical weapons into the conflict. Without condemnation of the Russian General, Kellogg stated:

"There are rules of warfare, and there are certain things that simply are not done...For example, usually wounded soldiers are not finished off on the battlefield, and non-combatants should not be killed either. When you kill a military general, admiral, or other major military figure in their hometown, you seem to expand (the battlefield. — Ed.). I don't think that's smart. You see, this simply does not comply with the rules of warfare. If you are a general, then you are a 'legitimate target' on the battlefield. Like what happened, it means to go too far, so you will have to hire mercenaries. I don't think this is a good idea," said Kellogg, quoted by the publication 'Country'.

"They are brothers, cousins," the Pope said, according to Vatican News. "Let them come to an understanding! War is always a defeat. Peace to the whole world!"

Some believe the pope's use of the terms 'brothers' and 'cousins' is in reference to the Kremlin's framing of the Russia-Ukraine war as its mission to reunite the two nations as 'one people,' according to the Kyiv Independent. Russian President Vladimir Putin even wrote an essay on the subject in 2021, stating that "Russians, Ukrainians and Belarusians are the heirs of Ancient Rus, which was the largest state in Europe."

December 25, 2024

New Year's Reflections

When observing the New Year, a person should take stock not only of what happened and affected humanity in general, but also of personal views and one's behavior, that is, how affected was one by events of the prior year, how he/she reacted, to what degree was one's perception flawed, and did events justify expectations. In that regard, I must confess that I was seriously more wrong than right. Events rarely justified my expectations or forecasts. I must add that I am an optimist by nature.

I am a bit of an amateur political analyst, like everyone else, even the pretentious ones posing as professional pundits. There are no experts. I must admit that 2024 was one of my worst years. Perhaps this is because I am a Ukrainian born in America, where I take an active part in public life. I root for my homeland, Ukraine, because that is how my parents raised me, and in particular because it is in a struggle for its very existence.

This is not just a noble component on my part, but somewhat even selfish, because for me, Ukraine is a big part of my existence and ordinary life. How today's struggle will end in my mind is not only the work of the Lord, but it depends much on the efforts of the Ukrainian people and the people of Ukraine. I belong to the first of these. To tell the truth, I even have personal interests in Ukraine, and I want to expand them.

I never expected what happened in America on November 5, 2024. For me, Donald Trump is a clown and evil incarnate. By the way, he confirmed this for me once again recently on Christmas Day 2024, when he presented himself through his communication networks as simply mentally ill with his narcissism and passions. He was emotionally distressed that the Baby Jesus was getting all the attention.

Frankly, I was not as surprised by his sacrilegious jealousy as much as by his election by stupid white Christians in particular. I apologize for the word 'stupid,' but it fits. Faith is a beautiful virtue in the Judeo-Christian tradition. It is also very dangerous when it is exploited by charlatans. The Lord gives people free will. Unfortunately, this affords a great opportunity for charlatans.

Today, there are no more evil charlatans in the world than Vladimir Putin and Donald Trump. They rule their population by exploiting human weaknesses. Putin uses the Moscow culture of the glory of the great empire. This culture of strict rule is also in Trump's mind. We laugh at recent Trump comments about encroaching on Panama, Greenland, and even Canada. Perhaps his simple, stupid statements should be regarded as the painful reasoning of an abnormal person. However, we must realize that this abnormal person was elected by a relatively large majority of the American electorate. Anyone who says that this is not who we are as Americans needs to reexamine the American electorate. Add to this total control in both houses of Congress and the Supreme Court, with no Code of Ethics.

Living in America, I meet people, especially women, who say that they do not talk to their husbands about these topics because their husbands are rabid MAGA supporters. Others talk about the religious factor, saying that she or he voted for Trump because they felt that he protected Christian moral values. I shake my head in disbelief when I hear the combination of the two words Trump and Christian morality.

I never imagined Trump winning the election. After the election, I thought that even Trump was capable of becoming semi-normal. I was very wrong about this again. Donald Trump is basically an evil caveman who does not read or pray. Those who voted for him are not much better.

World politics has proven to be a bitter disappointment, at least for me. At the helm is an international network at least eighty years old, that is, international institutions promising the possibility of the rule of international law. There has been little, if any, progress. Sure, more institutions have sprouted, but the rule of law has not advanced much.

Perhaps this effort has been marred by the populism that has taken hold in the USA and is attempting to make advances in Europe. Worse, the world leaders of international organizations are not individuals suited to their positions. They are simply chosen for the sake of inclusion or because of a rotational system. Striking examples are the UN Secretary-General Antonio Guterres, who, by the way, was once highly praised by my friends from the Permanent Mission of Ukraine to the UN. Sure, he was amiable as a low-level dignitary. What transpired? The UN Secretary-General went to Kazan to meet with Putin and others during the Summit of the so-called BRICS countries. What did he think would be the consequences? He didn't think at all. There is a UN (International Criminal Court) arrest warrant against Putin. Guterres did not go to arrest Putin. He went to support him in his isolation.

He is not the only one. The Holy Father has compromised himself and the Catholic Church several times in 2024, with misplaced words of wisdom such as Ukrainian-Russian brothers and panegyrics about the mordant, murderous Russian emperors, perhaps manifesting support for that mantle to be placed on the current Russian Criminal Vladimir Putin. The Council of Europe has been compromised many times in the last six months by its rotating chairman, Prime Minister Viktor Orban. After Orban, Slovakia's Prime Minister, Robert Fico, went to Moscow. Two very cowardly leaders met with a criminal convicted under the UN Charter, and yet Hungary and Slovakia enjoy membership in the European Union and NATO without consequences. The rule of law practically died in 2024.

Yes, 2024 was bad. It was even worse because it left consequences for 2025.

December 28, 2024

Inside Russia – Kazan Tatars

A federation is a group of states with a central government in which, at least in theory, by contract, those states may maintain independence in internal affairs. The Russian 'Federation' is not that kind of 'federation.' It is, in essence, an empire accumulated over half a millennium by the ruling center with direct or surrogate central authority over all aspects of the affairs of constituent states. Today, this central authority is involved in a war against its neighbor due to its own aggression. Russia's conduct of this war utilizes the constituent nationalities primarily as its infantry or cannon fodder. Should Russia not prevail on the battlefield, it may have to face disastrous results with the Federation. Thus far, the Federation has been kept in check at significant expense through a policing mechanism. Very few, if any, of the federated states remain within the Federation willingly.

One hundred fifty nations comprise the 'Federation,' among them are the Kazan or Volga Tatars. Their land, now Tatarstan, was forcibly invaded and occupied by the Muscovites, now known as Russians. This is the story of these people, perhaps the largest national minority within the RF, numbering more than seven million. Recently, the BRICS (Brazil, Russia, India, China, and South Africa) Summit was held in Kazan, the capital of Tatarstan. Pictures of guests, such as the Secretary General of the United Nations being greeted upon arrival by smiling, attractive Tatar women, were widely used by Moscow for propaganda purposes. This was a Potemkin summit organized by Russia's strongman, Vladimir Putin, who is under an arrest warrant from the International Criminal Court and could attend a summit in any of the more than 120 countries that respect the Court's jurisdiction.

The territory of Tatarstan, a Republic of the Russian Federation, was inhabited by different groups during the prehistoric period. The state of Volga Bulgaria grew during the Middle Ages and, for a time, was subject to the Khazars. The Volga Bulgars became Islamic and incorporated various Turkic peoples to form the modern Volga Tatar ethnic group.

The region came under the domination of the Kazan Khanate in the 15th century.

In 1552, after many days of fighting during the siege of Kazan, the army of Ivan IV (known as the Terrible) stormed the city, plundered, and then burned it. The male population of the city was completely slaughtered, and women and children were driven into slavery. Muscovites tied the naked corpses of the brutally murdered residents of Kazan to 50 logs and launched them down the Volga. Not a single village remained within a radius of 60 kilometers from Kazan itself. All of them were devastated and burned along with the inhabitants.

The Kazan Khanate lost its independence in 1552. The capture of Kazan did not mean the fall of the entire state, although its army was destroyed and the khan was captured and sent to central Russia. The Tatars actively resisted for several more years. The Khanate was abolished in 1708. This period from 1552 to 1708 was marked by the settlement of the area by Russians and attempts at conversion to Orthodox Christianity, provoking a number of rebellions among the Tatars and neighboring groups.

In the late 18th and 19th centuries, industry developed, economic conditions improved, and Tatars achieved almost equal status with Russians. Tatar national consciousness was growing, and with the October Revolution of 1917, national institutions were established, and independence was declared as the Idel-Ural State. After several years of civil war, the Soviet government suppressed independence and established the Tatar Autonomous Soviet Socialist Republic within the Soviet Union.

The Russians pursued a policy of genocide and ethnic cleansing in the occupied lands. The Russians' calamitous policy forced the Tatars' migration from the Volga to the eastern parts of the Kazan

Khanate. In this region of the former Kazan Khanate, the Russians did not rule until the beginning of the 18th century. Whereas the territories along the Volga and the city of Kazan were inhabited by Russians. The Tatar population was forbidden to settle along the Volga River for 200 years. In the 18th century, peasant uprisings began, which were supported by the Tatar population.

The first Russian revolution was actively welcomed by the Tatars. The Tatar population was among the most educated among the Muslim peoples of Russia. Therefore, the Tatars were represented in all political currents of that time. However, the czarist government, by amending the laws, created difficulties for Tatar voters. Thus, the majority of Muslims of Central Asia could not take part in the elections to the Third Duma, and according to the results of the elections to the Fourth Duma, the Kazan province became disenfranchised.

During the Soviet era, all activities of civil society were tightly controlled by the authorities. At the same time, the activities of organizations that did not recognize Soviet power and communist ideology were banned (legally or semi-legally; such organizations existed only in the early 1920s and reappeared in the late 1980s).

Under Soviet rule, there was a famine followed by a progressive decline of the Tatar language, culture, and religion, both Christian and Muslim. The discovery of large petroleum deposits helped to promote further major growth in industry. Around the time of the fall of the USSR in 1991, there were again moves for independence, but in 1994, the region, under the name of Tatarstan, became a constituent republic of the Russian Federation. In 2008, a national assembly, the Milli Mejlis, declared Tatarstan independent, but this status was not recognized by the Russian government or the United Nations.

The lack of support for independence movements by the global community, particularly at the UN, is a very grave problem. It was recently manifested in no uncertain terms by the bizarre participation of Antonio Guttieres, the UN Secretary General, at the

BRICS Summit in Kazan. It shows how little the UN has evolved since its formation in 1945, when it was forged by coconspirators strongman Josef Stalin and President Franklin Delano Roosevelt, who delivered Eastern Europe to Stalin as part of the conspiracy.

In the early 1990s, two ideological currents began to form in Tatarstan: the Tatar national movement and the Russian-inspired federalist pro-Russian movement. The peak of their political influence occurred in the early 1990s. On August 24, 1990, a rally was held in Kazan demanding the adoption of the Declaration on the State Sovereignty of Tatarstan. Five days later, the Supreme Council of the TASSR began to consider this issue. A lively discussion ensued. On August 30, 1990, the Supreme Council of the Republic adopted the "Declaration on State Sovereignty of the Tatar Soviet Socialist Republic." However, the Tatar national movement insisted on the adoption of the Declaration of Independence.

By the beginning of 1991, the situation in the USSR had become critical. The central authorities began to lose control over the union republics, and the Union entered a period of apparent disintegration.

In the autumn of 1991, the Tatar people gathered at their rallying site, demanding nothing less than independence. On October 15, 1991, an attempt was made to storm the Tatarstan parliament. On October 24, 1991, the Supreme Council of Tatarstan adopted a resolution on the act of state independence of the republic, preparing for a referendum that was supposed to reinforce the previously proclaimed state sovereignty.

The Chairman of the Supreme Soviet of the Russian Federation, Ruslan Khasbulatov, in an interview with the Izvestiya Tatarstan newspaper, promised to deliver the leaders of the Tatarstan republic 'in an iron cage'.

The situation escalated. Russian authorities agitated people to ignore the referendum, to vote 'No.' The Republic of Tatarstan was flooded with leaflets calling for a boycott of the vote. This was the subject of a televised address by Russian President Yeltsin. On Saturday, the day before the referendum, the prosecutor of Tatarstan personally brought to the Chairman of the Supreme Council of the TSSR a notification that if the popular vote did take place, the head of the parliament would be held criminally liable on the basis of the decision of the Constitutional Court of the RF.

The Referendum on March 21, 1992, was an important step toward determining the status of the republic. The question was: "Would you like the Republic of Tatarstan to be a subject of international law, a sovereign state with the right to establish relations with the Russian Federation and other republics and states based on equal treaties?" 81.7% of Tatarstan citizens took part in the referendum. 61.4% of them voted 'yes'.

On November 6, 1992, the Supreme Council of the Republic of Tatarstan, based on the will of the people, adopted the Constitution of the Republic of Tatarstan. Tatarstan was the only one of all the republics within the Russian 'Federation' that refused to sign a new federal treaty. They cited the Declaration of 1990, the results of the Referendum, and the new Constitution, thus demanding that it secure a special status in its relations with Moscow.

Pressure on the leaders of the Tatar national movement and, in particular, the government, increased. A disinformation campaign ensued. Statements of the Tatar leaders were distorted. Disinformation spread among the population that one of the leaders of the national movement spoke of the inferiority and 'illegitimacy' of children from mixed marriages and the need to exterminate them. This 'modus operandi' of spreading disinformation and accusations is now well recognized by the global community. One recalls that Russia invaded Ukraine full-scale in 2022 to 'denazify' Ukraine and its Ukrainian Jewish president.

The Tatarstan government began to gradually 'voluntarily surrender' sovereignty. First, sovereignty provisions were relaxed in the 1992 Constitution, then even more so in a 1994 Treaty with Russia.

In February 1994, the leadership of Tatarstan signed an agreement on the delimitation of powers between the authorities of Russia and Tatarstan. The agreement provided for special conditions for the Republic to join the Russian 'Federation,' which seemingly relieved tensions between Moscow and Kazan for years to come. For this compromise, Tatarstan was granted fairly broad rights of a sovereign subject, for example, the opportunity to conduct foreign economic relations and, to some extent, foreign policy activities.

With Putin coming to power in 2000, the complete rule of Moscow was restored. All regional specifics were brought "in compliance with the legislation of the Russian Federation." By 2017, the special relationship between Moscow and Kazan was terminated. Putin prohibited the study and teaching of national languages in all the federated national republics. The decision was justified by the numerous complaints of Russians living in Tatarstan and other republics that they were being forced to learn a language other than their own. For Moscow, this was to be the final nail in the coffin of the Tatar language and culture – a cultural genocide. This is the way that the Kremlin operates.

However, the Kazan Tatars are very much alive both culturally and politically. Recently, the State Council of Tatarstan decided to take a 'demarche' against Putin and the Kremlin. Moscow revealed this but enveloped this in some diplomatic language: "could not come to a consensus on this issue. 'The Security Council and the State Duma.'" (Parliament, although it has none of the characteristics of a legitimate parliament) of the Russian Federation decided that migrant children could not be educated without knowledge of Russian. Still, the Tatarstan parliament decided not to impose a ban on the education of these migrant children. This appears to be a significant issue for the people of Tatarstan. While it is a complicated one for the Kremlin, Putin, as a strongman, no doubt will attempt to resolve it by force. There appears to be trouble ahead.

In any event, at some point and probably very soon, with Russia substantially weakened by its aggression against Ukraine, the struggle for the independence of Tatarstan and other nationalities within the RF will reach a boiling point, and the international community will be asked for support. Feckless international leadership will have to step aside for more resolute action.

Russia has put Kazan and Tatarstan at the front of the war with Ukraine. The nationalities in the RF are cannon fodder. The Russian version of the Shahed-136 drone is currently being manufactured in Tatarstan.

On the morning of December 21, 2024, at least seven drones struck Kazan. Some hit residential buildings, including a 32-story luxury apartment block. The Russian authorities also reported a strike on an industrial plant in Kazan.

Andrii Kovalenko, head of Ukraine's National Security and Defense Council's Center for Countering Disinformation, said on Telegram that the Kazan Powder Plant is a key enterprise in Russia's military-industrial complex specializing in the production of explosives, rocket fuel, and other components critical to the Russian army. The plant provides the Russian armed forces with ammunition and materials they need to produce missiles of various classes and purposes, including Kalibr, Iskanders, and other missiles.

Divide et impera!

The Volga Tatars are too smart for that. They recognize who the real enemy is.

December 31, 2024

Jimmy Carter – Unlike any other – May he rest in peace

Ukrainian President Volodymyr Zelensky said that Jimmy Carter served as US president when Ukraine was not yet independent. Still, the Ukrainian president recognized that "his heart stood firmly with us in our ongoing fight for freedom. We deeply appreciate his steadfast commitment to Christian faith and democratic values, as well as his unwavering support for Ukraine in the face of Russia's unprovoked aggression. Today, let us remember: peace matters, and the world must remain united in standing against those who threaten these values."

I voted for Jimmy Carter twice, he first time in 1976 when I did not know him at all. I voted in condemnation of President Gerald Ford's ignorance of or callous approach to Soviet domination of Eastern Europe. In 1980, I voted for President Jimmy Carter, after four years, recognizing him as clearly a unique politician with a moral backbone and principles, who was a champion of human rights and the first American president to discard the American global mantra of appeasement towards the Russians. Here was a farmer from Georgia who saw right through the Russian soul. When Soviet Russia invaded Afghanistan, President Carter manifested America's disapproval by refusing to participate in the Olympics in Moscow. Countries followed because America was the moral compass. That compass was Jimmy Carter.

There was also a specifically Ukrainian element in my praising President Carter. The names of Ukrainian political prisoners, scientist Nina Strokata, philologist Viacheslav Karavansky, and historian Valentyn Moroz come to mind. They were released from Soviet gulags and permitted to emigrate. There were other prominent non-Ukrainian dissidents who were released and exchanged. Many Soviet Jews benefited from President Carter's principled and unwavering position as well.

Presidents Carter and Ronald Reagan did not bring down the Soviet Union, but they certainly were helpful in this regard. I respected Carter much more than Reagan because of his moral integrity. Reagan was an actor turned politician, duplicitous in his behavior and, in the case of the Iranian hostages, treasonous, delaying the hostage release until after his election. But he was effective in dealing with the Soviets to some degree because he dealt with a reformer, Gorbachev, not an idealist, but rather an opportunist.

The timing of President Carter's death could not be more glaring as America is entering an era of unbridled amorality. Ironically, America's attention is focused, albeit briefly, on Jimmy Carter, not only as President, but as a person who was a humanitarian, human rights activist, and Nobel Peace Prize laureate. The flags in America fly at half-mast at least until January 20, 2025, when the anti-Carter takes the oath of office. President-elect Donald Trump represents the complete nullification of Jimmy Carter. Trump was jealous of the baby Jesus on Christmas Day and is now jealous of President Carter as America and the world honor his memory.

To be fair, President Carter's tenure was not a big success because of high inflation and interest rates. For that and other reasons, his reelection was problematic. Nonetheless, the Carters, the President, and his wife spent the rest of their long lives doing good, helping those less fortunate, monitoring human rights abuses, and enabling peace throughout the world. Many of these good deeds have been long-lived.

The best that can be said about the 39th president is that he spent his life following the guidance of his Lord and Redeemer. His legacy and lifestyle should serve as an example for all of us and, in particular, for other political leaders. Unfortunately, among world leaders, he was an exception and not the rule. It has become even worse.

January 8, 2025

Anticipating January 20, 2025

An Aberration of Democracy

The Gulf of Mexico to be renamed, Panama, Greenland, and Canada to be annexed are all silly, yet dangerous halos. Perhaps none of these matters, because it is all so bizarre, but we are on the eve of an inauguration.

The psychotic mind is working non-stop. How do I become a strongman in a country that prides itself on democratic checks and balances? Is it possible to bring back the age of empires? Frankly, I do not know what that means because I have no knowledge of history. I have achieved the impossible - an overwhelming electoral victory while under three indictments and one conviction. I have fooled most of the people, at least this one time. I control all three branches of government. No one can stop me because I am unbridled. I cannot run again, so there is nothing in my way.

Ruminations of a madman or a democratically elected president.

This could never happen in America because this is not who we are, said the madman's predecessor. President Biden was so wrong. This is precisely what we have become. We just buried a president who spoke of helping others, working towards peace, and protecting the rights of all individuals. His mentor was none other than Jesus. His funeral was attended by Democrats and Republicans and all living past presidents. Even Donald Trump was there, even if he did not fit in.

For America, it is a time of much concern. Please put to rest the illusion that America is exceptional. There is nothing in its history to evidence that absurdity. Today, America is exceptionally primitive. That is the bottom line. One would have to go back to the 19th century to find a similar American president. Andrew Jackson comes to mind, but even he did not take the presidential oath as a convicted felon.

America has to overcome this. With all the wealth that God has bestowed, America should be at the very least democratic with a separation of powers and checks and balances as written in its Constitution. A moral component is a necessary element, but a fake religious zealotry or disingenuous sacrilege does not result in morality. Remember that part of Trump's presidential campaign was the publication of a Bible for sale at $60.

What is wrong with America? America's highest court has no code of ethics. Its lower legislative body is led by a self-professed religious zealot, in fact, a disingenuous pharisee, elected by less than one tenth of one percent of the American population. Its upper house will be presided over by a hillbilly. Its president carries only a diploma in real estate, and even his supporters acknowledge that he does not read anything. His primary supporters are the poorly educated, by his own choice and admission. Oh, sure, he has others joining his coteries for personal enrichment.

Donald Trump is a good option for Elon Musk and the rich. He will lower their taxes and arrange for less government regulation, all at the expense of the middle class and the poor. Government regulations are often overbearing, but mostly well-intended since few possess the assets of Elon Musk or Donald Trump, for that matter. Corruption in America will take on a new dimension. There will be a Trump hotel down the road from the White House (Trump is working on that), yet Ukraine will be told to clean up its corruption before entry into NATO or even the European Union.

January 20 will be the start, but the danger is so apparent. On January 6, 2025, exactly four years after Trump's treason at the Capitol, VP Kamala Harris confirmed his electoral victory. What irony! Except that this is how Democracy is supposed to work, but Trump does not know the meaning of the term "peaceful transition." It was so different in 2020 when Trump lost. No one stormed the Capitol this time. Now the Senate will take up its futile task of advising and consenting on the confirmation of many inappropriate members of the new administration.

This is a parody of America. Unfortunately, American leadership is the world in which we live. English is the global language. America is the leader of the North Atlantic Treaty Organization. America is the most formidable member of the G7. Yet America will be led for the next four years by a man who does not understand the basic meaning of the rule of law, forget the nuances.

Can we move on? One obsessed man, no matter the sycophants and American primitiveness, cannot dictate the norms for a global society, its own government, or its actions. International law has not evolved in almost one hundred years. This is a major stumbling block, unlike any in the last 100 years.

Yet, Ukrainian resistance to Russian aggression will continue, perhaps, ultimately to a victorious conclusion. How is that possible?

There is a non-calculated variable in any war that involves a nation's existence. With or without tangible American support, Ukraine will pursue the defense of its existence. Europe has engaged substantively and now will have to support Ukraine even more.

And then there are the subjugated nations of the evil empire. There are massive problems within the Russian Federation, also known as the Russian Empire. Besides Russians, more than 100 nations, many living on their own land except that that land is controlled by the Russians. At the same time, these people serve as cannon fodder in Putin's war against Ukraine. They do not want to be cannon fodder, nor do they want to help the Russians, because the Russians are their enemy as well.

There is much going on. Sure, America has drifted into an era of anti-democracy and the rule of a psychotic strongman. Yet, there will be no era of empire because, frankly, Trump has no idea what that means. Empires are not purchased on an open market. Greenland, Panama, Canada, or the Gulf of Mexico are not purveyed by a real estate agent. In each instance, these are elements that involve sovereignty, something which a primitive and antidemocratic Trump can never understand.

Believe it or not, the Russian Empire is falling apart. America may be in trouble as a democracy and global leader, but Russia's role as an empire is an anachronism.

January 13, 2025

The Nonsense of President Trump's Inauguration

There was plenty of nonsense, but most of it did not or will not matter except for the moment and only for those who applauded, standing up. Self-aggrandizement is the main affliction of psychopaths, and Trump simply showed this symptom again in front of the whole world. This is the first time in US history that world leaders were invited, but few showed up. They did not want to appear as clowns in this circus. Without a doubt, many viewed it silently or even with exclamations on various networks.

Trump did not catch them off guard. They got what was expected. That is, the most powerful state in the world has a sick psychopath as a leader. And not just an ordinary leader who can be controlled to some extent by the US Constitution. Is he dangerous? Without a doubt, because Trump sat on the Constitution and did not keep his hands on the Bible. America has transformed, through a democratic process, into an oligarchic system of government, and the oligarchs have realized that this is to their advantage. The danger is that all branches of power are in the hands of one psychopath with a delusion not only of grandeur but also of controlling and ordering everyone.

Trump spoke about the prospect of the future as a golden age of America, that is, insulting all his predecessors as usual. He spoke about geographical expansionism, which completely contradicts the policy of the last eighty years of America. America expanded back in the 19th century, but not at the expense of the sovereignty of other states, but only their colonies. When America takes Panama or Greenland (and maybe Canada, because madness allows everything), why can't Russia take Ukraine, Belarus, the Baltic States, Poland, etc.?

Trump repeated the nonsense about saving his life from an assassination attempt by the Lord himself because the Lord has a purpose for him, as if he were a messenger of the Lord himself. For this fable, not one but five prayers were arranged during the circus, two Catholic, two Protestant, with one dark-skinned representative because it was the symbolic birthday of Martin Luther King, and one Jewish prayer invoking the prophet Jeremiah as if Trump were a modern prophet, Jeremiah. Apart from the prayer of the Catholic Cardinal Timothy Dolan from New York, who actually led a prayer, everyone was mercilessly scrambling for the political benefit of the new President. The farce was so great that even Trump himself laughed.

The Capitol rotunda, ironically where Trump tried to stage a coup in 2021, was covered with Trump apostles, who know how many participated in the January 6, 2021, sedition, only now wearing a tie. They stood up and applauded every two minutes as America moved from democracy to dictatorship and oligarchy. They applauded at the greatest stupidities that their leader repeated. Then, Trump issued an Executive Order to pardon the criminals of January 6, 2021, as predicted.

It was truly a black day for America because, as Trump himself repeated several times, everything changed on election day. The majority of Americans voted for Trump, and Trump won in all the states where there was once a question of his support. This became proof of his version of the truth and the cleansing of all his sins, criminal charges, and a mandate for his dictatorship.

Trump emphasized not only his victory but the victory of the American people; that is, this manifestation of the will of the American people indicates the direction of this country. Americans are an Uber nation; all others are Unter, similar to Hitler's political doctrine. America will be guided exclusively by what benefits Americans; moral principles will be irrelevant. After all, this is American nationalism or, in fact, American neo-fascism. This gave new meaning to the term "the ugly American".

I must say that the absence of other world leaders in this farce is very indicative. The world sees before it a parody that must be addressed, but not approved. This spectacle, in one episode or image, showed how far America has slid to the nadir of its history.

There is no need to sympathize with America. Its long-standing arrogance has resulted in today's democratic ruin. Rather, it is necessary to fight such an America, especially from the inside. Silence means approval. Putin's Kremlin could not have arranged a better holiday for the world's imperialists.

Trump is almost 79 years old. If he lives or survives until 2029, he will be the oldest president in American history. But it is unnecessary to hope for a democratic revolt. God also does not help those who do harm to themselves. Next to Trump stands a second psychopath. Accepting this farce will mean that the farce of America will outlive its main actor. A dark era has begun for America and a little for the whole world.

January 21, 2025

Back in Ukraine

Warsaw, Rzeszow, Przemysl and City Line to Kyiv. Finally, I breathe Ukrainian air.

I came first to apologize to Ukraine and Ukrainians for America, for electing such a primitive as president, and to sense how Ukraine is enduring the first of Trump's Executive Orders. After all, a 90-day moratorium on humanitarian aid has been declared. Some are worried, others are unaware. In the end, I will figure it out on my own skin because it will be relatively comfortable, or I will freeze.

The third anniversary of the war is approaching, and the situation is quite grave, in particular on the Donetsk front near the city of the glorious composer Leontovych, Pokrovsk. Currently, Europe, and in particular Great Britain and Poland, are speaking out in word and deed about their support. Presidential elections are being anticipated in Poland. The Law and Justice party has nominated Nawrotsky. For now, it looks good. With Tusk and Nawrotsky, disparate as they may be, Polish support for Ukraine and its own safety is assured.

Meanwhile, in the US, Trump has pulled America out of the World Health Organization and the Paris Agreement on the environment, two institutions that help the whole world and should not be controversial to anyone. This is proof that America and Trump do not think about health or the environment, very clear signs of a primitive and amoral position.

In Poland, an Uber driver who is a supporter of Nawrotsky is not much concerned by Trump, but believes that America is on the verge of making big mistakes that will be felt all over the world. In his opinion, America owes this loss of international esteem to its arrogance. As an example, he cited the fact that American soldiers at the NATO base treat Poles with a level of contempt. He said that these are not the soldiers depicted in American films during World War II. He blamed a culture in America of American exceptionalism.

My main task in Ukraine is to meet volunteers through whom military aid is delivered, in particular, military aid, mainly drones, electronic detection systems, Jeeps, trucks, and optical devices. A large role here is played by priests, chaplains, and ordinary citizens, even older ones, who are unable to participate in the defense due to old age or poor health.

A lecture is also planned at four universities on the topic of the recent elections in America and what Ukraine can expect. This is meant to prepare students who will shape the future of Ukraine. The warning about America comes not only from the newly elected president but also from his appointed Secretary of State, the senior Senator from Florida, Marco Rubio (Little Marco, as Trump called him), who in the first week after the presidential inauguration spoke several times on this topic. The Senator's thoughts are quite disturbing because his presentation of the moral equivalence of the two sides is incomprehensible and, in fact, completely amoral. He asserted shamefully that both sides should surrender some interests, equating the morality of imperialism with that of defending its territory in order to assure its nation's existence, providing equal treatment for the aggressor with the victim, and rewarding the aggressor for bad behavior. Little Marko, in defense of the Russians, pointed out how much the Russian people have suffered, the cost of human lives, and economic difficulties.

The president was even worse, actually blaming Ukraine for precipitating the aggression by the Russians. This cannot be justified or ignored simply as psychosis or primitiveness.

I spoke in Kyiv with one Erzyan who leads a group of Erzyans in the Ukrainian international Legion, and was once the head of the Free Nations' League. He is surprised by America because there was much hope for America, not only from Ukraine but from the people enslaved in the Russian empire. He stressed that only Ukraine and its allies can mediate peace with Russia, and only when Russia becomes more modest because it has been defeated. America can in no case be considered an honest or objective mediator. No one is looking to President Trump and his version of America to save Ukraine or help the subjugated nations within the Russian empire.

He said that we must prepare for further struggle, which should lead to the economic collapse of the empire, internal revolutions, and, in its place, the emergence of independent states. Only then will Russia cease to be a danger.

January 24, 2025

Dear Ukrainian American Republicans

I write to you as a Ukrainian American maverick. I am currently a registered Republican intent on unseating a congressman, a former Democrat, now a sycophantic Republican from the Cape May area in southern New Jersey. I registered as a Republican only for that reason.

I believe that the Republican Party can be saved by running candidates who would defeat the Trump acolytes in traditionally Republican districts.

Perhaps the best President of the United States was a Republican. No, I am not referring to Ronald Reagan, but Abraham Lincoln. You would do well to look that far back. Ukraine was certainly not an issue in American politics in the 1860s, but the moral underpinnings of Lincoln certainly were. He freed the slaves based on his personal moral convictions. At that time, the Republican Party represented moral convictions, while the Democrats negotiated principles. Lincoln also managed to preserve the Union by manifesting justice and mercy.

Today, the Republican Party represents nothing at best and the formation of an oligarchy and dictatorship, an undermining of democratic principles, such as checks and balances. In my worst nightmare, I could never imagine Donald Trump returning as President of the United States. He is the anti-Lincoln. I am hopeful that talk of a third term will not become an issue, not because of the intelligence of the American voter, but by the will of God. This is how much we have declined.

Let's get to the point. America is important in our hearts and minds, but so is Ukraine, whose very existence is at issue. More than one Russian imperialist has voiced their position that Ukraine will cease to exist by the end of 2025. I know many of you are concerned with this possibility.

There is much trash also in the Ukrainian American Republican group, whom I consider traitors. But mostly, I believe you are both American and Ukrainian patriots.

For me, party allegiances mean very little. For many of you, they mean much for myriad reasons. There are ways, even under President Trump, for Republican Ukrainian Americans to aid Ukraine in its struggle for its very existence. There is no need to distance yourself formally from the Republican Party. There will always be a group disaffected by current policy. I recognize that the Lincoln Project and important individuals have been largely ineffective, although well-meaning. This is merely a sign of the times.

I would ask you to simply break with your party leadership. Donald Trump is evil in his very essence. There is no moral underpinning, there is no saving grace. Presidential pardons be damned! President Joe Biden pardoned many, including his own family and certain persons, preemptively, who should never be considered for criminal prosecution. Biden did the latter because of threats being voiced by his incoming successor. Donald Trump, on his first day, pardoned all the criminals who invaded the very building where he took his oath of office. They had been responsible for killings, injuries, and property damage and had been convicted by the American judicial system. The message here is clear: if you commit crimes in my name, you will be pardoned. That is not the rule of law.

I would not suggest that you save the party and steer it on a different course. But I am asking that you look out for Ukraine as a priority. The existence of Ukraine as a state is essential for the identity and well-being of the Ukrainian people.

I, personally, feel that Ukraine is an integral part of my and my family's joy and spiritual nourishment. My wife and I travel to

Ukraine three times a year. We meet with people, I lecture at universities, do media interviews, and enjoy the theatre and opera. During the war, we are more involved with assistance. There are many like us.

Ukraine is struggling for its existence. I would never disparage a longstanding, honorable, and proud political structure such as the GOP because of its current leader. But one man's distorted vision should not affect the many centuries' struggle of the Ukrainian people. As Ukrainian American Republicans, please prioritize Ukraine at this existential time.

Respectively,

January 27, 2025

Why Go to Ukraine at a Time of War

The last few days have been informative and inspiring. At night, my wife has psychologically battled ballistic missiles and drones while I mostly slept. One time, she did manage to wake me up because the targets were close to home, and the noise was unbearable. I went back to sleep almost immediately. I do sleep well in Ukraine, even with time zones and sirens.

We took an Uber to the PhD school at the Kyiv Mohyla Academy in Kyiv's Podol region. Our driver was Vitaly. We tend to converse intentionally and provoke our driver. He had come from the left bank of Kherson. He hadn't escaped Russian occupation. He and his wife simply left on a bus consisting of 10 people, by way of Crimea to Armenia, and then to Ukraine. The bus riders were thoroughly investigated or "filtered," as he said. The investigators were well informed beforehand. Three of the ten managed to make it through. Both he and his wife were among the three. Some really good fortune.

His Ukrainian language was not so good, but he tried very hard. If he even had an inclination to speak Russian, he had been cured of that affliction. He said that he had never seen such brutality. His friend was simply executed before his eyes. His refrain was that the Russians are not human.

Vitaly was not unusual. In conversations with people who came from the occupied territories, including non-Ukrainians, they have spoken with one voice. The invaders are brutal.

Mostly during my trips to Ukraine, I focus on learning experiences with university populations, which include the administrative staff and faculty, which are very informative, but the students themselves are very special. Administration and faculty are restrained in essence. If you are seeking genuine responses, then students are your best source.

I might add that I have found students in Ukraine to be not only very well informed but also very astute in political matters because politics affects their very lives.

What are the issues then for these little more than children? They despise the Russians. They love Ukraine. But they are tired of war. They speak well of America, but they are deeply concerned. They think that President Trump is evil and amoral. Frankly, they do not understand how the American people could have elected such a conman who represents none of the principles that made America a beacon of light for the world. They believe that Europe should make up the difference because their friends are dying to save Europe. They want peace, but not at any cost. They want a lasting peace where Russia is no longer a threat. They are quite sophisticated in interpreting Article 5 of the NATO Charter and see it as a guarantee, unlike the Budapest Memorandum. They want to be a part of the EU and NATO; they want it now, and they feel that they have earned it.

They did ask me provocatively because they saw me as a reflection of the Ukrainian American community, whether many Ukrainian-Americans voted for Trump. I minimized the reality because I was embarrassed. They asked me how I could be friends with those people. I said that I am not.

The bottom line is that students speak on behalf of Ukraine's future. There is nothing or little disingenuous about them. They are very straightforward, and more importantly, they genuinely care.

Get a feel for what Ukraine is about. It is about those young men and women willing to give up their lives for the future of their children. It is also about the University students who may be unsure about their future but are damn sure that they will be a part of it. The Ukrainian nation is an undying and unyielding spirit. There may be obstacles, but Ukraine's heart will prevail. They do seek assistance, and we are assured that the democratic world is with them.

That is why I am going to Ukraine at this time. I go to learn, to reach out, to help. There is no more revealing and real Ukraine than when it is fighting for its existence. Please try to help.

January 29, 2025

How is the American president perceived?

In the US capital, Washington D.C., near Reagan Airport in the Potomac River, 67 Americans died when a civilian passenger plane and a military helicopter collided. The President and his equally primitive associates took the grief to a new level by accusing their predecessors and the policy of diversification in hiring incompetent personnel, particularly in the air traffic controller's area. Not a single piece of evidence was provided for this accusation. In fact, it was more likely that this happened due to the inattention of the military in the helicopter. When asked how the president could say such things without the slightest evidence, Trump's impudent answer was "common sense." If anyone had any respect for this clown, then this press conference dashed any hopes that there is any sense in the White House today, common or otherwise. Among the accusers of their predecessors were the president, the secretaries of defense and transportation. Such a tragicomic circus could not have been imagined, but it was staged.

The next day, I gave a lecture at the Ivan Franko National University of Lviv using this bizarre example of what Ukraine can expect from today's resident of the White House, pointing out that this president is, at the very least, abnormal. There were students and professors in the hall who also saw this circus and who, by the way, speak English. They admitted that the behavior of the US President was appalling. I drew attention to the fact that they should direct such behavior to the tragedy of the war and Russian aggression, war crimes, and the attempted genocide in Ukraine. I asked what Ukraine could expect from such a president. We searched for the answer for two hours and still did not find it.

We agreed that we need to work with Europe and the US Congress, which, by the way, will change significantly in a short time. A positive phenomenon is that the first executive orders of

Trump imposing a moratorium on aid, which also relates to Ukraine, have already been enjoined by the American judiciary and by Trump himself rescinding the orders to save face.

Regarding Europe, I pointed out that none of the European leaders took part in Trump's swearing-in ceremonies except for the Prime Minister of Italy. Apparently, Europe does not accord Trump much respect or even concern.

It was our consensus that it is necessary to work hard on Europe, and in particular. France, Germany, as well as the apparent new Polish President, so that these countries increase aid and even pave the way for Ukraine to join NATO. Slovakia's Fico will retreat from opposition because of opposition to his pro-Russian policies by the Slovaks themselves, and Orbán and Hungary will be bought off by promises to pay out some of their withheld EU funds. Significant progress in Europe has already been made by the successful 100-year security agreement recently signed between Ukraine and the United Kingdom. Help will also come from the growth of frozen capital of Russian oligarchs in European banks. Also important is the expansion of the military industry with production in Ukraine, which has already shown that weapons produced in Ukraine are far more powerful in their dimensions than American long-range missiles.

Students in Ukraine are very idealistic. We have witnessed over the past 20 years two widespread revolutions. No other nation has shown such enthusiasm and democratic spirit during this time. These students are not only devoted idealists, but they are also very intelligent and informed. The level of education in Ukraine is very high.

I am not closing the page on the history of Trump's impact on and assistance to Ukraine. Let him come to Ukraine with Little Marco and see not only the ruin but also the courage and devotion of the people. I do not know if he will be impressed. I think not for someone like him, but we need to work even in this seemingly hopeless area. I wish those Ukrainians in America who supported

Trump would act today, but the students were told the bitter truth that Ukrainian Americans for Trump are traitors.

In the meantime, the bankrupt Russian economy should fail. We need to monitor sanctions, making oil and gas cheaper, so that Russia has nothing to pay either Russian soldiers or the police. Continuing the struggle on Russian territory also helps a lot, as defending Russian territory requires resources that otherwise would be used in Pokrovsk. The unrest of the nations enslaved by the Russian empire can bear great fruit. The Chechens. Tatars, Erzya. Kalmyks, Buryats, Bashkirs, and Circassians are ready to explode. They want their freedom.

What is important here is not to worry much about the evil clown in the White House. This is a deviant of history who does not have enough intellect, common sense, or integrity to change history. We will survive this as well.

January 31, 2025

Butterfly and Ukraine

My wife and I went to the Lviv National Opera named after Solomiya Krushelnytska to see "Madame Butterfly" seemingly for entertainment. But the opera provided a new political life experience, as is often the case with masterpieces.

American Lieutenant Benjamin Franklin Pinkerton practically raped a poor fifteen-year-old Japanese girl. Then he left for America. She gave birth to a child. When he learned that he had a son, he decided to return, end it with Butterfly, and take the child with him. The girl, deeply in love, had given up everything for him, including her faith, her family, and friends. Her countrymen shunned her, and she was left essentially without honor in Japanese society. Having neither dignity nor life, she committed suicide.

Friends and experts on the composer Puccini said that he wrote the role of Madame Butterfly for the world-famous Ukrainian singer Solomiya Krushelnytska.

Sitting in the audience, I recalled the words of the Ukrainian poet bard Taras Shevchenko from his poem "Kateryna", but not about a Japanese woman but a Ukrainian woman, and not an American lieutenant but a Muscovite soldier, with a similar plot of love, betrayal, and suffering.

"Make love, black-browed women, but not with Muscovites. Because Muscovites are foreign people, they will do you harm."

In my mind, Madame Butterfly is really Ukraine, and Pinkerton is America, and not only the contemporary version, but in relation to Ukraine, it is America with its deceptive policy of almost a century old. America, represented by President Franklin Roosevelt, essentially betrayed Ukraine in World War II at Yalta in 1945, giving it and other nations and states of Eastern Europe to the Russians under the guise of the USSR. During the Cold War, America worked openly and secretly all the time to support the principle of essential

Russian unity, considering Ukrainians as separatists. It declared Muscovites to be the indigenous people of the entire USSR. This apparent ignorance of America was completely disingenuous in order to appease the Russians. And this continued for 45 years. Until the last minute of the "Cold War", that is, in August 1991, the President of America, George Bush Sr., called on the Ukrainians to preserve the empire. After the declaration of independence of Ukraine, on August 24, 1991, and even the referendum on December 1, America did not immediately recognize Ukraine as a sovereign state until December 25, 1991, and this only after the resignation of Gorbachev and the formal liquidation of the USSR. There was little manifestation of goodwill, although Russia itself, represented by Yeltsin, had liquidated the USSR. Bush listened only to Gorbachev.

And even after the recognition, America continued to behave insincerely and even shamefully, deceiving Ukraine with lies, supposedly assuring security to get rid of nuclear weapons and uranium in favor of the Kremlin. The Budapest Memorandum was the essence of political fraud for which America was primarily responsible. Gullible Ukraine thought that America was guided by good faith. Recognition and disappointment ensued, but it came too late.

During Moscow's first invasion of Ukraine, that is, the takeover of Crimea in 2014 by Russian little green men, America told Ukraine not to fight. By the way, during the Revolution of Dignity, only two Senators, McCain and Murphy, came to Ukraine to show support. No Administration officials came. During the full-scale invasion on February 24, 2022, and for almost three years, America has helped. Still, Ukraine would not lose, but did not win either, without delivering the necessary weapons or with a lengthy delay.

And now America has chosen a cruel and primitive commander-in-chief to perhaps leave Ukraine for good, like Pinkerton did to Butterfly. All this is done with brazen disregard for morality, and in the case of Trump, with incessant lies.

But Ukraine is not Butterfly, who was in love and completely dependent on Pinkerton. Ukraine is not in despair, although it has suffered very difficult experiences affecting its very existence. Ukraine itself is strong, not only in spirit, but it has true friends and allies. Its own weapons are stronger and more far-reaching than those supplied by America. Its soldiers are the best in the whole world because they are of Cossack lineage and are fighting for the existence of their own nation. The whole nation is engaged. The Ukrainian nation, with its allies in Europe and the enslaved peoples in the Russian Empire, will ultimately win. There will no longer be the evil Russian empire.

On the other hand, America, together with its current version of the unscrupulous Pinkerton, the Trump circus, will become, if not already, the laughing stock of the whole world. At the curtain call, I jeered at Pinkerton. I jeer at Trump as well.

February 2, 2025

Poland

I traveled back home through Rzezow, Poland. At the airport, I asked my Uber driver to go around several times so that I could count the number of American Patriot Defense Missile systems. I counted twelve. Initially, I was upset as to why they were in Poland rather than in Ukraine, where they would be of great use. Later, I discovered that they were from Israel pursuant to an agreement among the United States, Israel, and Ukraine. And now meant for Ukraine. If only I could be sure that Trump would not embargo them.

Most of the people I meet and converse with in Poland are sympathetic to Ukraine. This has been the case for almost three years now. This time, there were several encounters of a centuries-old Polish psychosis, best represented in the last century by the extremist Roman Domowski, a voice from the past, a political figure, a so-called "national democrat", and a xenophobe. His affiliation was the National Democratic Party. My father spoke extensively about them. But he was a Ukrainian nationalist.

National democracy is a bit of a misnomer, as it means democracy, but only for the ruling nation. All others are excluded. It was this ideology that molded Polish statesmen. The alternative was Dictator Josef Pilsudski in the 1920s and 1930s. Those policies were also right-wing and resulted in almost twenty years of Polish lordship over Ukrainians in Western Ukraine. Ukrainians never had a chance in that democracy. So they fought back with civil disobedience and more, assassinations, etc., a revolution.

I took my place on the flight from Warsaw to Newark. As the crew recited the standard safety regulations, I said to myself, I hope there are no American military helicopters in the air at Newark Airport. My Polish-American neighbor immediately took issue with me, asserting that it was the incompetence of air traffic controllers who caused the recent tragedy at Washington's Ronald Reagan

Airport. He stressed that they had been hired by the Biden Administration. There was no need to rile me up. I immediately asserted that this tragedy was on Trump's and Hegseth's watch.

The short of it was that he was a Polish-American whose idols included Trump, Le Pan, Orban, and Fico. At first, I tried to explain that Trump blamed the accident on air traffic controllers because of their alleged diversity (DEI) in hiring, meaning, I suppose, that the non-whites were at fault. Trump's bigotry, racism, and white supremacy were all exposed during that press conference. Trump presented no evidence of fault. Then I realized that my neighbor was xenophobic.

I went further and tried to explain that Trump was not good for Ukraine or Poland. My neighbor's retort was that Ukrainian missiles had killed two Poles. This apparently had happened two years earlier, and it was questionable as to responsibility. He never mentioned the Russian threat and the need for a Ukrainian-Polish alliance.

I recognized the societal xenophobia that has been the shame of Poland for centuries, which was responsible for the 1947 attempted Genocide of Ukrainians in Poland, and more recently, attacks by the Polish Party of Law and Justice against Ukrainian peaceful processions to the Ukrainian cemetery with shouts of Poland without Ukrainians. I suggested that it's time to find cooperation in view of the current perils and to remember that Poles invaded Ukraine three times. No such invasion was made by the Ukrainians. The crew intervened, and we were quiet for the ensuing nine hours.

There remained plenty on my mind. I realized that societal irrational antipathy persisted, probably on both sides. I even suspect that Poles had not offered the Patriots to be delivered at least in part to Ukraine precisely because of this, besides adherence to any instructions from NATO, meaning America. They were only hurting themselves since the Ukrainian defense was defending Poland from the Russians as well. Oddly, old scores were more important than today's political survival.

I had gone too far. Several weeks from now, the Polish people will go to the polls to elect a new president since the current one is term-limited. The strongest candidate appears to be Karol Nawrocki, the Chair of the Institute of National Remembrance, officially outside the Law and Justice Party, yet supported by it. He has already made some questionable statements about Ukraine and its place in the EU and NATO, depending upon its remorse for alleged atrocities against the Polish population during World War 2 in Western Ukraine. The current president of Poland, Andrzej Duda, is a member of the Law and Justice Party and supports Nawrocki. Perhaps Duda should attend to Nawrocki's less-than-moderate tone on Ukraine's accession to both the EU and NATO.

Poland is a member of both the EU and NATO. Despite its history with Ukraine, it is a crucial ally. At a time of extreme and mutual danger, heinous traits such as xenophobia can only exacerbate that peril. Xenophobes, racists, and white supremacists probably cannot be cured of their afflictions. However, they must be made to understand that their psychoses work only for the benefit of the real enemy. Convincing such people of the common good is a battle within the war for survival. But that battle has to be waged.

February 9, 2025

Auschwitz and Today

My father, Evhen Lozynskyj, was arrested by the Gestapo on September 21, 1941, in the Western Ukrainian city of Stanislaviv, now Ivano Frankivsk. He was charged with treason against the Reich for proclaiming Ukrainian independence. Five others were arrested with him, including two brothers of the Leader of the Organization of Ukrainian Nationalists, Stepan Bandera, Oleksandr and Vasyl.

They were all transported to the notorious Lonskoho prison in Lviv, then Montelupich in Krakow. In the spring of 1942, they were transported by first transit from Ukraine to the German concentration camp outside Krakow, Poland. The camp was Auschwitz. In the course of their confinement, Bandera's two brothers were killed at the camp by Polish capos. My father survived. When the Germans learned at the end of January 1945 that the Soviets were near, they took reasonably able prisoners and conducted a march of death to nearby concentration camps. Anyone who fell during the march was executed. The march continued through camps at Mauthausen, Melk, and Ebensee. Finally, at Ebensee on May 6, 1945, the remaining prisoners were liberated by the American army. My father weighed 98 pounds at the time of his "liberation".

My father's friend and Auschwitz inmate Danylo Czajkowsky wrote his memoir in 1946 entitled "I Want To Live." Last year, it was translated into English and published in Toronto, Canada by the Ucrainica Research Institute. Here is an excerpt:

"A vehicle stopped at the gate to the Eleventh Blockhouse. It looked like a box, tightly sealed on all sides.

'Leave the engine running!' said the SS-man sitting next to Arndt, the driver. 'We'll load up and keep going.'"

He climbed out and walked over to the rear of the van. The driver's cabin was sealed off completely from the cargo bay. The SS-man checked the doors, tested them to make sure they opened properly, and then examined the space between the driver's cabin and the cargo bay.

'All in good working condition,' the SS-man reassured himself, 'the death compartment's ready,' and headed off towards the gate.

In a long hall of the basement, a special court was in session. A group of frightened, emaciated prisoners huddled by the door. The German words being read quickly from a piece of paper by one of the three judges were totally incomprehensible to the prisoners, as was, in fact, their entire stay in the basement of the Eleventh Blockhouse. The inmates peered at the judges, studied their insignia, and listened to their names being repeated in the judgment.

'Well, at least it's good that they've arrived. Maybe they'll let us all go home sooner,' an old peasant took solace in the thought.

With a heavy military gait, the judges left the room, chatting pleasantly amongst themselves. The sentenced group let them pass, moving to the side in an involuntary gesture of respect. The clerk hastily collected all the documents.

'Everybody out!' a voice called from the corridor. Obediently, like a string of lambs, the sentenced men walked toward the van. The SS-man stood next to the open doors.

'Ready!' he yelled to the driver, slamming the doors tight. The engine roared, spewing out the acrid smoke of burned gasoline.

The SS-man quietly took his seat next to the driver. The poisonous gases from the burnt gasoline hissed gleefully, making their way through a pipe into the cargo bay where the sentenced prisoners sat. The vehicle transporting death pulled away.

Most of the survivors found themselves in displaced persons' camps and were subject to severe scrutiny by the Allies. After all, the Soviets were allies. My father came to America in 1951 with his young wife and baby daughter. He was, in essence, imprisoned at Ellis Island before America would allow him to enter. He was a member of the Organization of Ukrainian Nationalists, an organization found on a list of inimical organizations compiled by the Soviets and utilized by the Americans. Following the summit at Yalta, Josef Stalin and Franklin Roosevelt, with his coterie of Soviet agents in both State and Treasury, were buddies.

Auschwitz Concentration Camp was set up for Poles, and Poles were the first political prisoners there. The number of prisoners grew steadily as a result of the constant arrival of new transports. In 1940, nearly 8 thousand people were registered in the camp. Almost all of them were Poles. There were also small numbers of Jews and Germans in the camp. At that time, the latter usually held supervisory functions as capos and block supervisors. In 1941, over 26 thousand people were registered in Auschwitz (about 15 thousand Poles, 10 thousand Soviet POWs, and more than 1 thousand Jews).

As a result of the inclusion of Auschwitz in the process of the mass extermination of the Jews, the number of deportees began to soar. About 197 thousand Jews were deported there in 1942, about 270 thousand the following year, and over 600 thousand in 1944, for a total of almost 1.1 million. Among them, about 200 thousand people were selected as capable of labor and registered as prisoners in the camp.

In this same period, from 1942 to 1944, about 160 thousand Poles, Roma and Sinti, Belorussians, Ukrainians, French, and others were registered as prisoners and given numbers. There were also more than 10 thousand people, mostly Poles, Soviet POWs, as well as Roma and Sinti, who were not entered into the camp records or given numbers.

The mass deportation of Jews to Auschwitz that began in 1942 radically changed the makeup of the prisoner population. After three months of deportation, in mid-1942, Jews already made up the most numerous ethnic groups, and their share of the population rose steadily from about 46% in June 1942 to about 68% at the peak of the camp's population, in August 1944. A total of about 400 thousand prisoners were registered: 195 thousand non-Jews and 205 thousand Jews.

Frankly, the anniversary of the so-called liberation or liquidation is not about either. Those who remained and were 'liberated' by the Soviets more often than not were executed by the Soviets on the spot or transported to Soviet GULAGs. It may surprise some readers, but the Soviet GULAG was the predecessor of the Nazi concentration camp. The GULAG served as a model for the Nazis.

Even more surprising would be the fact that Auschwitz was not closed after the war. Nor did it become a museum immediately thereafter. Communist Poland used the facilities at Auschwitz long after the war, and many Ukrainians, particularly of Lemko ethnicity, who found themselves in their native land only to discover that it was now part of Poland, were interned at Auschwitz during the infamous ethnic cleansing of Ukrainians that was a state policy of Communist Poland in 1947.

I refer back to my own father. There were many like him who received similar treatment by America after liberation. They found themselves in Displaced Persons camps and ultimately emigrated to America and elsewhere, but not without complexity and mistreatment. Post World War 2 America was a paragon of appeasement towards the Soviets. When it became finally apparent to America that the Soviets were the next enemy, America failed to identify the Soviet Union as yet another manifestation of the Russian Empire. For the longest time, the Russian nation was considered one of the nation's captives within the USSR.

The significance of the 80th anniversary of the liberation of the Auschwitz concentration camp is two-fold. First, that it was not a liberation, but merely a substitution of one tyranny for another. The second, and perhaps more important, is that all the liberators were complicit in one of the greatest travesties of fairness and justice in human history.

We can and should start with the Jews who were certainly most affected and mistreated by the Nazi regime. The Nazis simply wanted to obliterate all Jews. They failed, but not for the number of victims. The world was accommodating or reticent, but not forever. Today, the Holocaust is known worldwide as one of the most egregious attempts at genocide of a people.

On the other hand, appeasement of murderous regimes goes on. The Nazis were certainly not the last. In the XXI century, as for many centuries before, the Russians have carried on as they had before. The Russian Federation constitutes eleven time zones, all occupied through invasion. But even that is not enough for the brutal Russian imperialists. Those Ukrainian political prisoners in Auschwitz were precisely that. They sought Ukrainian freedom. In February 2014, Russia invaded Ukraine. But that was not enough. Russia invaded in full force eight years later. For three years, the battle has gone on. It has been an attempt to "wipe Ukrainians off the face of the earth." There has been much global support for Ukraine because there is no issue of right or wrong.

Is this about to change because America has once again reverted to its shameless role as the betrayer?

February 13, 2025

NATO Without America

It is a revolutionary concept, yet addressed more than once over the last few years, and in particular over the last few days. It has been framed in various forms, including a European military alliance or a military alliance within the European Union.

An interesting historical point is that only once has NATO's Article 5, about all for one and one for all, been invoked in its 75-plus-year history, and that was by the United States of America for a military operation to kill one man originally thought to be in Afghanistan and ultimately realized in Pakistan. The North Atlantic sphere of operation was significantly extended.

The NATO Charter reads:

"The Parties to this Treaty reaffirm their faith in the purposes and principles of the Charter of the United Nations and their desire to live in peace with all peoples and all governments.

They are determined to safeguard the freedom, common heritage, and civilization of their peoples, founded on the principles of democracy, individual liberty, and the rule of law. They seek to promote stability and well-being in the North Atlantic area.

They are resolved to unite their efforts for collective defense and for the preservation of peace and security. They therefore agree to this North Atlantic Treaty:"

America has become NATO's bully. Europe has to break away from bullying without damaging the structure, which has been damaged severely by American arrogance, hopefully not beyond repair.

The die has been cast. Ukraine's President Zelensky continues to pay attention to arrogant discourse from President Trump, his neophyte vice president Vance, his neophyte Secretary of Defense Hegseth, and the ultimate paragon of Washington buffoonery, Senator Lindsey Graham. The last one carried a certain level of decorum when he was decorated in company by the most Honorable American politician, the late Senator John McCain.

John McCain is gone, and so is any decorum attendant to American politicians. This is not about partisan politics. Ukraine and moral principles were abandoned many times in the last 100 years, beginning with Democrat Woodrow Wilson, Franklin Delano Roosevelt, Republican George H. W. Bush, Democrat Bill Clinton, Republican George W. Bush, Democrat Barack Obama, Republican Donald J. Trump, Democrat Joe Biden, and now, certainly the worst of the lot, Republican Donald J. Trump. No one can measure up to Trump in his amoral and anti-Ukrainian politics than perhaps Franklin D. Roosevelt, and Roosevelt was totally infiltrated by Soviet Russian agents.

And so Europe has to look out for itself. That message has been delivered resoundingly over and over again by American politicians. American eyes are on China, having more than once asserted that defense issues in Europe must be addressed by the European partners in NATO. More importantly, American duplicity has been overwhelming. Up north, Canada, as a member of NATO, contributes less than 2% of its GDP, significantly less than even currently prescribed NATO members.

The European side of NATO is beginning to recognize its own perils and responsibilities, and so it will no longer be subject to American amorality, arrogance, and bullying. Europe has to realize further that, instead of America, it is exceptional in terms of culture and achievements. Europe has managed to unite thirty or so countries in a continental European Union with a GDP and population greater than that of America. It has provided Ukraine with more military aid than America. America is struggling to rename the Gulf of Mexico.

Frankly, China, while certainly a factor in European trade, presents no security issue for Europe. There is always the moral principle with China that Europe cannot ignore. China perpetrates genocides against its Muslim population and utilizes slaves, including child labor.

And so the Munich Security Conference concludes with much serious discussion about the Ukrainian peril and Russian aggression. Long-term, America appears to be a non-player in Europe, Ukraine, or Russia. That was the entire purpose of NATO. I was born in America, but certainly, I am not proud of what America has become. Frankly, I do not know whether I love this America.

February 16, 2025

A Call to Revolution

President Donald Trump and his capos, VP J.D. Vance and Secretary of Defense Pete Hegseth, as well as Secretary of State Little Marco Rubio, are the newest versions of the ugly Americans.

Disparaging and blaming the victim, insulting our allies, and lending credence to and accommodating the aggressor are the most recent examples of bizarre deal-making.

In the course of 10 days, America has given little regard to every symbol of freedom that America possesses or represents by tearing it down. America has betrayed its friends and chosen new evil allies in an attempt to formulate a new world order, according to Trump, a convicted felon, and Putin, a convicted war criminal and murderer, devoid of morality, truth, justice, and everything for which generations of Americans have stood.

While some Republican lawmakers have refuted some of Trump's most heinous assertions, such as that Ukraine started the war and that Ukraine's president Zelensky is a dictator, mostly they have done so without distancing themselves from their 'great leader' or 'fuhrer'. Current VP Vance was prescient in 2015 when he saw this coming. But, instead of fighting this premonition, he joined for self-promotion.

Some unhinged and very primitive Ukrainian Americans have spun Trump's bizarre rhetoric as a bargaining ploy. In negotiations, if you agree to everything the other side asserts, you have relinquished any bargaining position.

Who is to blame for America having become a dangerous laughing stock and ultimately a pariah in the global democratic community? The answer is quite simple: the American people, including Ukrainian Americans, have betrayed their mothers and fathers. Hopefully, it is not too late.

It is time for Revolution! It comes at almost the two hundred fiftieth anniversary of the first one. We can only pray that this Revolution will not be bloody, but there are no guarantees. The bloody prelude of Proud Boys and Oath Keepers on January 6, 2021, and their subsequent pardons come to mind. America is no longer a country governed by the rule of law.

Ukrainian American supporters of Trump should be shunned and isolated. There is little distinction between a Russian asset and a Russian agent, so it is best to err on the side of caution. If these people have no role in the community, they will at least be neutralized and not represent a danger.

At all times, the focus has to be very clear – Trump and the White House. Any protests in Washington have to be located there. The Lincoln Memorial or other locations are not appropriate venues. Trump has to be called out by name. The State Department and the Pentagon are appropriate. Congressional offices should be fair game, in particular those of some of the more odious members of Congress, such as Senator Lindsey Graham, Representative Jeff Van Drew, etc. Certain think tanks, such as Heritage and CIA fronts, are appropriate as well.

Local venues should be addressed as well, particularly in red states or districts where the governors are most abhorrent, such as Texas. Democracy is a local manifestation, primarily even in presidential elections, because of the electoral system.

Individuals who are, in essence, Trump shills in positions of importance held currently or in the past, such as current American ambassador-nominee to the UN Elise Stefanik or former ambassador to Ukraine John Heerbst, should be shunned, certainly never invited to Ukrainian American events.

Since this tragedy of America has been precipitated by grassroots support for Donald Trump, the ultimate blame falls on the American people. They need to rise and right the wrong that they have done to Ukraine, Europe, Canada, and the entire global democratic community. Populist ignorance cannot be an excuse.

February 20, 2025

The Sleazeball

A New York City residential tenant telephoned his landlord seeking permission to renovate his kitchen at his own cost and expense. The landlord considered the request, saw dollars to be gained, and suggested that his managing agent visit the tenant at the apartment to work out the details. The following day, the managing agent visited. In the course of the conversation, he slips in a piece of paper which contains the landlord's consent, but also a rent increase. Without reading the document, the tenant, eager to begin work, signed it.

That is what happened in Kyiv twice between President Zelensky and two of Trump's agents. It also involved real estate, but only an assault on its minerals. Of course, there was significant fraud attempted as Trump's papers estimated Ukraine's debt to the United States to be 500 billion dollars, while the actual aid amounted to little more than 100 billion. Additionally, this aid was not a loan, but rather a contribution to the defense of Ukraine, Europe, and America appropriated by Congress. But that's clouding the issues with facts.

President Zelensky was astute enough not to sign the document. Still, it was a lesson learned. Even if Ukrainian intelligence had not warned President Zelensky, this one experience would have opened the eyes of the Ukrainian president as to Donald Trump and contemporary America. President Zelensky had an eye-opening experience with Trump as America's president in 2019. This is the modus operandi of Donald Trump, the sleazeball Landlord and the equally defrauding President of the United States. How shameful is that!

In my previous article, I called for a revolution against Donald Trump and his accomplices. After the subsequent confirmation of the new FBI director, ignominious Kash Patel, my wife warned me that the FBI would be coming to our house. I joked that I needed to check our liquor stock. She was not amused.

To add to my un-American transgressions, I recently viewed the hockey tournament of four countries, where the final game was Canada against the United States, held in Boston. I was ambivalent until I heard American spectators booing the Canadian national anthem, which, together with Trump calling Canada the 51st state, turned me against America. I rooted for Canada. Canada won 3-2.

Most recently, with the final outcome to be determined, America at the UN is opposing the Ukraine-Europe draft resolution commemorating three years of the full-scale war, condemning Russia, and insisting on its full withdrawal. America is insisting on its draft, which would whitewash blame.

There are moments of Trump's pure evil exhibitions elaborating on "squeezing" Ukraine. One has to wonder whether the 25th Amendment should be invoked, but that would require the action of an equally depraved Vice President.

And then there is Trump's current accomplice in crime, Elon Musk, threatening the removal of Starlink unless Ukraine accedes to the mineral steal.

There is a serious problem in diplomacy when the adage about keeping your friends close and your enemies closer is applicable in a perverted form. Today's Ukraine-America relations are blurred. America may no longer be Ukraine's ally. Time and events will tell.

However, there is no doubt that Trump is one of Ukraine's enemies. Before the final verdict on Ukraine-America relations, all efforts must be focused on removing the convicted felon and sleazeball from the White House. So, the revolution must proceed.

February 24, 2025

America and Russia are officially Allies

Today, on the anniversary of Russia's full-scale invasion of Ukraine, at the United Nations General Assembly, the United States of America and the Russian Federation together voted against a joint Ukrainian and European resolution condemning Russian aggression in Ukraine and demanding Russia's immediate withdrawal. This was perhaps America's most shameful day in its almost quarter of a millennium existence, certainly in the 80-year history of the UN.

While sanctions against America will not be imposed by anyone, the entire democratic world should consider boycotting American products and increasing the purchase of European and Canadian products.

For me, this will be relatively easy since I have always detested American beer.

Is this a turning point or simply an aberration resulting from the last presidential election of essentially an evil fool to lead America?

Either way, it requires a reaction from everyone in America.

The tally of the votes indicates that America at this point has few allies in the world as it changes its allegiances and friends. Even Iran and China refused to fall on the Russian and American sword.

America's Permanent Representative to the UN was glaringly absent. The American vote was cast by Ms. Stafanik's undersecretary. I cannot believe that Ambassador Stefanik was otherwise engaged. While it would have required real courage for the Ambassador to have voted other than as instructed by Trump, she would have had to resign her position, as she serves at the mercy of a thug, and she had given up a congressional seat and committee designations.

However, she is certainly responsible for the American vote. At this point, any Trump sycophant, frankly, anyone on his so-called team, should be considered fair game for severe criticism and manifestations of disaffection in myriad lawful forms.

A UNGA resolution does not change global security dynamics. However, given the vote tally of 93 for and only 18 against with 65 abstentions, it was a profound humiliation for the United States, portending additionally that America was no longer the leader of the world.

Besides America, Russia, Hungary, Belarus, and Israel, the remaining negative votes belonged to third-world countries beholden to Russia. The Hungarian vote should result in repercussions at the European Union, which currently holds frozen sanctions money earmarked for Hungary. Enough playing games, that money should be released, but not to Hungary, rather to Ukraine for its defense. Prime Minister Viktor Orban has not been a loyal participant in the EU, and his recent half-year presidency of the Council was deliberately offensive to EU policy. Forfeiture of money may teach the Hungarian people a worthwhile lesson.

French President Macron and British Prime Minister Starmer are separately meeting with Trump this week at the White House. Both certainly are prepared with their message for Trump and the American people. They certainly will be circumspect so that all bridges are not burned. Yet, they must stress that American global leadership is in jeopardy. It is not their job to correct the mistakes of the American people, nor is it within their power.

This brings me back to the American people. How could we have become what we are today? I was born in America, and while I am not complicit in this travesty, I am sympathetic, but not forgiving, unless efforts are made to rectify one of the worst deliberate acts of America in almost two hundred and fifty years. This alliance with Russia, a manifest criminal and killer, Vladimir Putin, ranks up there with the annihilation of the native people, of which Trump's hero, Andrew Jackson, was so proud, and the enslavement of black people and continuing that discrimination for 100 years after the theoretical emancipation.

America had this coming because of its arrogance, considering itself exceptional. Trump cannot be rehabilitated or changed. He has to be removed. That in itself will begin the rehabilitation of America.

February 24, 2025

The Betrayal

On the heels of America's shameless vote with the Russians at the United Nations General Assembly, which, aside from exposing America's lack of morality, also manifested global opposition to America's latest foray into the world of bullying and imperialism, the White House staged a Kremlin-scripted ambush and sabotage. It turned out to be a bizarre Oval Office press conference.

It was Trump at his most ignorant, forgetting historical facts, financial details, strong-arming, and talking over his guest. He was surrounded by his sycophants for support.

The primary takeaway is that Ukraine and Europe now realize that the free democratic world needs a new leader because America has joined the enemy camp, the camp of Russia, Iran, and North Korea. Even China has been reluctant to join.

I suppose that it was a decent run for America with achievements, but many betrayals. America will be remembered for both. As long as America is wealthy, achievements will be embellished while betrayals will be attributed to overwhelming circumstances.

The framework for a Ukraine-U.S. Reconstruction Investment Fund was to be the subject of the White House meeting between the Presidents of Ukraine, Zelensky, and of the United States, Donald J. Trump. It never got that far. President Zelensky was ambushed by Trump and his VP Vance, and the rest of the program was canceled.

Trump's worldview, his intellectual capacity, and thuggish behavior were on full display. VP Vance was personally and actively invested as an appendage, certainly not according to any accepted protocol. Still, the hillbilly Vance may be a quandary until such time as he becomes an independent actor. After all, he once called Trump a Nazi. Until then, he is simply a sycophant, but loud, brash, and offensive.

I was reminded of a characterization of Trump given by a British expert on Sky News after the Trump-Starmer meeting. He stated that Trump had a butterfly mind. He explained that his mind or focus was fleeting. Trump could not say the same thing twice. He could not remember that he had called Zelensky a dictator. Nor could he remember that Putin broke a ceasefire in December 2019 pursuant to a Paris agreement. This happened on Trump's watch.

The butterfly suddenly gains focus when it comes to Putin. Like a parrot, Trump kept reiterating his long-standing relationship with his friend Putin. Trump stated unequivocally that he was not on Ukraine's side. Since there are only two sides, the only conclusion can be that Trump and, I suppose, America is on Russia's side.

If ever there was doubt as to whether Trump is a Russian asset, it may have been dispelled. This may be a subject for another analysis following serious investigations. However, the circumstantial evidence surrounding Trump, his first wife, Ivana, and Russia through its KGB is certainly more than enough for a grand jury indictment.

For me, there is only one outtake from this latest event. The democratic free world, including Ukraine and Europe, needs a new leader. Following this latest fiasco, European leaders made that point very clear. The United States of America, the bastion of liberty and democracy, is very much afflicted with cancerous growth – Trump. This cancer has metastasized throughout America's political body.

Later that evening, President Zelensky appeared on Fox News. Three times, the interviewer Brett Baeir suggested that Zelensky had somehow offended America and should apologize. This script must have been taken from 'The Godfather.' Don Trump may have instructed Fox to make that suggestion.

President Zelensky had been treated discourteously as an enemy contrary to any international protocol, but he stood his ground. When asked rudely whether he would resign, he calmly replied that he was elected by the Ukrainian people and their will shall prevail.

Ukraine and Europe lost an ally, but no one came away more disturbed than the American people.

March 1, 2025

The Bottom Line

The British news channel Sky News offers a British perspective on global affairs. Its journalists, including its guests, offer a fresh view, often critical of the colonies. Almost invariably, they call their prime minister Sir Keir Starmer, Ukraine's President, President Zelensky, but refer to America's President simply as Trump. Is this a clear or subconscious expression of disrespect?

Respect is an interesting reaction and manifestation because very often it is simply a process of protocol, especially in politics. It is very rarely earned because of actual deeds or behavior. Most often it comes with one's title.

As a civilian, Donald Trump often stated that during his presidency, he and America were highly respected. Frankly, nothing could be further from the truth. The world rued for the America of old rather than what it had become under Trump's first term, often laughing behind Trump's back, yet very much concerned for global security, but believing in America's democratic system of checks and balances, and hoping that Trump would be kept in check by the grown-ups in his Administration. And there were some grown-ups.

It is interesting to note that none (zero) of Trump's cabinet has returned for his second term. Many have written books on the subject of their disapproval of their previous leader. Trump has casually dismissed their criticism. What is amazing is that following this almost unanimous reaction, Trump managed to win the 2024 election. That says much about the electorate.

The second term is somewhat more disturbing because Trump is unbridled. The Trump Cancer has spread throughout the Republican party and permeated other unexpected parts of America's body politic. A simple review of the new cabinet exemplifies that. Many of the nuttier or sycophantic members of Congress now serves in the Cabinet. Trump has chosen the Speaker of the House, three members of the Supreme Court, so that now the Cancer is in stage four and the body politic is withering.

Trump is an evil clown, but as President of the United States, he is very much in control and very dangerous to the point of even being able to use the American military against Americans. 'General' Hegseth will give the orders to shoot at Americans. Hopefully, the American soldier will recognize that he has become a tool of the enemy.

President Zelensky is a statesman and very patient. Despite his unpardonable treatment at the White House, where he was actually, perhaps non intentionally, physically assaulted as he sat next to Trump, and Trump often flailed his right. VPVance was a witness and could testify truthfully if under oath. President Zelensky kept his focus on the needs of the Ukrainian people and withstood this disrespect for their benefit. He will continue to do so for as long as it takes.

Will America come around? I am not suggesting that America come around and resemble somewhat what is envisioned in its Constitution. I am referring to the America of the last one hundred years, where it was the leader of the free world, often standing on principle and only sometimes betraying its friends and allies. Now it sells out its friends indiscriminately.

America boasts of its contribution to NATO, but only once has Article 5 been invoked, and then for the benefit of America only. America messed that up by not including in the withdrawal negotiations the Afghan government it had propped up in the withdrawal negotiations. The specious negotiations took place under Trump. America also forgot to thank its fellow NATO members.

In my opinion, America will return to some form of normalcy, but not in the near future. After Trump, and assuming he is not succeeded by Vance, America will have to undergo a period of rehabilitation. The recent vote with Russia at the UN GA, the ambush of Ukraine's President at the White House, the more recent suspension of offensive cybersecurity measures against Russia, and the suspension of arms delivery to Ukraine are all symptoms of a deep-seated, severe, and debilitating affliction. America will have to undergo a revolution, a catharsis if you will. A new generation will have to come to save America.

With that in mind, Ukraine and Europe have to assume the mantle of leadership. The population of Europe is five times that of Russia and more than twice that of America. Europe's general GDP is a bit greater than that of the United States. America is much greater in per capita terms. The only thing missing is the will to take on NATO or global leadership.

That includes the will to take on more expenditures at the cost of some social programs. While people enjoy social programs, they are more afraid of war and the loss of freedom.

While European presidents and prime ministers continue to soothe on a part-time basis the savage beast in Washington, they must focus, as they have recently, on their security. There is no comparison between Europe and America as far as civilization and numbers are concerned. It's all about will. Trump and America have done Europe a favor by Trump's bad behavior. Today's America is almost not even a Democracy.

March 4, 2025

"We Both Have A Police State In The Good Sense Of The Word."

These words were uttered by a purported Russian journalist, Yevgeny Popov. He hosts a television program (yes, 'Sixty Minutes') which is the most popular daily political broadcast on Russian state television. He did point out that American weapons were killing Russian soldiers on Ukraine's battlefields. One of his guests, a firebrand lawmaker, Aleksei Zhuravlyov, known for threatening the United States with nuclear annihilation, said last week that Russia 'could make friends with America and rule the world...Trump needs us. Do we need Trump? We do. Do our interests coincide? They do. Against whom? Against the European Union.'

This was reported by The New York Times.

French President Macron recently spoke to the French people, but broadcast globally, stating rather resolutely that, since America is proving to be an unreliable partner, without giving up on America, we need to make France much stronger than it is. Perhaps more importantly, he expanded France's nuclear umbrella. He said France was ready to extend its nuclear deterrent to EU partners in the 'new era' in which Europe faces a growing military threat from Russia. He announced a plan to host a meeting in Paris of the chiefs of general staff of countries willing to ensure future peace in Ukraine.

In the meantime, Trump and America are behaving more and more badly. Trump stopped intelligence sharing between Ukraine and America. He has threatened to expel, beginning in April, some quarter of a million Ukrainian migrants who have entered the United States. There is talk of lifting sanctions against Russia.

As Trump ravages Ukraine, Putin has increased his military assault. As a result, there have been greater civilian casualties, in particular because of the lack of Patriot interceptors and the lack of sharing of intelligence. Perhaps Trump's next step will be to announce the shipment of American military supplies to Russia. That is not so far-fetched.

There is much to the allegations that Trump and his first wife, Ivana, were KGB assets and continue to work with former KGB Colonel Vladimir Putin. The undisputed evidence remains largely circumstantial in time and place, but only because no investigation is taking place.

America does have a history of KGB agents infiltrating its ranks, and, frankly, much of it had been covered up and finally investigated long after the damage had been done. Imagine it were to be revealed that a sitting President of the United States was working for a foreign state, and an evil one with an international warrant for the arrest of its leader. I am not sure that sycophantic Republicans would vote to impeach.

Donald Trump fancies himself a 'stable genius,' particularly in economic matters, which is surprising since his educational level is only a bachelor's in real estate. During his initial fifty days, the stock market crashed, and unemployment increased. The economy is very volatile, with inflation set to skyrocket as soon as his tariffs are in place.

The war in Ukraine is no closer to peace or a ceasefire. In fact, a traditionally neutral country like Ireland has joined the side of Ukraine. The Gaza hostages remain, with only very few living hostages released despite Trump's deadline. America has lost its Mexican, Canadian, and European friends. The land grab for Greenland, Panama, and Canada has gone nowhere. Trump has imposed tariffs only to retract them. America has lost the respect of the world, retaining only a sliver of tolerance because of its wealth. Certainly, no one likes America. Or what it has become.

Suffice it to say that Trump's first fifty days have been disastrous.

March 7, 2025

Piece of Hillbilly Garbage

The following was posted by hillbilly garbage VP Vance on X:

"Today, while walking with my 3-year-old daughter, a group of 'Slava Ukraini' protesters followed us around and shouted as my daughter grew increasingly anxious and scared. I decided to speak with the protesters in the hopes that I could trade a few minutes of conversation for them leaving my toddler alone. (Nearly all of them agreed.) It was a mostly respectful conversation, but if you're chasing a 3-year-old as part of a political protest, you're a shit person."

Nice language from a VP.

Except that this did not happen. There is a video also on X showing this fact. The demonstrators are fixed in one place, far removed from the VP. The road upon which his house sits is closed to pedestrian and vehicle traffic. There are as many local police and secret service as there are demonstrators. There is no meeting between the protesters and the VP. These are the facts, unless you cannot believe your eyes.

What kind of garbage would try to provoke a controversy by using his own three-year-old? That kind of garbage works in tandem with another piece of garbage, his boss, Donald Trump.

Vance has been particularly offensive and clearly deliberate, so, as an attorney, he should be aware of the limitations of his office. Beginning with that shameless meeting ambush in the Oval Office, Vance has been downright uncivilized. Any educated individual, even one with the educational level of Trump, and in particular, an attorney, should be aware of protocol. That protocol mandates that at a summit meeting of presidents, the vice president of one of the sides, if present, should remain silent, particularly where that side hosts the meeting. Perhaps Vance feels that Trump is too primitive and poorly educated to hold his own.

To borrow a term from those who, when not possessing an argument or any evidence, often refer to common sense yet possess none of their own. Aside from the obvious protocol, that is common courtesy. At the meeting, Vance went not only beyond what was expected, but additionally rudely shouted over the White House guest. No one but President Zelensky spoke from the Ukrainian side.

When Trump chose Vance as his running mate, many, including me, wondered why. Ohio was pretty red. I finally understood that he was chosen for two reasons: he was certainly a groveller, entirely based on self-aggrandizement, which Trump appreciates very much. Secondly, he was a security guard. Having Vance next in command, no American patriot would try to remove Trump from office. Vance is, in fact, the greater of two evils, though not as sophisticated in mendacity as Trump and so much less threatening.

There is a third member of this evil triangle, all visibly onstage during the State of the Union as a warning, who happens to be third in command. Mike Johnson as Speaker of the House is a travesty, having neither the skill nor experience to run the House of Representatives.

Vance was in his first term as Senator. Johnson had two completed terms as a congressman when he was elected Speaker. Neither had any legislative accomplishments on their resumes. Good fortune and sycophancy have been the motor for their rise to power, and certainly no one, not even the crazy MAGAs, would want them leading the country. I suppose that their expertise in politics is greater than that of Trump before his election in 2016.

This is an old methodology for autocratic rule. Surround yourself with largely unknown weaklings, and your dominance is assured. Putin has always done that. So did Josef Stalin. This happens in the Mafia as well. Trump is following that script.

March 9, 2025

A Travesty of a Deal

The alleged master of deal-making has been exposed once again. The purported writer of 'The Art of the Deal', six times bankrupt, has been proven to be inept. KGB Colonel Vladimir Putin, whose negotiating skills were honed in the Soviet and Russian secret service as well as by his experience as a dictator and killer for more than twenty years, certainly not a negotiating master, has shown himself far superior to his American pupil and perhaps Soviet underling. Putin accepted none of the terms of the proposed ceasefire, instead proposing his own terms of mutual restraint on the energy infrastructure, which benefits only Russia. Ukraine's main targets are the Russian energy grid extending deep into Russian territory.

After an apparent two and one-half hours, the pseudo master walked away, characterizing the negotiations as productive. Sure, productive to Russia, but Ukraine cannot agree to these terms. There are Ukrainian children in Russian captivity. Russia will continue to target civilians, women and children, hospitals, and maternity wards with one difference. Putin believes that Russia will now be considered the side that offered the olive branch.

Donald Trump is not adept at either deal-making or remembering historical events and innumerable personal mistakes. He has stated on many occasions that if he were president at the time, the Russian aggression against Ukraine would not have occurred. The only thing that he seems to remember about the war and his first term is that he authorized sending Javelin anti-tank weapons. Naturally, he does not accord any appropriation credit to Congress on this account.

He also does not remember such glaring errors of commission and omission which took place during his first term: in July 2018 he met with Putin in Helsinki and proceeded to side with Putin against American intelligence; a ceasefire between Ukraine and Russia which was brokered in Paris in December 2019 which Russia breached almost immediately with no reaction from the Trump White House; that the 'disastrous' American withdrawal from Afghanistan was negotiated by his administration not with the legitimate government of Afghanistan, but rather with the Taliban. The implementation of that withdrawal could not go smoothly. Afghanistan today is back where it was before the American incursion. Yet Trump considers all of these events as "winning."

We are roughly at the 60-day point of Trump's newest term. So far, he has been enjoined in his activities more than 80% of the time by the courts, the streets of America are overflowing with demonstrators, his approval rating is well below 50% and the stock market is in shambles. His promise to bring peace to Ukraine is nowhere to be found. Few presidents have had a more depressing beginning.

The reason why Trump goes on, even boastfully and arrogantly, is because he is deranged. His supporters have attributed a derangement syndrome to his opponents, but there is no doubt that their hero is the one who is deranged.

There is no possibility that Trump will recover or recognize his affliction. He is to be 79 years old this year, and his mind is not getting any sharper. Nor are his delusions about to abate. The world knows this.

Ukraine's behavior in this regard should be to play along, encouraging American military support, intelligence sharing, European enhanced support, and building up its own military prowess. There is no point in confronting Trump.

America, on the other hand, has to work overtime to rid America of this not only affliction, but inherent evil. The more Americans recognize the evil within, the more rapidly they will remove the cancer. Donald Trump is both sick and evil. Fortunately, he is not a king. He can be checked by the other two branches of government if they are willing to do their Constitutional duty, the media, and most importantly, the American people. Democracy relies upon the people to right their own wrongs. Resistance is the remedy. It takes many forms. That process is already in the works. It simply requires more participants.

March 20, 2025

A Gracious Moment

President Zelensky faces a very challenging conundrum. He either plays along with America's President Trump or he loses American military support and intelligence sharing. Or he can be straightforward and direct and rely strictly on the Europeans, who are stepping up in their support and increasing their capability.

Zelensky has told Trump many times that Putin does not want peace and that he has breached numerous ceasefires even during Trump's prior term. Trump feigns amnesia, or is it ignorance? European leaders have confirmed that opinion on many occasions. Trump denies the obvious, alluding to some long-term relationship with Putin, perhaps in the KGB.

Trump insists that he wants to stop the killing. Judging by Trump's indiscriminate support for Israel's Prime Minister Netanyahu and Netanyahu's approach to killing Palestinian women and children, killing is the least of Trump's concerns. More than 50,000 Palestinian civilians have been killed in Gaza, mostly civilians. Trump's concern for the Palestinian people is belied by his own initiative of their ethnic cleansing in Gaza.

Europe is on the doorstep of current and future Russian aggression and has a vested interest in Ukraine and certainly a more reliable ally than MAGA America. But why relinquish long-term American support even though a primitive, skinned narcissist is in charge temporarily?

Zelensky is an intelligent man, as he has shown over and over. Unfortunately, the American man in the White House is a neanderthal surrounded by sycophants of his own choosing. His main envoy on the Middle East and Ukraine issues appear to be even worse. Trump's friend Steven Witkloff recently applauded Putin's religious devotion, stating that Putin actually went to Church and prayed for the health and safety of Donald Trump after his assassination attempt.

"Russian strongman Vladimir Putin claims he rushed over to his local church and prayed to God for President Trump's safety after he was nearly assassinated at a rally in Butler, Pa., last July."

Witkoff met with Putin last week while trying to advance peace talks with Moscow, and the Russian leader described Trump as a 'personal friend,' according to the special envoy.

And so, Putin prays for Trump, and we can assume, perhaps, that Trump prays for Putin, although the truth is entirely different. Neither of them has prayed in the last fifty years.

Witkoff has also manifested ignorance on Ukraine's geography, referring to the four regions that Ukraine has to give up as Crimea, Donbas, and Luhansk, proving once again that just because you are a billionaire in real estate does not mean that you are well-informed or have done your homework.

But clearly, Ukraine is in a precarious situation. Its people, including women and children, are dying. Yet, its President has to humor and appease an ill-elected fraud, retain a semblance of normality because of America's wealth and military capacity.

But Ukraine is not alone. Europe and Canada have recognized the immediate problem, and they understand that, at least for the time being, it needs to be addressed gingerly. America cannot be treated as an outcast or an enemy. It has to be treated as a friend and shown respect despite the fact that it deserves none currently.

My wife and I traveled to Canada last week. We felt compelled to apologize to great applause among Canadian Ukrainians for the 'idiot in the White House.' Frankly, I made that reference to both Canadian and American border control. I could not have passed both controls more expeditiously. This assured me that the circus is only a matter of time, and with each passing day, fewer are taking Trump seriously. Unfortunately, much harm has been done, including the killing of innocents.

I have been informed that some intelligence circles consider Trump's mediation of peace a futile exercise geared to present his case for a future Nobel Peace Prize. In the meantime, Vladimir Putin humors Trump by delivering a portrait of Trump to Trump's special envoy. Steven Dummkopf opines, 'A gracious moment.'

March 25, 2025

Exceptionalism

When Russia's full-scale aggression into Ukraine began on February 24, 2022, much of the world stood by, anticipating a disastrous albeit brief conclusion. Russia attacked from many sides, including from Belarus, directed at Kyiv itself. That part of the invasion was thwarted because of the heroics of Ukrainian forces, less than one hundred miles from Kyiv in Mezhyhirya. A Russian tank did reach the City of Kyiv, where it was destroyed. The Russian air attack was stymied, and the caravan of tanks was stalled. The latter became easy targets for Ukrainian artillery, American Javelins in particular, as they were mired in the early Spring mud.

In fact, most military experts predicted Russian overwhelming superiority in the air and on the sea. Ukraine had no fighter jets or drones to speak of. The jets it had were antiquated Soviet models, and the drones had been acquired from Turkey. Those Turkish Bakhtiyar drones proved to be very effective. But on the Black Sea, Ukrainian vessels were captive in the ports of Crimea under Russian occupation.

To date, precisely in those two areas in the air and on the sea, Ukrainians have proven to be exceptional.

Since 2022, Ukrainian-made drones in the air and on the sea have enabled Ukraine to survive. Russia is limited now to the eastern portion of the Black Sea and ground incursions in four regions of Eastern Ukraine. Ukrainian water drones have inflicted major damage on the Russian fleet. Ukrainian-made air drones and missiles have reached as far into Russian territory as the City of Kazan in Tatarstan and Moscow itself. Each is more than 500 kilometers from the Ukrainian line.

Russian missiles and drones continue to attack power grids and civilian sites throughout Ukraine, killing innocent men, women, and children, targeting hospitals and maternity wards. Still, there is little danger that any of these locations will be invaded by the aggressors.

Ironically, Ukrainian exceptionalism in courage and particularly drone manufacture wherewithal has been spurred by American disingenuity and dilatory tactics even under President Biden. The first F-16s arrived in Ukraine in mid-2024, during the third year of the war, and not from the United States but from its allies. Under Trump, that support has been practically non-existent.

There are only five American Patriot missile systems in Ukraine. These systems are the most effective defensive systems in Ukraine, but there are very few of them. There are twelve such systems sitting idly at a NATO base in the Polish city of Rzeszów. There may be more. I myself saw the twelve. Their transfer to Ukraine is not imminent, even though they have been earmarked for Ukraine for almost one year.

So what's the point? The lack of American exceptionalism in aiding Ukraine has spurred Ukrainian exceptionalism so that today, about 60% of all weapons used by the Ukrainian forces are produced by Ukraine itself. Today, Europe is supplying almost 70% of all aid to Ukraine. No one can be certain of what is supplied by America.

Ukraine's President Zelensky, during his ambush in the Oval Office, profusely thanked the United States for its support. Nevertheless, both ungracious hosts, Trump and Vance, accused Zelensky of being ungrateful and disrespectful. All of Europe sided with Zelensky. Theories have abounded about Trump's alliance, agency, and even familial relations with Putin.

Ukraine has accepted the terms of an American-mediated ceasefire. Russia has declined. Trump has threatened new sanctions against Russian oil by imposing an additional tariff on those countries that continue to buy Russian oil, including banning their imports. Frankly, I don't know what that means since Trump has threatened tariffs on every country, friend and foe alike. In the case of China, I doubt that there will be Chinese products in the United States. What will happen to Ivanka's licenses and trademarks in China?

American exceptionalism has always been a myth. Under Trump, it has proven to be a brazen lie. Resistance has come and will continue to grow, and not only at the ballot box. The irony is that in the midst of all that is happening, including a recession in the American economy, Trump is "threatening" a third term. There are checks provided in the Constitution. Trump is also 78 years old. Perhaps the best check will come from the Almighty. We can only pray.

April 2, 2025

Resistance in America - Resistance in Ukraine

Cape May Courthouse is a mid-sized town in the southern part of New Jersey by the shore, some 150 miles south of New York City. It is the government hub of Cape May County, where the courts and government offices are located. In recent history, it is generally acknowledged to be a Republican country and even MAGA.

On Saturday, April 5, 2025, a crowd of close to 1000 people gathered on Route 9 near the corner of Mechanic Street in Cape May Courthouse. They held flags and signs. The flags were American and, perhaps surprisingly, Ukrainian. The signs read 'Dump Trump', 'Dump Van Drew', 'We will defend Democracy', 'No Tyranny', 'Save Medicare and Social Security', and even 'Give me liberty or give me death'.

I mingled in the crowd, urging them on with a bit of a cynical exhortation, 'It's about time!' and spoke to two of the protesters who displayed Ukrainian flags. I simply asked whether they were Ukrainian. In both cases, they said "no" but added 'we love Ukraine', 'Ukrainians are protecting us and the whole world from tyranny.' I was obviously very proud and acknowledged my Ukrainian background. They showered me with accolades about the courage of the Ukrainian people and how the entire world owes them a debt of gratitude.

Cape May County went for Donald Trump in the last presidential election by what is considered a landslide, 59% to 41%. Jeff van Drew, the congressman from the 2nd congressional district of New Jersey, which includes Cape May County, won by 58% to 42% over his Democratic challenger. As noted, he was an object of disdain as well.

Van Drew has never voted in support of aid to Ukraine and is considered one of the more sycophantic members of Congress. I had on one occasion visited his lone office in New Jersey. Since then, I have written to him many times with only proforma replies. I have inquired about a town hall meeting with no response. He is also an unprincipled renegade, having once been a Democrat similar to his hero, Trump. To be fair, I should not criticize him for that since I am now a registered Republican in his district, intent on making his life miserable.

I stepped into a public library located some two hundred feet from the corner where many of the protesters had congregated. As I reached for The New York Times, I said to myself, 'Let's see what else the idiot did.' Frankly, I often vocalize my thoughts. It gets more frequent with age. A man of roughly my age asked to whom I was referring. He then acknowledged that he had been a Trump supporter, and while he was not participating in the protest, he was proud to be an American because here people can protest. I submitted to him that there are protests in authoritarian countries like Turkey against the dictatorial President Erdogan, so America is not that exceptional.

After a brief chat, including my lesson on the level of Trump's education and the nefarious background of both Fred and Donald in New York City real estate, he admitted that he was watching the protest and was not quite sure where he stood at this time. He did confess that Trump's first 75 days have concerned him. He also acknowledged that his own wife and daughter were among the protesters.

Protests like this one are taking place not only all over America, but all over the world. Loss of jobs, inflation due to rising tariffs, a stock market crash because of all of this, and the uncertainty in the future have made Donald Trump a global and national pariah. Bad economic policies, arrogance, circumventing the Constitution, and the other branches of government have made Trump the least popular American president of the modern era. Resistance to tyranny is a formula that has been in use for centuries. For me, unlike most Americans who have been hit greatly by essentially evil (this cannot be only stupid) Trump economics, there is much, even more important solace. The American people have not forgotten and continue to support and even applaud Ukraine and the Ukrainian people.

April 5, 2025

The Art of the Deal (with a terrorist state)

An American citizen of Russian descent and citizenship, which is strange since the U.S. Constitution does not provide for dual citizenship except by treaty with individual countries. On whatever grounds, but in all likelihood moral ones, she opposed the Russian aggression in Ukraine, which was totally unprovoked and included the murder of innocent civilians, including the kidnapping of children. She contributed a symbolic $51 towards humanitarian aid for Ukraine through an American not-for-profit.

She then decided to visit her grandmother in Yekaterinburg, Russia. She was arrested for treason and sentenced to 12 years. She pleaded guilty to the charge upon the advice of Russian counsel, since only convicted prisoners are swapped. She appealed the sentence, but it was upheld.

About one year later, through the efforts of Russia's President Putin and his friend, the American president now sitting in the White House, she was swapped in a prisoner exchange for a Russian-German smuggler of military components from the United States to Russia, essentially a Russian spy. Russia does not have a legitimate legal system, but the one it does have seems to work for the state very well, although it has nothing to do with the rule of law.

A few words about the prisoner released by the United States. His name is Arthur Petrov. He is a Russian citizen. On August 9, 2024, the Associated Press reported:

"Arthur Petrov, 33, made a brief appearance in Manhattan federal court, where he agreed to remain detained. He was arrested last August in Cyprus at the request of the United States and was extradited on Thursday. Attorney Michael Arthus, Petrov's court-appointed lawyer, declined to comment on numerous charges brought against his client, including multiple conspiracy counts and smuggling goods crimes. The charges collectively carry a potential penalty of over 150 years in prison."

The lack of moral equivalence of the two political prisoners is stark. Nevertheless, the man in the White House is lauded by his supporters for the art of the deal. This is normal in today's America. America has gone rogue or simply stupid. The man himself becomes even more full of himself, boastful of yet another 'perfect' deal. To have a better understanding of how bizarre this was, some distinction is necessary. The woman was not a political prisoner. She was a kidnapped hostage. America not only negotiates with terrorists and hostage takers but actively strives to enhance relations with them. This paints a clearer picture. Obviously, buoyed by his 'perfect' deal in this matter, Trump sent his special envoy, Steve Witkoff, to meet once again with Vladimir Putin, the leader of a terrorist state.

RT (Russia Today) reported on April 11. 2025:

"'The discussions between Russian President Vladimir Putin and White House special envoy Steve Witkoff on Friday involved aspects of the settlement of the Ukraine conflict,' the Kremlin has announced, declining to provide further details. Witkoff visited Russia on Friday and met with Putin in St. Petersburg. The meeting lasted over four hours, and the content of the talks has been largely kept under wraps by Moscow and Washington. However, White House Press Secretary Karoline Leavitt addressed the issue during a press briefing earlier in the day when asked by a reporter about the purpose of Witkoff's visit to Russia. According to Leavitt, the visit was aimed at facilitating direct US communications with the Kremlin as part of a broader effort to negotiate a ceasefire and eventual peace agreement in the Ukraine conflict.

The Trump administration faced growing internal divisions this week after Witkoff allegedly proposed a ceasefire plan that would recognize Russian control over four eastern regions claimed by both Moscow and Kiev (sic-ASL), Reuters reported on Friday, citing anonymous sources. During a White House meeting with President Donald Trump last week, Witkoff argued that recognizing Russian ownership of Lugansk, (sic-ASL) Donetsk, Zaporozhye, and Kherson was the swiftest path to halting the war, the outlet's sources said. General Keith Kellogg, Trump's Ukraine envoy, reportedly pushed back, stressing Ukraine would not accept full territorial concessions. (ASL - Kellogg went on to carve up Ukraine into zones like Germany after World War 2).

The meeting reportedly concluded without a decision from Trump, who has repeatedly said he wants to broker a ceasefire by May. Witkoff subsequently traveled to Russia on Friday for talks with Putin. The episode has deepened rifts within the Trump administration, as officials debate how to resolve the Ukraine conflict, Reuters wrote. Witkoff's approach, previously outlined in a March interview with Tucker Carlson, has reportedly alarmed both Republican lawmakers and US allies. 'They're Russian-speaking,' Witkoff told Carlson of the eastern territories. 'There have been referendums (ASL - Russian held at the point of a gun) where the overwhelming majority of the people have indicated that they want to be under Russian rule.' Several Republicans reportedly contacted National Security Adviser Mike Waltz and Secretary of State Marco Rubio to raise concerns about Witkoff's stance, criticizing him for echoing Russian rhetoric. Despite criticism, Witkoff retains strong backing from Trump and some administration officials. Waltz praised his efforts, citing his business background and recent diplomatic activity, including securing the release of US citizen Marc Fogel from Russia."

Trump's personal envoys Witkoff and Kellogg continue to echo Russian rhetoric. These are Trumpian American proposals that could be the basis for another 'perfect' deal. In fact, they are echoes of Russian diktats. In the now-famous words of the Greenlanders, Make America Go Away (MAGA), Ukraine and the entire democratic world should echo those words. The dealmaker is evil and stupidity incarnate. That's what makes him so arrogant.

During this Easter Holy Week, let us pray, please, God, make Trump and America go away.

April 12, 2025

From Genocide to Genocide

On Sunday, April 13, 2025, the world's media, including the leading American network CNN, reported:

"Russian missiles hit residents who were gathering for a Sunday church service in the city of Sumy in northeastern Ukraine, killing at least 34 people in the largest attack of the year. According to the State Emergency Service of Ukraine, among the dozens killed in the strikes on the city center were two children, and 117 people were injured." A bus carrying passengers returning from a service was also hit, killing everyone on board. The bus was transporting people from a Palm Sunday service.

Although this news story was not much different from other news stories about Moscow's attacks on Ukraine during the war, this strike probably caught the attention of world opinion a little more than others, perhaps due to the number of victims and also the ambiguity. The enemy simply destroyed the Ukrainian population without a specific military strategy.

On February 24, 2022, Russian troops invaded Ukraine from many sides. Many Russian leaders, including the Primates of the Russian Orthodox Church and individuals from the Kremlin, voiced the position that the purpose of this invasion was to 'wipe Ukraine off the face of the earth.' This completely contradicted the instructions given, saying that we were going to protect the Russian-speaking population of the eastern lands of Ukraine. By the way, this is exactly the lie that the Kremlin tried to sell to the world at the International Court of Justice in Gaza.

This criminal intention to 'wipe Ukraine off the face of the earth' is the intention of Genocide, as outlined in the 'UN Convention on the Prevention and Punishment of the Crime of Genocide.'

Russia's actions in Ukraine over the past three or so years strongly confirm this intention. Russia has targeted its artillery, missiles, and drones both at civilians, including women and children, and at military and strategic targets. When Russia is accused of attacking civilians, it is simply lying. Today, almost no one believes the Russian explanations. This is very clear on the screens of the United Nations Security Council meetings, although the UNSC is helpless due to the Kremlin's illegitimate veto.

For more than three years, the International Court of Justice has been considering a lawsuit filed by Ukraine two days after the invasion, alleging Russia's attempted Genocide in Ukraine. In March 2022, a preliminary injunction was issued against Russia to stop the invasion, which Russia has not only ignored but has also clearly done so in word and deed. The Kremlin has declared that it will not comply with the court's preliminary injunction. The Kremlin's behavior and proclamations were brazen evidence of the component crime of Genocide, that is, intent.

In the margins, perhaps, one should make a remark about the weakness of the very instances of international law. The ICC is acting very slowly, despite the fact that people are dying and Moscow is increasing its brutality. The preventive measure is not being implemented, and the Kremlin even publicly condones it. Unfortunately, this is evidence of the weak evolution of modern international law and institutions. The world is far from the rule of law or justice, even when it comes to the highest crime - Genocide.

Even China has refrained from demonstrating support for Russia, although it strengthens Moscow by trading and purchasing Moscow's oil. Only Iran and North Korea, global pariahs, and countries dependent on Moscow in Africa and Central and South America have sided with Russia. The biggest surprise is Israel, which often votes against Ukraine in international forums. This is already a matter of immoral opportunistic politics.

Support for Ukraine is global, morally and in words, although not enough in practice. The aid was mostly inadequate and delayed, supposedly so that Ukraine would not perish but would not win. This was until the day of the inauguration of the new US President.

The glaring lack of support has arisen recently from the United States and its new President Donald J. Trump, who, having declared himself a friend of the criminal Vladimir Putin, sentenced by the International Criminal Court, offered himself as a mediator, often demonstrating a lack of understanding of the seriousness of the Moscow invasion, as well as sympathy for the same authoritarian leader of the aggressor state.

Ninety years ago, in the territory of modern Ukraine, Russia, acting under the guise of the Union of Soviet Socialist Republics, introduced a program of collectivization of land and punishment of Ukrainian farmers, which led to the death of an estimated 7-10 million Ukrainians from starvation, a third of whom were children. Although collectivization was supposedly an economic program spread throughout the USSR, part of it, which included severe punishments, the seizure of grain and produce, and the closing of borders, was limited to Ukrainian territory and parts of Russia with a concentration of Ukrainians, such as the Kuban (formerly Ukrainian lands). Stalin's correspondence with Kaganovich, the Five Ears of Wheat Law, and directives closing the borders of Ukraine and the Kuban indicate that the starvation program was directed against Ukrainians.

This Holodomor of the Ukrainian farmer was preceded by a Kremlin police crackdown on Ukrainian intelligentsia, a show trial in Kharkov, the capital of Soviet Ukraine, and the liquidation of the Ukrainian Autocephalous Orthodox Church, followed by further repressions and murders in the Yezhov region and the liquidation of the Ukrainian Greek Catholic Church in 1945, the arrests of hierarchs and clergy, and their deportation to Siberia when the Soviets occupied Western Ukraine.

Raphael Lemkin, a Jew, was born in Poland and educated as a lawyer at the Ukrainian National University in Lviv. He is often called the father of the UN Genocide Convention. He was the drafter of the Convention and often referred to the famine of Ukrainians in 1932-33 as the quintessence of the meaning of genocide. He published an article about this genocide. The Holocaust was also on his mind. He made sure that the definition of Genocide in the Convention included the words "in time of war or in time of peace" so that it was clear that the Holodomor fit the definition of the Convention. The Jewish Holocaust was during a time of war, and the Holodomor was in a time of peace, but not for Ukrainians.

Because it was even the founder and neighbor of Muscovy, and also with a much longer history of statehood and culture (Kyiv was founded in the 18th century, the Kievan state in the 9th, Moscow was founded in the 12th, and the Muscovite state became independent only in the 15th century), which aroused Muscovite vanity and envy, even its name and religion were stolen or appropriated. Ukraine and Ukrainians have been victims of Muscovy's cruelty for centuries. The Russian Empire was established by Peter I, taking the name of Kyivan Rus.

Over the past 100 years, two very brutal political, police, and military attempts at genocide of Ukraine and Ukrainians by the Muscovites have taken place or are taking place. Attempts at cultural genocide have been rampant for over 300 years, starting from the destruction of Baturyn in 1708. Russia replaced the Ukrainian language with its own language and banned Ukrainian in its empire, used its state religion as a weapon to destroy religion in Ukraine, destroyed the Zaporizhian Sich, introduced serfdom and, after the restoration of Ukrainian statehood, constantly interfered in Ukraine's internal affairs, including elections, at one time even successfully involving its own agent to become the president of Ukraine, similar to Lukashenko in Belarus.

Ukrainians, unlike Belarusians, resisted these Russian methods through national revolutions and today through the nationwide defense of their country and culture. They say that every Ukrainian grandmother has her role and Molotov cocktail, so Ukraine is invincible, but the war will continue until the collapse of the Russian Empire and its dismemberment into independent states of the peoples who are today prisoners in it.

It is important to note that although Ukraine and Ukrainians managed to gain a certain level of sympathy from the democratic world in both cases of attempted genocide, this sympathy lacked real support. In 1933, at the height of the Holodomor, America, under the leadership of President Franklin Delano Roosevelt, ironically, formally recognized the USSR as a legitimate state and exchanged diplomats. Attempts by the Ukrainian-American community to seek the intercession of the President's wife, Eleanor, were in vain. The American media, including The New York Times, was largely silent and even echoed the Soviet line. Its notorious lead reporter, Walter Duranty, coined the Stalinist mantra of collectivization, saying, "You have to break a few eggs to make an omelet."

Today, following the tragedy in Sumy, retired General Keith Kellogg, the problematic (who wants to divide Ukraine into zones) special envoy of US President Trump to Ukraine and Russia, posted on social media: "Today's attack by Russian forces on civilian targets in Sumy on Palm Sunday crosses all lines of decency. There are dozens of civilians killed and wounded." Kellogg, drawing on his military experience, unequivocally stated that the Russians were clearly targeting civilians.

Attacks on civilians during wartime are a war crime. In the context of many statements by Moscow leaders, including clergy and their hierarchs, about the merging of Ukraine off the face of the earth, this is also an element of the crime of genocide.

President of Ukraine Volodymyr Zelensky stressed regarding the Sumy tragedy: "It is very important for everyone in the world not to be silent, not to remain indifferent. Russian strikes deserve only condemnation. Pressure is needed on Russia to end the war and guarantee the safety of people."

While other Western leaders have made strong statements against Russia over the brutal attack, which once again targeted unarmed civilians, US President Trump made a cool statement aboard Air Force One, the US presidential plane, when a reporter asked him about the attack: "I think it was terrible, and I was told they made a mistake. But I think it's terrible. I think the whole war is terrible."

The only hope is that the world today is very different from 1932-33, because the Muscovites are still the same murderers they were. Unfortunately, the US President seems to be absent from the civilized democratic world and has gone over to the enemy.

April 15, 2025

List of sources used:

Starosolsky, Vladimir, Theory of the Nation, U. Starosolskaya. 1991B New York,

Zapisnik Sovarystva im. Shevchenko

Convention of the League of Nations

ungeneva.org/en/about/league-of -nations/overview

Charter of the United Nations

un.org/en/about-us/un-charter

United Nations, Statement by the Secretary-General to the 16th BRICS Summit, 24 October 2024

International Court of Justice

icj-cij.org

International Criminal Court: Russia: International Criminal Court issues arrest warrant against Putin, United Nations Novygy, 17 March 2023

International Court of Justice, Ukraine v. Russian Federation, Press Release, 31 January 2025

"On the Protection of Property of State-Owned Enterprises, Collective Farms and Cooperatives and the Strengthening of Public (Socialist) Property", 7 August 1932

Stalin and Kaganovich. Correspondence 1931 - 1936. - M., 2001. - P. 273, 274).

August 11, 1932

Resolution of the Central Committee of the All-Union Communist Party (Bolsheviks) and the Council of People's Commissars of the USSR on the prohibition of the departure of starving peasants of the Kuban and Ukraine to Russia and Belarus, January 22, 1933

The Tragedy of the Soviet Village. Collectivization and Dekulakization. 1927 - 1939. - M., 2001. - T.3. 1930 - 1933. - P. 634, 635.

The America of Trump, Vance, Little Marco, and Steve Witkoff

It has been suggested by some, both Catholics and non-Catholics, that the Holy Father succumbed to a cerebral hemorrhage on the Monday morning after Easter because he had been visited by the Devil himself on the day before. That diabolical apparition was the Vice President of the United States, J.D. Vance. While this seems far-fetched, it may be appropriate to note that Jesus Christ, himself as a human being, was persecuted by Satan while he prayed for forty days in the desert.

That same day of the Holy Father's demise, VP Vance's boss instructed his underlings to submit an ultimatum to Ukraine. Vance and Little Marco both vocalized that the Russian diktat, now in the form of a Trump peace plan: Surrender to Russia. Throughout all of this, Russia's assault on Ukraine has not abated. It has become even more severe not only in terms of the number of missiles and drones, but also in terms of the targets, which have become almost exclusively residential civilians. Recent massacres in Kryvyi Rih, Sumy, Odesa, and most recently Kyiv, with twelve civilian deaths, have been Russia's response to so-called peace efforts.

When criticized for demanding concessions from Ukraine only but not Russia, Trump once again displayed both his ignorance of the matter at hand and his lack of respect for Ukraine by stating that Russia could have taken all of Ukraine's territory. The old saying has been on full display before the global community that if Ukraine has a friend like the United States, it does not need enemies. America has completely gone over to the other side. Russia's crimes go unpunished. Perhaps because Trump is accustomed to his own crimes going unpunished.

On Thursday, The Wall Street Journal published an editorial somewhat critical of Trump's ultimatum to Ukraine, and suggesting that Trump was wrong to do so since it would be viewed by the rest of the democratic world as a loss for American leadership. The morality of attempting to pressure and even punish the victim while benefiting the aggressor, which should embolden other aggressors, was marginalized by the Journal. The following day, the Wall Street Journal published a more even editorial and ended by stressing that Trump's one-sided treatment of Ukraine in favor of Russia would tarnish Trump's legacy. The moral imperative was absent once again. That was disappointing but understandable given the Journal's ownership and proclivity.

So, what is Ukraine to do? Certainly not accept the joint Russian-American ultimatum. President Zelensky may continue his tireless diplomacy because hope springs eternal. The rest of the world should, at the very least, express its disappointment and even shun Trump and America. A most telling reality of Trump's global credibility was when Trump stated recently that America and China were in trade talks, and China called that fake news; the majority of the world believed China and not the American president. Further defending his economy, Trump stated that the price of eggs had decreased by 87%. That would mean that the price of a dozen eggs in America is currently 50 cents. He went further to underscore that the price of gasoline is less than $2.00 per gallon. Not a single one of the 50 states enjoys that price.

Resistance is the only solution. Many Americans have taken to the streets with protests. Ukrainian Americans have been largely remiss in this regard, and yet they have the most to lose. The man in the White House is no longer simply a liar and a buffoon. He is the devil himself. His acolytes are pure evil. As a result, America today is evil. It is a pariah, pretty much despised by the entire world. Foreign tourists are shunning America. American products are boycotted. No country in the civilized democratic world respects America.

Only Americans can undo what they have done. This is truly a tragedy because the 'land of the free and the home of the brave' has become a travesty, and the American people are responsible.

Contributing in part to that travesty, the Ukrainian American community has either not been focused on the real problem or worse has appealed to Trump's psychoses (vanity, narcissism, mendacity). Immediately following the shameless display of American lack of hospitality and even ugliness towards President Zelensky at the White House, the Ukrainian American community staged a rally at the Lincoln Memorial in Washington, D.C., with no focus aimed against Trump, the major perpetrator. That rally, of course, received no media attention. Another rally held in New York City at Astor Place, of all venues, chanted "Thank you, USA." For what? For selling out Ukraine. Granted, some Ukrainian American shills for Trump, including several clergy, have been remorseful, but with no substance.

The people in Ukraine live under the illusion that Ukrainian Americans are both sophisticated and well-intentioned. Unfortunately, nothing can be further from the truth.

My message to good Americans, including some good Ukrainian-Americans: it's really time to join the resistance against the evil that has permeated America today.

April 25, 2025

The Case for Ukrainian Crimea

One of the ridicules that Trump has suffered since he entered political life has been, "How do you know when Trump is lying? His lips are moving."

In many instances, the lying is a result of ignorance. Trump watches television, but he does not read much and very often assumes the credibility and accuracy of his last adviser. Bear in mind that his advisers are chosen by him. Essentially based on fealty. Assuming that the advisor is someone as poorly versed in world politics as Steve Witkoff, it's no wonder that Trump has no clue about Crimea.

His arguments for suggesting American recognition of Crimea as a part of Russia are two-fold: Crimea has historically been Russia, and Ukraine gave away Crimea to Russia in 2014. Both arguments are specious. Trump is not simply lying, as is his norm, because frankly, he has no reason to know the history of Crimea except that presidents of important countries should learn the facts before speaking.

Crimea historically is neither Russian nor Ukrainian. Russia's initial connection to Crimea took place only under Czarina Catherine II of Russia, who simply conquered it in 1783, like most of the territory of today's Russian Federation. Until that date, there was no Russia-Crimea connection. Today's RF is an amalgam of militarily conquered territory.

Kyiv's connection with Crimea is significantly older, and more benign, in fact dating back to the IX century based on trade. The Kyivan Prince Volodymyr, who baptized the people of Kyiv and the surrounding areas in 988, was himself baptized in Chersonesos, originally a Greek colony, then belonging to the Byzantine empire. Chersonesos (Sevastopol) is in Crimea.

Until the Russian invasion of 1783, it belonged to the Mongol Golden Horde, then the Ottoman Empire, and ultimately the Crimean Khanate.

By 1975, at the time of the Helsinki Accords, which is considered the timeline for the determination of borders, Crimea was a part of the Ukrainian Soviet Socialist Republic. And so it was in 1991 when the Ukrainian SSR became Ukraine, and the Russian Soviet Socialist Republic became the Russian Federation.

In December 1994, the Russian Federation provided security assurances to Ukraine, including the inviolability of borders pursuant to the Budapest Memorandum, when Ukraine voluntarily gave up its nuclear arsenal. In 1997, Ukraine and the RF signed a friendship treaty, which further recognized existing borders.

Vladimir Putin came to power as President of Russia, succeeding Boris Yeltsin in 2000. In the first few years, he worked to crush the Chechen uprising in the RF. But by 2004, he turned his attention to Ukraine by manipulating presidential elections to elect his surrogate, Viktor Yanukovich. The Ukrainian people responded with a revolution (the Orange Revolution). Yanukovich was out.

Putin had to relinquish power in the RF briefly to his surrogate (Medvedev), but worked to rehabilitate Yanukovich in Ukraine, setting the stage for the next election in 2010. Putin managed to insert his surrogate, Victor Yanukovich, as Ukraine's president in February 2010, not unlike Lukashenka in Belarus. If there was any doubt as to Yanukovich's allegiance, that was clarified within two months. In April 2010, Yanukovich, as President of Ukraine, extended Russia's fleet lease in Sevastopol, Crimea, for an additional twenty-five years.

Yanukovich continued to serve his master well. In 2013, he declined Ukraine's accession to the European Union. This resulted in a second revolution (Revolution of Dignity). Yanukovich was forced to flee Kyiv. However, by that time, he had managed to deplete the Ukrainian military.

In February 2014, when Russia surreptitiously took over Crimea with 'little green men with no insignia,' Ukraine had only six thousand able men in its military. There was no way for Ukraine to fight back. Additionally, President Obama told the Ukrainians that there would be no Western support.

Russia's war against Ukraine began not in 2014. It began in 2004. Actually, it never stopped since the XVII century. I certainly do not expect Donald J. Trump, with a bachelor's degree in real estate, to know or understand the historical facts. That would require some serious reading. Bloviating requires less.

April 26, 2025

The Next One Hundred Days

Apparently, Trump's next one hundred days are beginning much better than the first. Granted, it's a very low bar. On Wednesday, April 30, Ukraine and America signed something that is akin to an agreement. The Ukrainian side appeared encouraged.

"Truly, this is a strategic deal for the creation of an investment partner fund," said Prime Minister Denys Shmyhal. "This is truly an equal and good international deal on joint investment in the development and restoration of Ukraine between the governments of the United States and Ukraine."

Ukraine's economy minister, Yulia Svyrydenko, flew to Washington on Wednesday to help finalize the deal.

"Together with the United States, we are creating the Fund that will attract global investment to our country," she said in a post on X after the signing.

"This agreement signals clearly to Russia that the Trump Administration is committed to a peace process centered on a free, sovereign, and prosperous Ukraine over the long term," Treasury Secretary Scott Bessent said in a press release. "President Trump envisioned this partnership between the American people and the Ukrainian people to show both sides' commitment to lasting peace and prosperity in Ukraine. And to be clear, no state or person who financed or supplied the Russian war machine will be allowed to benefit from the reconstruction of Ukraine."

Whatever the reading or the details of the agreement, Ukraine and the United States are now jointly concerned about the future of Ukraine. In order to protect its investment, America has to supply arms and share intelligence. Furthermore, inasmuch as Russia is the aggressor, it is the only force that may interfere in this mutually beneficial relationship; Russia now becomes potentially an enemy of the United States, irrespective of the distance or the natural barriers such as the ocean.

A better or fuller understanding will come once the actual agreement is available for review. However, even for Trump, someone who has no moral compass, a vested financial interest is very significant and, frankly, the only type of interest that a 'businessman' like Trump can understand. He now has a business interest in Ukraine.

Politics is the art of the possible. Under the circumstances, this was a 'perfect' resolution of the many differences between America under Trump and Ukraine. There are even more significant or equally significant ramifications. The Senate under Republican leadership will not move to sanction countries that are trading with Russia. The price of oil, because of this and because of Trump's total disregard for the environment, will drop even further from its current mid-sixties' dollars per barrel.

Any agreement is bound to be successful when both parties are equally satisfied or dissatisfied. In this case, satisfaction will be the glue that holds this deal together.

There is so much more that has to happen in American-Ukrainian relations, but in the opinion of one skeptic and unbridled Trump critic, this is a 'perfect', to use Trump language, beginning in his second 100 days.

May 1, 2025

The Replacement of the Ugly American and Europe's Epiphany

The process for 'habemus papam' was relatively short in duration, but the election was surprising unless one had insider information, and even then. The conclave is as secretive as the word conclave (with a key) implies, with little obvious electioneering.

Anyone who suggests what Pope Leo XIV will do during his tenure is not being honest. This is not the same Catholic altar boy from Chicago. This is the spiritual leader of more than one billion people, men, women, children, old and young, of diverse political and sexual orientations. The position changes people and has almost invariably in the past.

I am a practicing Catholic, albeit a discerning or even critical one. Not everything the Pope says is dogma. Nor is it necessarily correct. Many times, the leader of the Church, because he represents diverse communities, will delve into matters that place him on the wrong side of history or even the teachings of Christ as to good and evil, with no capacity to discern. That was very often Pope Francis's problem, whether due to poor advice or his own simplicity and lack of information. The role of the Holy Father is to recognize the truth, distinguish between good and evil, and manifestly condemn evil by naming it and advocating, if not working against it.

While Pope Francis was very much sensitive to humanity and love for all of God's children, he often fell victim to political calculations that he should not have done. Because he was the Holy Father, many in the Church considered his words and deeds to be infallible, although the Church is clear that the Holy Father is infallible only in matters of faith. Unfortunately, the average person falls victim to the position. My one wish from Pope Leo XIV is that he follows his predecessor in humanity but recognizes his own human intellectual frailties.

In any event, the election of an American as Pope is symbolic for me, particularly in this day and age. America is on the verge of becoming a pariah because of the words and deeds of one man who, until the election of the new Pope, was arguably the single most important American in the world and even more important in his own mind. Now that an American is the Holy Father, Pope Leo's humanity, spirituality, and love should overcome and replace the current image of the ugly American, who is an imperialist, a predator, and yes, a felon.

Some twenty years ago, I traveled to Bulgaria to meet with the Ukrainian community as well as Bulgarian officials. By chance, I happened to meet with a Bulgarian attorney who, after being told that I was his professional counterpart from America, insisted on relaying his view of America. He said that Bulgaria is now an ally of the United States, so we should be wary. I asked why, and he replied, because Bulgarian alliances are mostly doomed. Bulgaria was an ally of the Roman Empire, the Ottoman Empire, Nazi Germany, and the Soviet Union. None of these exist today. I laughed.

In retrospect, he did foresee the demise of the American empire. Unless you live in the hills of Kentucky, from where J.D. Vance's family comes, and read nothing but the local herald, you must be aware that America today lacks respect throughout the world.

Not immediately of its own volition, but fearing a Russian exploitation of this void, the leading countries of Europe have stepped up, not only in defense of Ukraine, but in an attempt to make Europe self-sufficient and capable of defending itself. America's decline was a dark cloud, to a large degree self-formed, but there is a silver lining. This silver lining is, after all, better for Ukraine because Ukraine is an integral part of the European community in history and culture.

The recent ridiculous parody of force in Moscow was shunned by the European community, except for the prime minister of Slovakia and the president of Serbia. No one else from Europe attended. Prime Minister Fico of Slovakia has significant internal opposition in Slovakia, as does the President of Serbia. Serbia is not a member of the EU, and certainly, this escapade by its President will not help in that endeavor. Romania will be holding a second and final round of its Presidential election. The leader in the first round was a pro-Russian extremist; in fact, some consider him an agent of Russia. And then there is Viktor Orbán, Prime Minister of Hungary, whose term is long overdue.

These are all issues that Europe needs to address, but the message from Europe is that it is ready to take on the mantle of world leadership.

The message for Americans is that world leadership comes and goes. In the interim, America needs to address its own Constitutional crises.

May 10, 2025

Understanding China

The People's Republic of China is one of the most powerful and complex countries in the world. To understand even its name and essence is a major undertaking. Is it communist? No one can answer with certainty. Perhaps the best description is that it is a capitalist state under full state authoritarian control.

How it is a people's republic when democracy is non-existent is one of the conundrums of politics. What we know is that it is powerful in terms of the size of its population and economy. In fact, according to the world ranking, it is the second richest country in the world, but its population probably does not experience this wealth.

There is probably no country that does not trade with China. The indisputable fact is that its products are relatively good and also inexpensive by comparison. They can be purchased anywhere in the world. Since the imposition of tariffs has now been postponed by America for ninety days, with only 30% of the tariff remaining. China will certainly maintain its economic prominence.

The Chinese people are essentially well educated and resourceful. The culture is also at an extremely high level. This was brought to the attention of America's vice president when he called the Chinese peasants, and they reminded him that Chinese culture is five thousand years old, while America is only reaching its 250th anniversary. Even the Chinese cuisine is probably the most popular in America. And perhaps to a lesser degree all over the world.

The evident problem is that China was Putin's main guest at the May 9 parade in Moscow. Not only did the Chinese leader sit next to Putin during the parade, but he spent four days in Putin's company. I use the term "leader" when I write about the Secretary of the Communist Party of China, President, Dictator Xi Jinping. He has many more titles. This is also important because it is known that when he speaks, he cannot be contradicted. By the way, in this respect, he and Putin are similar because their power or titles cannot be defined.

Chinese troops are not formally fighting on the side of Moscow in Ukraine. But they constituted the largest contingent in the parade besides the Russian troops. Even the dictator of North Korea was not present in Moscow on May 9. Without exaggeration or doubt, it can be said that Putin's choreography was to present to the world that Russia and China are the closest of friends. It is clear that a photo with the Chinese leader is more significant for Putin than a photo with the relatively clownish leader of North Korea, whose soldiers are actually on the ground and his missiles in the air in Russia's war against Ukraine.

China claims that it does not transfer weapons or military equipment to Moscow. There is much evidence that contradicts this. China sometimes diplomatically abstains from voting in the United Nations Security Council when Moscow votes against. A resolution. This so-called neutral position is only because the Kremlin does not need China's vote, since Moscow illegally uses its veto. One vote is enough to impede any action by the UNSC.

One might think that China, with its self-proclaimed neutrality and limited manifest bravado, is not as aggressive or brutal as presented by the West until one gets acquainted with what is happening inside China, the repression of its own people. Any opposition and the press, brutality, and in particular towards various other groups or ethnicities, starting with the Muslim Uighurs. There is a genocide going on within China that the whole world sees but somehow tolerates because it does not affect it directly. China takes advantage of this. Inexpensive products are the reward for silence or at least acquiescence.

As for Ukraine, the biggest fault of China against Ukraine is that China is the largest consumer of Moscow's oil and gas. China and India together enable Moscow's war economy. Only limited personal and sectoral sanctions have been imposed on China by Ukraine, Europe, and America. Ukraine, in fact, with its war economy, cannot afford an embargo against China. The average Ukrainian with a low salary buys Chinese shirts, watches, etc. There is no alternative.

With the exception of two cases where Ukraine accused China, albeit diplomatically, of delivering munitions and parts to benefit the Russian arsenal and a relatively small number of Chinese mercenaries fighting on Moscow's side in Ukraine for Moscow's money, Ukraine maintains relatively even relations with China. Here, politics as the art of the possible plays a key role. China is playing, and Ukraine participates in the diplomatic game lest China join the other side.

President Zelensky is one of the smartest leaders in the world. So far, he has managed to outwit Ukraine-hater Donald Trump, who would like to be in the Putin and Xi club, but for now, American courts are getting in the way. True, this may only be a temporary phenomenon. Trump is still supplying Ukraine with weapons and intelligence. That can change, so President Zelensky continues to appease the American leader primarily with flattery.

China remains a mystery. A mystery is better than an enemy. The most important thing is that it is not a threat to Ukraine, and also that, in the final calculation, China and Russia may become less friendly. There are territorial and other conflicts between them that are not currently inflamed. In this case, the potential enemy of my enemy can also become my friend. President Zelensky's game with China is correct and well played.

May 15, 2025

Moral principles of politics and the mood in Ukraine

Morality is perhaps the least utilized consideration in political activity. Politics is fundamentally the art of the possible and is only very rarely influenced by moral or ethical factors. This does not mean that there have never been principled, honest, and moral politicians in world history. However, such politicians were rare. Perhaps because such factors as morality and ethics sometimes negatively affect success, which is measured in self-aggrandizement.

However, America's current president, like other authoritarian leaders, lowers morality to a new level. This is particularly disturbing because America has long represented freedom and democracy at the highest level. There have been principled and ethical presidents in America. Over the past hundred years, perhaps the most distinct example of this was the relatively politically unsuccessful President Jimmy Carter. Others had their virtues but also serious vices with greater or lesser political efficacy.

President Trump's last trip to the Middle East was a success of unknown quantity. However, it will only be measured in dollars. Trump counted among his successes the personal gift of a $400 million airplane from Qatar. Only Trump did not see gross corruption in this. Access to the President of the United States costs that much.

Business transactions took place without any mention of such problematic issues as respect for human rights, women's rights, or even the condemnation of the murders of political opponents. It is clear that states such as Saudi Arabia, Qatar, or the United Arab Emirates are not interested in such issues. They interfere with business as usual and more so with business at an enhanced level. President Trump, with a single mind to make a financial profit, easily found his interlocutors without the slightest hesitation or consideration for the morality of it all.

Returning home, Trump had to consider non-business matters and realized that the meeting of the delegations of Ukraine and the Kremlin in Istanbul was not a success, except for the exchange of prisoners. Trump insisted that he had to have at least a phone conversation with his partner in authoritarian rule, Vladimir Putin. The phone conversation led to nothing, but Trump characterized it in a similar way to Putin, that the conversation was useful and sincere. Excuse me, but even a primitive like Trump could not believe that any conversation with a criminal could be sincere.

Trump is a consequence of national populism, where a leader can say whatever he wants, and his followers not only approve of him but also promote his ideas. However, it is already apparent that this direction of false populism is running its course. This has become evident in Germany, France, Romania, Hungary, Slovakia, and even in Poland. The latter is very significant because the Poles are fundamentally chauvinistic by culture. And although they are threatened by Moscow almost on their border, it is difficult to change. People such as Prime Minister Tusk are a modern democratic outlier. A candidate for President of Poland, Karol Nawrocki, albeit independent but very conservative in his views, was in first place just a few months ago. Recently, he came in second place in the general elections. The mayor of Warsaw, of a moderate direction, ran first. The final elections in a week will show the inclination of the Poles.

Returning to the USA and President Trump, who constantly claims that his authoritarian behavior was approved by American voters with a large mandate, giving him a very big popular victory. This is just another lie, because the difference in votes between Trump and Biden in 2024 was the smallest in the last 24 years, that is, in the last six American presidential elections.

Trump continues to lose in the courts. America's role as a world leader has been assumed by Europe. Among Trump's allies are Putin and Kim from North Korea. True, some world leaders continue to shower praise on Trump, but Trump does not understand that this is a political game. The indisputable fact is that America has not had such a primitive and immoral president since the time of Andrew Jackson in the first half of the 19th century. Jackson was infamous for the genocide of the indigenous population in America.

Among Trump's sins in the first four months of his presidency, and there are many, was a major offense against international law. Apparently, Trump could not understand this because crimes against American law are beyond his understanding, and he has no understanding of international law. The International Criminal Court issued an arrest warrant against Israeli Prime Minister Netanyahu for war crimes and crimes against humanity. So far, the Israeli Armed Forces have killed 52,000 Palestinians, among them probably 90% innocent men, women, and children. It is true that the war was started by the Palestinian terrorist group Hamas, which killed 1,200 Jews and took 251 hostages on October 7, 2023. However, Israel's response far exceeded the norms of war under international law.

In February 2025, Trump imposed sanctions against the chief prosecutor of the ICC, a British attorney. This order by Trump was not only without precedent but also manifested his complete disregard for international law, which is already slow to develop due to the ill behavior of the world community, its leaders, and the lack of goodwill.

The Holy Father Pope Leo XIV has already spoken out on the topic of Trump's behavior, particularly regarding immigration, several times, the last time, although not by name, during his sermon at his installation as head of the Universal Church. This is also significant. And it should be added that today, only 39% of Americans approve of the behavior of this president. Where is the mandate? Even Americans are starting to wake up. It's not too late.

I went to Ukraine, because there are more important issues of today.

May 23, 2025

Understanding Ukrainian Doggedness

I arrived in Lviv, a Ukrainian city of very beautiful Western architecture founded by the Ukrainian King Danylo in 1256 and named after his son Lev. I like to irritate my Polish friends by reminding them that Lviv is one year older than the pearl of Poland, the city of Krakow. Lviv is marked not only by its old architecture but by the strong will of its people. I call it Ukrainian doggedness.

I was reminded of that strong will on day one when I visited a bank and a store where I purchased light bulbs. At the bank, I asked the teller to yell because I was hard of hearing. She refused, reminding me that in Lviv, they do not yell at their customers. Because I am as dogged as she, I went to the next teller. At the store, the young man selling light bulbs offered a variety of regular and economical bulbs. I asked him what the difference was, and he replied that the economic ones last much longer. I simply said, I don't know about that. He replied, but I do,

I love these people even though they often annoy me. I probably annoy them. It's this type of attitude and mutually annoying congruence among Ukrainians that has allowed the Ukrainians to overcome centuries of great difficulties, which persists to date.

There is a tale about God and the creation of various nations and the distribution of lands. God conferred with the angel and suggested that he would create a people and a land. The women would be remarkably beautiful and the men very strong. The land would consist of great fertility so that if one were to spit, a tree would grow. The angel pointed out that this creation would be unfair to other people. God replied, wait till you see their neighbors. And so, like it or not, Russia is Ukraine's neighbor.

Lviv is considered the piedmont of Ukraine, the source of its outspokenness and strong will. I am hardly objective when it comes to the Ukrainian people, but it ought to be pointed out that I do find fault occasionally.

My bank in Ukraine is a state bank. There is no reason for service to be amiable. Rarely have I seen a teller smile. The worst are the managers. They are incompetent and unfriendly, but mostly women. The difference in America is that bank personnel are incompetent, but friendly. There is an exception: those who somehow have stepped up the ladder to compliance. They are both incompetent and unfriendly.

Banking in Ukraine is problematic. President Zelensky is making good on his promise to fight corruption, but with the war and Ukraine's need for money, there are great conflicts between money transfers for legitimate purposes and money laundering. Legitimate customers have to be very patient.

The description of Lviv and its people should not detract from other parts of Ukraine. Simply put, Eastern Ukraine had been under Russian domination for more than three hundred years. Russia has always been authoritarian and brutal. Western Ukraine was under Polish, then Austrian, then Polish, and finally Soviet Russian rule. Since World War 2, Polish rule was semi-benign by comparison with the Russian rule. Austria was significantly more benign than Poland.

In Lviv, I met with my Kharkiv liaison, a volunteer who was in the West visiting his ailing mother. We discussed the most urgent needs, in particular, drones and their interceptors, including the most expedient procurement and delivery. I was to travel to Kharkiv, but our meeting saved me that trouble.

As I walked out of my apartment at 9AM on Friday, I was met with an announcement, apparently, throughout Lviv, encouraging the people of Lviv to honor the memory of those heroes who had given up their lives on behalf of Ukraine. I was struck by the discipline as both vehicles and pedestrians stopped in their tracks to remember and honor the heroes.

It was a brief moment, but most inspirational. I noted consciously that this nation will persevere just as it has over the last 375 years. It will persevere because, despite turmoil, tragedy, and attempts to destroy it, as the Russians say, "to wipe Ukrainians off the face of the earth," Ukrainians remain undaunted and seemingly invincible. I am sure that God is on our side, even though He keeps testing us.

We are a deeply religious nation, sometimes to the point of accepting the teaching of our various churches as opiates. We manifest our faith by kneeling and kissing the ground. For me, that is just too much. But this form of religious adoration persists.

It is interesting to recall that under Soviet atheism, the only nationality that remained insubordinate was the Ukrainians. The Soviets gave up and set up their own version of churches in Ukraine. Ukrainians picked up the mantle to a ridiculous extent so that the imposed Orthodox Church of the Moscow patriarchate reaped the benefits well into Ukraine's independence.

Eh, Ukrainians needed to pray. They always distinguish, but they are doggedly Ukrainian and believers in God and Ukraine. Russia has no shot.

May 24, 2025

Ukraine's Future

I had the good fortune to lecture at two of the preeminent universities of Lviv. That is always a favorite part of my trips to Ukraine – a dialogue with students, which, in my opinion, offers an opportunity to see the future.

I recently published an English-language book entitled "Russian Crimes in Ukraine". It had been published in the United States earlier and is available at various outlets. In Ukraine, the publisher was the Lviv National Ivan Franko University, and the books were disseminated free of charge to libraries and ten of the largest universities in Ukraine.

My purpose is to interest the students in some basic aspects of international law and encourage them to study English. The Ukrainian language is very important, but English is indispensable as a second language, especially as Ukraine moves closer to the European Union and NATO. It is also a replacement for people who have long been oppressed and compelled to use only the Russian language to the detriment of their own. It's time to bury at long last the Russian language, which was a weapon of the oppressor, today offers nothing, and is a dead language everywhere except the Russian empire.

During my two presentations at the Lviv National and Lviv Polytechnic universities, I was once again very much impressed with the level of the students, who exhibited keen minds with original critical thinking and dynamic ideas. The representation was varied with graduates and undergraduates, and in various fields from history to law. There is a particular interest in the law, perhaps due to the fact that under the Soviet Russian oppression, the law was not based on justice but on giving the regime justification for its brutal rule. I often remark that the rule of law means the rule of justice, because laws can be enacted by repressive regimes to further their purpose.

International law, as it stands today with its relatively feckless institutions and almost powerless execution, can be considered merely a dream, but it certainly is the most significant aspiration of the modern era and dare not be abandoned. It must be reformed, however. Empires, for the most part, are evil phenomena of the past, with the exception of the Russian Federation (read Empire), as it encompasses almost 150 different nations, persecuted by one, the Russian nation, who had acquired its territories mostly by imperialistic invasion. The culture of the colonizer has not mellowed, but has put its own people outside the civilized democratic world. Before any consideration is given to changing the mindset of that nation, the empire must be dissolved.

The most significant Institution of international law is the United Nations, which, unfortunately, despite the addition of covenants and institutions, has failed to change in essence, with perhaps its most significant organ, the Security Council, largely intact, allowing aggressors to take advantage and very often render it null and void. Of course, the problem was in its founding documents, but eighty years later, the condition of lack of efficacy remains and is exploited by bad nations. There are bad nations forged by their culture. Strangely enough, a Russian mother is more often than not an imperialist.

The purpose of the UN, its covenants and institutions that followed, is expressed in the preamble to its Charter, from 1945, to prevent wars. That makes the UN Security Council its most important and most flawed institution. One very significant option would be to eliminate the veto power of the five permanent members. Three of the five today should initiate such reform. Unfortunately, today, three of the five may refuse to act. A Trump America is a quandary.

Assuming a joint Ukrainian-European winning conclusion to the war in Ukraine, which was the prevailing mood in the two auditoriums, Ukraine's future appears bright, precisely because of its next generation. That future is much more oriented towards Europe than America, which is a major distinction from previous outlooks. As an American by citizenship, I am fine with that, although very disappointed with my country of citizenship.

May 25, 2025

Recognizing the Past and Looking to the Future

I left Lviv and traveled to Ternopil. The city and region generally are pretty safe from Russian brutality, but just before my arrival, the city had been bombed. Fortunately, there were no fatalities, although there were injuries.

The region of Ternopil is a tourist attraction because of its medieval fortresses, its general safety, and its administration, which has reached out to locations in the West, establishing partnerships and even sister city relationships. Even during this war, tourists, partners, and investors come.

I lectured on the topic of International Law and the need for the study of English at the Ternopil National Pedagogical University. The enrollment is roughly 6000 students, which has increased during the war because of the region's relative safety. It now hosts proportionately more than its share of migrant students. It ranks 48th out of 192 universities in Ukraine and is the leading pedagogical institution of higher learning in Ukraine.

As noted, one of the purposes of my lectures is to impress upon both the faculty and students the importance of learning English. This is one of the strongest points of the Ternopil National Pedagogical University. There was a wide response from the students when I used an English language phrase or description. English is offered as a second language throughout the curriculum. Many students are at least moderately versed in English.

I had the opportunity to visit my mother's birthplace with the mayor who heads the community of the Township of the City of Kopychynci and 11 villages. The total population is 14,000. I was informed that English is available from the very first grade of elementary school. The mayor (33 years old) and the township council are very young and dynamic. The council is also very female.

Certainly, there is no glass ceiling here. It was shattered long ago and many times over.

Thereafter, I traveled to the oldest Eastern European Institute of higher learning at Ostroh in the region of Rivne. The Collegium was initially founded, and then the Academy was founded in 1576. The name was derived from its benefactors and location, the Ostroh Academy or Academia Ostrogiensis. It is a National University, established in independent Ukraine in 1994.

"The original Academy was based on the traditional Western European education system, presupposing the simultaneous study of languages to interpret the Holy Scriptures - Greek, Latin, and Biblical Hebrew. Ostroh Academy preserved the study of Latin and Greek and supplemented them with the local, bookish Slavic language...In addition to languages, Ostroh Academy studied the seven liberal arts."

Those included grammar, rhetoric, and dialectic, arithmetic, geometry, astronomy, and music. Philosophy, theology, and medicine were also taught.

Today, Ostroh Academy National University has 3000 students distributed among three institutes and three faculties. There are twenty majors. Students have access to dozens of international educational, volunteer, and exchange programs. The geographic backgrounds of the students are very diverse. Ostroh today is a small town. More than 90% of the student body comes from outside.

International Relations is one of its faculties, so my lecture was received with much enthusiasm. I came away feeling very good. International relations, if not international law, as well as the need for English language dialogue, were well established.

May 29, 2025

Dissolving the Real Evil Empire

A Ukrainian victory in the war can only be achieved with the demise of the Russian Federation. Assuming Russia's military and economic prowess, a prolonged war could last for decades. Russian leaders couldn't care less about the numbers. They, as Stalin once said, are merely statistics.

There must be an alternative to war in the end. Diplomacy is hardly the answer since Russia has, over the years, manifested total disregard for bilateral agreements or multilateral treaties and covenants. Russia is far from being a civilized state. A diplomatic conclusion to the war may result in a new war within six months.

Thus, what remains as a legitimate option is the dissolution of the Russian Federation as an empire. The formula for that is Russia's economic bankruptcy, where Russia is not capable of paying its military or police. That process is currently in place, as due to the current price of a barrel of oil, the Russian economy is not doing well. The current global price of a barrel of oil is $60. The Russian profit margin is based on a fixed cost of $30 per barrel. Should global production decline to $30 per barrel, the Russian energy industry would be bankrupt.

With that in mind. America's current mantra, however, ecologically not unfriendly, of drill, baby drill, as well as Arab production, would render the $30 level a reality. Additionally, India, as the second-largest consumer of Russian energy, being sanctioned through American legislation, would assist in the decline of Russian energy.

Furthermore, termination of the Russian shadow oil commerce would make Russia even weaker. An economically bankrupt Russian economy would make it impossible for Russia to pay its military and police personnel. At the very least, a revolt would ensue with different powers vying for the Kremlin throne. With no way to pay his guards, Putin may fall victim literally to the sixth-floor Russian tradition. The next Putin will not be any better than the current one because Russia and its imperialist culture made Putin, and similarly will make the next one. However, in the interim, there will be turmoil and chaos.

And in the midst of that chaos, the enslaved nations within the Russian Federation may rise. Chaos is good sometimes, particularly to bring down authoritarian regimes and empires that are based on an obscene order.

I attended and participated in a panel discussion at the Kyiv National Shevchenko University about passing legislation by Ukraine's parliament in support of the liberation struggle of the nations within the Russian Federation, aka the Russian empire: the Chechens, the Buryats, the Bashkirs, the Kazan Tatars, the Sakha, the Kalmyks, the Erzya, and the Circassians. I can go on because there are more than 100 such nations. That legislation is long overdue. There are movements in Ukraine, Europe, and even the United States advocating support for the liberation of these nations, thus dissolving the Russian empire.

I then went on to the Drahomanov National University in Kyiv and lectured the law students there on the subject of International Law and this proposal as a solution to the 'Russian Empire problem.' I was received with general, albeit critical, approval. We discussed the intricacies, the need for precision and legal support for everything to fall into place, and most importantly, for the nations of the Russian Federation, long subjugated, to rise. International Law does not anticipate such a process. However, International Law has proven to be feckless at all organs of the United Nations, the preeminent international institution.

The UN has been stymied by the inability of the Security Council to get anything done despite overwhelming condemnation by the UN General Assembly of Russia's aggression, war crimes, crimes against humanity, and even genocide. Putin remains under an arrest warrant by the International Criminal Court, yet UN Secretary General Antonio Gutteres sits with him in Kazan at the BRICS summit. The fecklessness of International Law and its institutions is so manifest.

With all the paradoxes and challenges, my audience of law students agreed that it can be done. The Russian Empire can and will be dissolved.

May 30, 2025

Still Chauvinists After All These Years

I cannot deny my conviction that the result of the latest presidential election in Poland is troubling. Recently, Poland has been on a path of democracy and diversity, which has included economic growth. Now it appears Poland is headed for strong rule, xenophobia (homogeneity), and isolationism.

Newly elected President Karol Nawrocki represents a Poland, long detested by its eastern neighbors. For Ukrainians, it is the Poland of Dictator Josef Pilsudski before the war. Even worse, the Communist Party in 1947 attempted to ethnically cleanse the newly acquired territories of Eastern Poland of Ukrainians living there for centuries and forcibly resettle them on newly acquired German lands. Being a Ukrainian in the Communist era was very difficult. There is no way to sugarcoat this.

The once Ukrainian city of Przemysl, Poland, sits as a stark reminder of the Polish past and Polish reluctance to right historical wrongs. There stands on top of a hill the Polish church of St. Theresa, operated by the Carmelites. That Church was once a Ukrainian Catholic Cathedral. Immediately below that structure sits the current Ukrainian Catholic Church of St. John the Baptist, turned over to the Ukrainians as unfair compensation. Even the Holy Father Pope John Paul was unable to convince the Carmelites to do what was both fair and Christian - return the Church to its rightful owners. At least that is a version suggested by the Vatican.

Several hundred meters below the churches sits the Ukrainian national home, returned by the Poles to the Ukrainian community two decades after independence, after intense petitioning.

Polish society has often been little more benign to the Ukrainians in Przemysl or anywhere else, for that matter, than the Polish Roman Catholic Church or the Law and Justice party. Upon more than one occasion, Polish demonstrators have appeared at both Ukrainian venues with placards, chanting Poland without Ukrainians. Often, they have desecrated Ukrainian cemeteries.

This reversal of Polish understanding of both mutual relations between nations based upon international justice, as well as a blindness to its own security concerns, is very serious. Ukraine is fighting a global enemy on behalf of Europe, at least. Unfortunately, this Polish reversal towards extremism may become damning for both Ukraine and Poland.

Polish-Ukrainian relations had blossomed over the last few years, particularly during the war years. Sure, there were outbursts from the Party of Law and Justice. But these were kept in check by Poland's prime minister, Tusk, and the party in power in the Polish parliament. During the war years, Ukrainian migrants were welcomed into Poland in greater numbers than into any other country.

President Karol Nawrocki is dangerous for Ukrainian-Polish relations, reconciliation, and cooperation. He was largely supported by the Law and Justice Party. More importantly, he is the Director of the Institute of National Remembrance. He has spoken out against heroes of Ukrainian history, branding them terrorists and denying current aspirations of Ukraine to join the European Union and NATO. He has declined to consider Polish troops on the ground in Ukraine as peacekeepers. Sure, all of these positions may change when he hears or sees Russians at Poland's doorstep.

This is clearly a step back for Ukrainian-Polish relations as well as Poland as a member of the civilized European community. Europe does not need extremism. That role is played by Orban in Hungary and Fico in Slovakia. No one needs an extremist Nawrocki in Poland.

Ukraine's President Zelensky must step forward as he has done very often during the war years to affirm the current Ukrainian-Polish alliance despite its many sore points in history and Polish historical chauvinism or extremist populist leadership, such as in the United States. Taking the high road is not unknown to the Ukrainian president, but for the relationship to endure, his overtures must be reciprocated by the other side. The task at hand is to salvage Ukrainian-Polish cooperation if only to defeat the common enemy.

June 2, 2025

The Ugly American

Coming back from Ukraine, I naturally traveled through Poland. The procedure is generally the same at points of entry and departure. I wanted to experience the pedestrian route near the current Polish, once Ukrainian, city of Przemysl or Peremyshl, since I was told that this was the simplest way to go to Poland.

A Ukrainian military chaplain with whom I work drove me to the border. I make a point of this lest someone accuses me of abusing the assistance we, meaning the Ukrainian Free University Foundation, provide to the Ukrainian military. This was not payback time. It gave me the opportunity to discuss various items of assistance. I swear we spoke about assistance all the way from Lviv to the border. In fact, we agreed upon several items and their cost, which I will wire on Monday.

Walking through Ukrainian customs and passport control was a breeze. Polish customs and passport control were a different story. It was simple for European Union passports. I lamented that I was not from Europe. As usual, I tried to sneak in through the EU line but was rebuffed with some determination and told that Americans, Brits, and Ukrainians are treated the same, and not as Europeans. As if I needed further affirmation of my non-special status, a Ukrainian on the not EU line asked me why I thought I should be treated differently.

I wasn't really glad that I was among my fellow Ukrainians because the line was lengthy, but being loquacious and full of some dad-like sense of humor, I began conversations with many. Surprisingly, they were not taken aback, but quite responsive. I suppose they were amused.

Americans are no longer liked by Ukrainians. I insisted that I was different because I was a Ukrainian American and a Trump hater. That helped little. One man from the Lviv region, the city of Stryj, well known for its nationalist underpinnings, simply asked me how

I could have voted for such a primitive president. I responded that I didn't. That did not help much.

I was mildly humbled. I responded apologetically that America did in the past substantially assist Ukraine with arms and would do so in the future, despite Trump, that Americans are good people, basically, if not misled by populist lies and slogans. I pointed out that some countries in Europe, including Poland, had most recently gone the populist route, but that I was sure that this was a bizarre anomaly. All of this turned into a good-natured banter where we maligned both Trump and Karol Nawrocki, the recently elected populist Polish president.

After one and a half hours, I reached Polish customs and then Passport Control. The experience could not have been more receptive, albeit of some duration, since both the customs and passport control officers wanted to talk and not about my luggage or passport. I recognized that the Poles were equally critical of America because of Donald Trump. To the detriment of the people behind me, they spend probably ten minutes discussing American abandonment. They were less critical than the Ukrainian throng, but certainly, equally displeased. They stressed that Europe is the way for the future for both Poland and Ukraine. They were very much pro-Ukraine and insisted that the newly elected president of Poland would come around.

I came out on the Polish side of the border feeling pretty good. Time spent seemed to me well spent, and I look forward to the future. Poland is Ukraine's closest neighbor, most affected by Russian aggression, and essential to Ukraine's success and security. The historical past will not be forgotten as my Ukrainian fellow travelers pointed out on my way to the taxi stand, but differences aside, cooperation has to ensue for the benefit of both nations. I agree.

I do realize that this is all anecdotal, but life and relations are a series of anecdotes.

June 5, 2025

ZRADA

Zrada is a Ukrainian term which essentially means a betrayal, betraying or forsaking one's convictions, one's loved ones, which could mean family, wife, or children, as well as one's country. In the broader political sense, particularly for Ukrainians in their often-tragic history, it also encompasses betraying or forsaking one's friends or allies. In the latter sense, there usually exists no formal binding bond because even under international law, bonds, treaties, or covenants are not enforceable. It's more of a moral concept, and precisely where Ukrainians have been exposed on many occasions. The exposure is often a result of mendacity or a naive willingness on the part of the betrayed to be misled. Oftentimes, the betrayer is mendacious. Here is an excerpt from the United States State Department archives immediately following the end of the war in Europe.

"14 May, 1945

TO:

Secretary of State-

This morning, a delegation of American citizens representing the Ukrainian Congress Committee of America called and presented the attached memorandum on the Ukrainian situation.

I received this memorandum on your behalf and said that in due course it would come to your attention. It is respectfully recommended that the document be referred to the Eastern European Division of the State Department. During the conversation this morning, the delegation remarked that the United States was the champion of oppressed peoples and that they felt confident of American official interest in the cause of Ukrainian nationalism. I answered that the interest of the people of the United States in all who felt themselves to be oppressed was well established in history, but I pointed out that it would not serve anybody's interest to create an impression that the United States government was the unreasoning champion of the discontented. It was necessary above all at this time to work out a friendly accommodation with the USSR. Nothing should be done to disturb that effort. The delegation professed to agree. (sgd.) De Witt C. Poole, Associate Public Liaison Officer"

Certainly, one cannot accuse the said De Witt C. Poole of misleading the Ukrainian delegation. Nevertheless, the document proves two things: that America was a willing albeit naive friend of the Soviet Union and thus an enemy of Ukrainians, and that Mr. Poole lied to his superiors, as there is no way that the Ukrainian delegation "professed to agree." This, however, was not considered a brazen lie. For the unacquainted, it was and remains spin.

Following World War I, US President Woodrow Wilson, the architect of the League of Nations, an organization meant to ensure peace and prevent further wars, decided to appease Polish imperialists by allowing Poland to take over Western Ukraine. This was Poland's third occupation. Despite current propaganda by Poland's newly elected president, Ukrainian Polish historical differences are largely one-sided. Ukrainians never invaded Polish territory.

In 1933, at the height of the Soviet orchestrated Genocide of Ukrainians (the Holodomor), when 7-10 million Ukrainians perished by famine, US President Franklin D. Roosevelt recognized the Soviet Union as a state and exchanged diplomats.

Twelve years later, an ailing FDR, accompanied by his aide Alger Hiss, a Soviet agent, sold out all of Eastern Europe to Josef Stalin in Yalta, which included Ukraine. Roosevelt's administration was deeply infiltrated. These sell-outs continued for the period of the Cold War and even at its apparent conclusion. In August 1991, US President George H.W. Bush travelled to Moscow and then Kyiv, stressing his staunch support for his friend Soviet strongman Mikhail Gorbachev President Bush warned Ukrainians to beware of suicidal separatism and to maintain the Union. Ukrainians did not listen and proclaimed independence some three weeks later, and then held an unprecedented referendum on December 1, 1991, ratifying that proclamation by more than 90%. Canada and Poland rushed to recognize that independent Ukrainian state. Who was first is still a matter of dispute. Some 150 countries followed, and only on December 25, 1991, following Mikhail Gorbachev's public resignation on the air, did the United States lend its own recognition to the Ukrainian state.

Perhaps all of these events may be attributed to American shortsightedness or a policy of appeasement. Aside from 1812, America has never had a foreign war on its soil. World War 2 and Soviet Russian atrocities on the field of battle should have opened up some eyes, but America was not in a position to complain about the Russians, given American war crimes in Japan, Hiroshima, and Nagasaki being the prime example. Much was learned during the post-war period, as Soviet Gulags, invasions into Czechoslovakia, and Hungary should have opened some eyes to a lesson. Still, even the Hungarians on Russia's doorstep did not learn much, given Prime Minister Orban's and Fidesz's long-term tenure in Hungary today. But the Hungarians sided with the Nazis in World War 2. The Slovakian behaviour as manifested by Prime Minister Fico today may be harder to explain, but Soviet tanks crushing the Prague Spring was not against the Slovaks, but the Czechs. The betrayal continued. In December 1994, at the insistence of the United States, Ukraine signed the Budapest Memorandum, not only giving up its nuclear arsenal, the third largest in the world, but later transferring its enriched uranium to its mortal enemy – Russia at American insistence. Many have suggested that this was a grave mistake on the part of Ukraine. Ukraine was young, idealistic, and eager to garner Western support.

Too few, however, have blamed America not only for the pressure but also for the betrayal. A brief sidetrack is important here. The English language text of the Memorandum includes the words 'security assurances', but not 'guarantee'. The document was signed in three

languages: English, Ukrainian, and Russian. In both Ukrainian and Russian, the word 'guarantee' appears in the heading. A semantical difference is very significant. Assurance refers to one's own behavior. Guarantee pertains to the actions of other parties to the agreement. One may assume that Ukraine was duped by reading only the Ukrainian or Russian versions, and the Americans acted in good faith by providing assurances of their own behavior. America knows what Russia was about, even under the drunken control of Boris Yeltsin, so America certainly does not deserve a pass here. The Russians are irrelevant to this discussion as to intent because personal assurances or guarantees are irrelevant. Russia never had nor has any intention of complying with international agreements, treaties, covenants, etc.

Furthermore, there is much more here than a misunderstanding of terminology. The Budapest Memorandum is a clear message to any state considering acquiring or in possession of nuclear arms or capabilities. That message is that without nuclear arms, you will be at the mercy of nuclear states. Why would any country agree to dispose of its nuclear capability or weapons, whether current or in the future? American duplicity towards Ukraine continued. In May 2004, American President George W. Bush met with Russian strongman Vladimir Putin. He came away saying &, I looked into his eyes, and I saw a soul. I trusted him. Six months later, Russia tried to steal the Ukrainian presidential election but was thwarted by a huge evolution inspired by Ukrainian youth known as the Orange Revolution. Five years later, Russia succeeded in putting its man in power in Ukraine. Once again, the Ukrainian people rose and ousted him in February 2014. In the interim, Russia destroyed the Ukrainian defense and in February 2014 attacked the Ukrainian peninsula of Crimea. President Barack Obama condemned the takeover and subsequent annexation but did nothing. In fact, he advised the Ukrainians not to fight back and supplied them with no arms.

President Joe Biden deserves some mention inasmuch as he was considered a friend of Ukraine. As Vice President, he traveled to Ukraine seven times. His boss never visited Ukraine.

He promised and delivered much to Ukraine as president and probably deserves only a little criticism despite the fact that often delivery was dilatory and much restricted. The problem also involved advice received from alleged American generals who suggested what Ukraine needs despite never being in Ukraine.

And then there was and is President Trump. Never in modern history involving America-Ukraine relations has there been an American president so ill-disposed not only to Ukraine but to such basic concepts enshrined in America's Declaration of Independence as freedom and justice. America has never had a strongman or authoritarian leader with no moral principles or soul. A glaring picture of President Trump is one from the summer of 2018, as he stands at a podium next to Vladimir Putin in Helsinki, stating quite clearly that given a choice between his own American intelligence and the words of a criminal thug, he chooses that of the criminal. Trump often refers to his approval of the sale of Javelin defense missiles to Ukraine in 2019. Until then, US aid to Ukraine for the war that started in 2014 had been strictly non-lethal. The operative word here is sales. Being unprincipled and amoral, this was entirely transactional. Sure, it benefited Ukraine, but for Trump, this was strictly a sale. Naturally, Trump did nothing to stop the war during his first term. His second term began with bluster even prior to his election. He stressed that the war would never have started had he been president, and then guaranteed to end it within twenty-four hours, and then one hundred days after taking office. Both terms proved to be exercises in futility. Ukraine agreed to a thirty-day ceasefire and signed a minerals deal. Russia did neither. Trump manifested disdain for Ukraine by ambushing Ukraine's President in the White House Oval Office in early February 2025. President

Zelensky took the high road, however, and persisted diplomatically. Trump then voted with Russia and against Ukraine at the United Nations General Assembly. Trump's collaborating Secretary of State Marco Rubio wished Russia a Happy Russia Day on June 12, 2025, and equally sycophantic Secretary of Defense Pete Hegseth included Russian colors of white, blue, and red on America's official banner for Flag Day.

Little Marco, as Trump called Marco Rubio, is a particularly interesting political animal, having predicated his entire political career on his staunch anti-Communist position, retelling the story over and over again, how his parents had to flee Fidel Castro's Communist Cuba. Fidel Castro came to power in Cuba in 1959. The Rubios left Cuba in 1956. Brazenly (because he had heretofore offended every one of the G7 members), Trump traveled to Calgary, Canada, for the G7 Summit on June 15, 2025. But cut his participation short because of the Middle East crisis. He did bemoan that the structure was no longer the G8 and insisted that Russia would never have started the war against Ukraine had it not been ousted by Presidents Obama and Trudeau. While Trudeau was not the President, but the Prime Minister, and the ousting was the work of President Obama and Prime Minister Harper, in fact, Russia was ousted after and because of its attack on Ukraine in 2014.

Having stood up for Putin and Russia once again, and displaying no knowledge of the facts due to a lack of information or cognitive decline, Trump left his G7 allies.

"Zrada" is being manifested throughout Trump's first year of his second term. There is a silver lining. Since America's European allies have recognized this, they understand the need to take on the mantle of global leadership. But no additional sanctions were imposed on Russia by the G7 at their Canada summit. Russia continues to bomb Ukraine at an unprecedented rate. The G7 issued no statement on Ukraine because of Trump's pushback. Ukraine's fierce defense and its ability to do the unthinkable by striking Russian military airports and facilities, blowing up key bridges in Russia itself, has left Russia so focused on defeating Ukraine that, in the interim, Russia could not protect its interests in Nagorno Karabakh, its surrogate or port in Syria, or its ally Iran. At least with the demise of strongman Assad and the prospective denuclearization of Iran by Israel, if not regime change, hopefully by the Iranian people, Ukraine seems to have done substantially more for global security than its erstwhile ally, the United States of America, with its strongman Donald J. Trump.

Source for U.S. State Department quote: US National Archives, BG 226, Entry 100, Box 98. UK351-360 Anglo-American Perspectives on the Ukrainian Question 1938- 1951, A documentary Collection, Lubomyr Y. Luciuk and Bohdan S. Kordan, The Limestone Press, Kingston, Ontario, 1987.

June 18, 2025

The Irony of the Russia-Iran Conundrum

On January 17, 2025, Russian President Vladimir Putin and his Iranian counterpart Masoud Pezeshkian presented what was seen as a breakthrough in relations between the two countries. There had been years of collaboration between the two countries. Iran had supplied its deadly Shahed drones to enable and enhance Russian aggression in Ukraine. Russia seemingly had Iran's back in the Middle East. Given the technology, Russia began to produce and utilize its own version of the Shaked with some success.

When Israel attacked Iran most recently, the prevailing view was that Russia, as Iran's ally, would hasten to Iran's aid. Nothing was further from reality. Russia's strongman, Vladimir Putin, did not hesitate to assure the world and America in particular, that the January treaty was not a mutual defense military alliance and did not require any direct obligations from either party. Instead, it simply formalized the close ties between Iran and Russia that have developed since the full-scale invasion of Ukraine in 2022.

That was Russia's signal to the United States and its Russia-obsessed President that Russia was fine with America bombing Iran's nuclear sites. After all, there was much benefit for Russia. The focus would shift from Russian aggression in Ukraine to the Middle East because America was now involved in a war at its own initiative.

Aside from its own Revolutionary War and the Iraq fiasco of George W. Bush, America had never initiated a major war. Furthermore, this war will help Russia immeasurably since the cost of a barrel of oil should spike, which will only enhance Russia's ability to conduct the war in Ukraine.

I am certainly not advocating the nuclearization of Iran. Clearly, Iran is the most brazen and aggressive player in the Middle East. Iran should never reach nuclear status. Even the idea of an Iran with nuclear energy status, which Iran has argued is its right as a sovereign, is beyond the pale since Iran has more than 10% of the oil resources in the world. Ecological concerns matter little by comparison with any grade level of uranium. Capability is a clear and present danger to the entire region of the Middle East and Iran's neighbors, and in particular Israel, which one should assume would be peaceful without its hateful neighbors.

A nuclear and militarily sophisticated Israel, the greatest recipient of U.S. Military aid, is an adequate answer in that part of the world. Israel has the right to exist, and if that means that Israel is the most sophisticated military state with a nuclear capability, then so be it. Israel's capacity makes the world a safer place, at least in that troublesome part of the world. The situation does not call for further American grandstanding.

No reason has been provided for the American premature bombing of Iranian nuclear sites. Trump had suggested a two-week period either for cooling off and a return to negotiations or a span to judge the efficacy of Israeli air prowess. He reacted in two days.

I submit that Trump's hasty actions were inspired not by a genuine concern for lives to be lost in Israel or Iran, since the attacks on both sides had been somewhat muddled in terms of targeting military or civilian sites. Both Israel and Iran have a history of war crimes, targeting military and civilians almost indiscriminately, including hospitals.

Trump wanted the world to know that he was still in charge. An Israeli military victory as inevitable as it is would not enhance his presidential biography. And then there was probably the factor that this helps his buddy Vladimir. Ukrainian lives are the furthest thing from his mind, but good relations with Russia and a Trump Tower in Moscow are always there. Medvedev's threats about Iran's allies arming Iran with military weapons are empty. Medvedev is simply and always has been Putin's clown.

At this point, we need to pray that both the people of Ukraine and the people of America will survive this latest stroke of unadulterated stupidity, at best on the part of a man ill-equipped to be president.

For the Ukrainian people, this is now an even more difficult war. For Americans, there is a tangible possibility that, through myriad terrorist activities, the war in the Middle East may be brought to American shores.

June 23, 2025

The Trump Press Conference

President Trump often boasts that no president has provided more access to the press. That is true. However, Trump's press conferences resemble nothing presided over by his White House predecessors and are more suited to a Fellini script than an opportunity for the press to get real information. So often the press piles on, not genuinely seeking the truth, but intent on humiliating a person of very sparse intellectual capacity and absolutely no regard for the truth.

A recent press conference from the 'Hagu' following Trump's participation in the NATO Summit was a prime example and certainly not an outlier. Aside from calling Federal Reserve chair Jerome Powell stupid, threatening to overcharge Spain on any further business transaction for refusing to spend the requisite amount on defense, and attempting to humiliate individual CNN reporters, Trump was entertaining, taking on more questions than usual, but offering no facts. Hyperbolic statements resounded, but there was a feeling in the room that no one really cared or was even there to get any real information.

The constantly repeated refrain was the American "obliteration" of the Iranian nuclear resources and capability despite many intelligence reports, including a leaked American one that suggested that Iran had suffered only a several-month setback to its nuclear program. The bottom line is that there is no evidence that 900 pounds of Iran's enriched uranium was destroyed in the American attack. No intelligence report, except for the White House and Trump himself, had asserted that accomplishment.

In any event, the military action on the part of the United States in Iran was successful. The issues here are to what degree and whether it was necessary for America to intervene. The amount of damage to the Iranian nuclear program, which was inflicted beyond any doubt could and would have been inflicted by Israel alone, whether it used American equipment currently in Israel's possession or availed itself of American bunker bombs.

Donald Trump is a psychologically disturbed person. For him, it is important to become legendary in history, and that has to include accomplishments, whether actual or fake (Trump terminology). His self-proclaimed motivation to bring peace is not a genuine moral desire to terminate suffering and killing, but most importantly, to be recognized as a peacemaker, resulting in a Nobel Peace Prize. This is blatantly evident in his press conferences as well as the public statements of his sycophants. All accomplishments are attributed to the President and very often to the Commander-in-Chief, which is proper terminology according to the U.S. Constitution, yet somewhat laughable when it refers to Donald J. Trump, who had five military deferments.

Is the mainstream press, American and global, an enemy of Donald Trump? Yes, but he brought it upon himself. He coined the term 'fake news' and continues to ridicule representatives of the mainstream press at every opportunity. Similarly, he is considered a buffoon, and every press conference is an opportunity to humiliate him. The extremist right-wing press that supports him indiscriminately does so in glaring fashion. FOX News, which is the originator of Trump sycophancy, has no program that may be considered remotely objective. Even "Hannity" is not the worst of the bunch.

This is not a healthy political environment. Trump is a bully and the mainstream press has taken a position to fight back, justifying its role as absolutely necessary when dealing with a primitive deeply flawed human being who fashions himself to be not only a president of a democratic country, but the smartest, ablest person in the room, intent on governing by imprimatur rather than the will of the people. He has 'bloviated' (to use a term popularized by his sycophantic followers) the mandate of his election by a margin of two million popular votes, not recognizing that this was the smallest presidential margin in twenty years.

A Trump press conference is satire, often replayed on Saturday Night Live. Both the mainstream press and SNL are only doing their jobs.

June 27, 2025

Summits

At first glance, two major global meetings in June seem to have forgotten Ukraine. Ukraine's President Volodymyr Zelensky attended both in Calgary and the Hague. President Trump attended the G7 Summit, albeit briefly, and the NATO Summit for much of the duration, even presiding over a press conference.

Neither convocation made any new or dramatic declarations regarding Ukraine. In fact, the NATO meeting failed to reaffirm its commitment to future Ukrainian membership. But essentially, that omission is as relevant as the previous declarations about membership since Bucharest in 2008. That was seventeen years ago.

The G7 meeting was marred by President Trump's ignorance regarding Russia's G8 membership and his inexplicable obsession with Russia. This occurred early so that his swift exit was welcome. The NATO Summit was somewhat different.

President Trump came to the Hague looking to be the center of attention after his bombing of Iran's nuclear sites. And he was! His insistence on greater input by NATO members was heard. All of the NATO members seemed to step up, except for Spain, which remained firmly based in reality. Given the fact that it took much time for two-thirds of NATO members to reach a goal of 2% of their GDP for military spending, an agreement to reach 3.5% for actual spending and 1.5% for infrastructure by 2035 seems out of reach for many members. Nevertheless, while it may not be a realistic goal, it is a target.

Even without perfunctory declarations, this was good for Ukraine. So was President Trump's promise to supply by sale or aid more Patriot defense missiles to Ukraine. Ukraine understands that this promise was made by Donald Trump in a private meeting. This is hardly a commitment. But it is something. President Zelensky and Europe have learned how to handle the current President of America.

That is the takeaway from the two summits. The essence is that Europe is stepping up. We can add Japan and Canada to the equation. The global community, even in Southeast Asia, is beginning to understand the peril that Russia represents, if not directly then through its allies.

South Korea sees North Korea as a Russian ally shored up by another authoritarian regime, China, which can become a danger to the world. Neighboring conflicts are always highlighted. Even India has to be circumspect as its future should be aligned with the West and not with Russia, and clearly, its most imminent enemy is not necessarily Pakistan but China. Trade with Russia sends the wrong message.

Politics is not a game, even if Trump has very often described it in terms of kids fighting in the streets. That description is not only inapplicable but also offensive to people who have suffered and witnessed so much death. Iran is intent on eliminating Israel. Russia is intent on eliminating Ukraine. Fortunately for Israel, it is well set up on defense and supported without question by the United States. Israel is a clandestine nuclear power not subject to any inquiry because of its great influence. Israel is defended by America even on issues of war crimes, and Israel is guilty of many.

Ukraine does not have the luxury of indiscriminate support, and, frankly, Ukraine is above the war crimes issue morally. Ukraine is persistently seeking assistance because the aggressor is bigger and stronger in military might, but not in spirit. Almost every instance of Ukraine's aggression on Russian territory has involved strictly military or energy targets, but not civilians.

The war in Ukraine, nonetheless, has been devastating and debilitating. For Ukrainians, it is a war for the existence of a country and its people. Few in the global community and even less in America can appreciate that. Very few people in Ukraine have not suffered tremendous tragedy and hardship because of the war. Most people in Ukraine that I have encountered are greatly affected by Russian aggression and have become involved in the defence.

Children are growing up in the milieu of learning or playing games, interrupted by the necessity of seeking shelter.

I have met the children of today's Ukraine. I am not a psychologist to determine whether they will be permanently scarred by the war. But I do know that their childhood is very different from mine. It's just not normal to constantly ask your mother whether you are going to be safe.

One of the seemingly safest parts of Ukraine is the western city of Lviv. I have been there many times during the war. What I will never forget is a funeral procession and the father who was burying his wife and three young daughters, killed by a Russian missile in their home. I do not know how he is now, but at the funeral, he was an empty shell. In my lifetime, this was one of the saddest events I have ever witnessed.

That was Lviv. Can you imagine how many children have died in Donetsk, Mariupol, Luhansk, Kharkiv, Kherson, Zaporizhzhya, Dnipro, and Kyiv? Unfortunately, the people of Ukraine do not need to imagine.

June 29, 202

Trump's Solution To The War In Ukraine

Is President Trump working on ending the war in Ukraine? You can say that. Since he took office, he has not imposed a single sanction on Russia. He has removed several sanctions, allegedly as they pertain to Syria, but they affect some of the same companies that enable Russia to conduct the war in Ukraine. He has stopped aid and intelligence sharing with Ukraine. He resumed it only to stop it again. Most recently, at the NATO Summit, Trump promised more Patriots for Ukraine. Now the Pentagon announced that some equipment earmarked for Ukraine will be going back into America's stockpile. In summary, the Trump administration has enhanced Russia by depriving Ukraine. Russia has amassed 50,000 troops on Ukraine's northern border and has boasted that it seeks to take over and annex five additional Ukrainian regions. It would appear that Trump's strategy to end the war is a Russian victory.

"As far as we understand, the reason for the decision was empty warehouses, but the fewer weapons supplied to Ukraine, the closer the end of the 'special military operation,'" Russian presidential spokesperson Dmitry Peskov said.

If you can't believe Peskov, you cannot believe Trump. Trump is an evil human being, as I have often remarked, so his predisposition for dictators such as Putin is not surprising. His mendacity is inveterate and psychotic. Ukraine and President Zelensky have to continue playing a game of political hopefulness. The rest of the world and America itself have to be more challenging.

The recent votes in the Senate and the House on the 'Big Beautiful Bill' are somewhat hopeful. The fear of primary armor is acquiring chinks. At least three members of the GOP in the Senate not only voted their conscience, but voted for their constituents rather than bend a knee to what they know to be evil. Initially, nine

Reps in the House withheld their votes so the Bill could not proceed in a timely fashion. Those nine are shrinking. Rewarding the rich and punishing the poor is a manifestation of amorality.

With Trump as president and the GOP scared, America has become one of the most corrupt countries in the world. Trump had a university that defrauded people. Now he is sold out to the cryptocurrency industry, and his holdings constitute 80% of all his ill-gotten assets. His presidency has monetised. He is selling Bibles and cologne. Can he be stopped because 2028 seems far away, and three and one years is an ample opportunity to destroy a democracy?

There is another factor here that should be addressed – the Ukrainian American electorate that voted for Trump. Some have jumped the MAGA ship after seeing what their 'Napoleon' from 'Animal Farm' is doing. Often, they joke about their newfound remorse. However, the damage caused by Trump is not a joke. I, for one, am unable to forgive them, irrespective of whether they were inspired by personal greed or stupidity. They will always be traitors as far as Ukraine is concerned.

I believe that Ukraine will survive this American debacle of democracy and evil. Ukraine and Europe have already stepped up. Ukraine supplies more than 50% of its military hardware, and the spirit of the Ukrainian people is remarkable. Europe is spending significantly more on defense.

I am really not concerned about the Republican Party, but the Party is in serious trouble, and a legitimate two-party system is important. The fringes will remain that - fringes. One man caused the Grand Old Party to become a travesty of itself. Its immediate future will be reflected in the midterm elections in 2026. That, however, will not be determinative since all parties decline in the next election after they assume substantial power. In due course, I assume that some morality and concern for constituents will prevail. But that will take some time. Morality has never been a strong characteristic of politicians.

On the eve of America's Day of Independence, it is important to consider its future. The future of America as a beacon of light is of great concern. While America was never exceptional, as Americans often say, it was a model for many nascent democracies. That model is very much broken. There is a Constitutional crisis in America as the three branches of government, meant to serve as a system of checks and balances, are in the evil hands of one thug. The undoing of what has been done will take some time, but the Constitution will prevail even if it is threatened by the current regime.

July 3, 2025

In Memoriam – Ihor Kalynets

Ihor Kalynets, a prominent Ukrainian poet, dissident, and political prisoner, a member of the 1960s movement known as the Shistydesiatnyky, passed away at the age of 86 on June 28. 2025. He was a political prisoner for six years in Soviet camps (among them the notorious Perm) with an additional three years of exile from 1972 to 1981. On July 1, 2025, Ihor Kalynets was buried next to his wife, Iryna, at the Lychakivsky Cemetery in Lviv. Iryna Kalynets, who predeceased her husband by thirteen years, was also a prominent poet, dissident, and political prisoner. A contemporary of the Kalynets family, Iryna Kliuchkovska, who currently chairs the International Institute of Education, Culture and Diaspora Relations of Lviv Polytechnic National University, founded and chaired initially by Iryna Kalynets, posted the following: "Who among us does not know Him, this God-given poet? Are there those who have not tasted his words, Muse awakened and Muse of the slave's an image, an association. Who has not felt the color of his word and at the same time the great power capable of awakening thought, protest, and the quest for change. And who among us has not entered his fairy tale – a joyful and mysterious land of childhood, where love, goodness, and justice reign, which the poet depicted so generously. Or maybe someone does not know that Kalynets' poetry sounds equally compelling in German, French, English, Polish, and other languages?

There are among us masters of literary criticism and historians, young researchers who deeply study his life path and creativity. There are also ordinary readers who try to understand the beauty and power of his language and words. And that is why his numerous literary awards are so understandable to us: the public prize named after Vasyl Stus, the National Shevchenko Prize, and many, many others. Ihor Kalynets was nominated for the Nobel Prize and was among the top ten finalists. Let us assume that the Committee had not grown up sufficiently to understand the depth of this man. 'After

1981, I fell silent as a poet,' he wrote. But we know very well that sometimes silence is more eloquent and louder than words. Ihor Kalynets was from Khodoriv, the son of Myron Kalynets and Efrosyna from the house of Huley. '... from there,' he wrote, 'came the source of my inspiration – there now in the cemetery are the people who gave me life and raised me with a strong national spirit. I also could never forget that I was baptized in the Ukrainian Catholic rite, and that my mother's brother, a student at Lviv University, was tortured in June 1941 in the prison on Lonskoho Street.' These roots of his native land were so strong that they grew into a strong core and formed a citizen and a patriot, a Christian, a faithful husband for a like-minded person and friend, the unforgettable Iryna Kalynets, and a sensitive father to his daughter Dzvinka. It gave him the strength to challenge the system, to go through interrogations, arrests, and exiles with dignity and not remain silent! He was strong in spirit, like steel, and at the same time very sensitive.

Having the good fortune to see him and work with him every day for 20 years at MIOK, I can testify that this man genuinely loved people. He reacted very subtly to their pain. I saw his tears when the boys died on the Maidan, and how he experienced the death of each soldier. He helped everyone in need. Not for show, but quietly and calmly, he supported those in need. Here is a small touch to his portrait: for a decade, he shared his pension with a poetess from the south of Ukraine. And there are many such examples, because his soul, which lived in harmony with the Almighty, yearned to help.

Have we forgotten about Kalynets the Christian? No, we must remember how much effort he put into ensuring that our Ukrainian Greek Catholic Church, after years of prohibitions, torture, and humiliation, came out of the underground and became what it is now – strong spiritual support for millions of Ukrainians in our globalized world. Ihor Kalynets was awarded the Order of Freedom because Freedom was his essence. We know Kalynets well as a public and political figure with instant reactions to everything that happens in our country. There are hundreds and thousands of good deeds, carried out according to the values that were vital to him - Truth, Freedom, Love for Ukraine, and Faith in the Almighty. Oh, how many did not like it, especially those who lived with a complex and guilt because they did not have the courage and manliness to stand up to evil. He did with Iryna Kalynets, with Vasyl Stus, with Vyacheslav Chornovol. I often clench my teeth so as not to betray the pain when brainwashed people scold us: "Why are they making heroes out of themselves?" - he wrote. And even today, some young people allow themselves to shout: 'You are interfering in our quiet lives.' Ihor Kalynets said, 'The story of my life is part of the story of my homeland.' And there is a lot of truth in this. This was his path. The path of a dissident, political prisoner, stoker, hammer, participant in the camp resistance movement, editor of Yevshan-zillya. This was the path of Truth.

I was very moved by one photograph. Ihor Kalynets at night in the square in front of the Shevchenko monument in Lviv, in the early hours when the Revolution of Dignity began. In the cold autumn, he came with a stick and stood alone on the empty square. He and Shevchenko. Later, people would come and fill this square with life and protest. I read deep symbolism in this photograph. He was always first, both at a time when Ukraine was sleeping and at a time when it was waking up. Yes, he and Shevchenko, to whose maxims he was faithful forever, and which became his guiding light.

Ukraine needs Kalynets so much today! In times of war, the aggression of Russian forces, the threat of new totalitarianism, when mobilization of all healthy Ukrainian forces is so necessary, when landmarks have been drowned in social networks, in FB, Twitter, when positions are lost, and values are discarded. We need Kalynets today. He never betrayed himself, nor Ukraine, neither in creative words, nor in deed. We do not need to invent myths and steal someone's history. We have our own heroes and our own history to draw upon, to shape new generations. Ihor Kalynets will be needed in the future as well. The writer Yevhen Malaniuk once wrote: 'The most important task for us as a society was, is, and will be to know ourselves. And so we must know ourselves to recognize the strength of Ihor Kalynets, who walked the path of a Ukrainian in Ukraine. This applies to Ukraine as a whole. Lastly, I should like to say: We are lucky to have had and still have him in our memories and in his writings, to have been able to talk to him, see him on the streets of Lviv, share a cup of coffee with him, listen to his speeches in the squares of Lviv, and read the carefully organized works of Iryna Kalynets by Ihor Kalynets, along with his own works. We live in the era of Ihor Kalynets. And this era is forever as long as Ukraine lives! "Unfortunately, the era of the persons who made up the "Shistydesiatnyky" is slowly receding. There remains only a handful. Their influence on contemporary Ukraine, its independence, its democratic ideology, concern with human rights, and the heroic struggle going on today against the Russian aggression cannot be overstated. With the exception of the Baltic states, Ukraine is unique among the former Soviet republics. It's the only one that is truly democratic and has manifested the will of the people and their freedoms again and again, including through two popular uprisings -revolutions in the 34 years of its independence, and more than ten years of active warfare against a brutal aggressor. The people of Ukraine present an unwillingness to accept anything less than freedom and democracy. People like Ihor Kalynets were exemplary of this undaunted spirit.

July 4, 2025

Stories Both Funny And Sad

Sunday night, I watched a soccer game between the United States and Mexico. It was a championship game for the North and Central American countries. This was not a new phenomenon, but it seemed strange compared to the Copa Americana. I suspect that South America was not included because neither America nor Mexico could ever hope to defeat Brazil or Argentina.

The US scored first very early. But I felt no rush of joy. I actually hoped for an equalizer to make the game more interesting. Mexico scored, and the half ended at 1:1. It went to the 77th minute, and now I was really hoping for a goal from either side as I detest overtime and even more so penalty kicks.

Mexico scored again. Ultimately, Mexico prevailed 2:1, and an irrational joy overcame me. I have no relationship with or to Mexico. Why was I happy? I took a shot of vodka to clear my mind and better help me understand.

I finally came to the conclusion that I was incapable of rooting for a bully and that this was payback for the Gulf of Mexico naming fiasco.

This happened to me, who was born and has lived 73 years in America. This is the country of my citizenship, although I will not be certain of that until the October Supreme Court term, since I was born in 1952 and my parents were immigrants who had not been naturalized until well after my birth. It is a scary proposition to have your rights decided by people like Thomas, Alito, and Kavanaugh. I would rather see a majority opinion written by Sotomayor, Kagan, or Jackson.

I assume that the entire world rooted for Mexico. This is what Donald Trump has done in less than six months. One British psychologist called this mental condition arising from victimhood 'victim to victim' syndrome. It is based on Trump's paranoia that he

201

has been a victim of, at the very least, an uneven press and justice system, to his imposition of strong-arm tactics on the entire world as President. Whether Trump's America is respected throughout the world is besides the point. It certainly is not liked by Mexico, Canada, and Greenland at the very least.

On the subject of Trump, victimhood, a recent use of a trope by Trump in one of his speeches (in Iowa) was branded antisemitic by such haters as Representative Jerry Nadler.

Nadler used to be my congressman when my family lived in Manhattan's East Village, and my children attended St. George Ukrainian Catholic elementary school. He had a reputation for being totally non-receptive to the Ukrainian community located in the district he represented. I experienced that first hand when I attempted to have a school and children crossing sign posted on the corner of East 7th Street and Shevchenko Place. I sought the intercession of Mr. Nadler. Frankly, all I asked was a letter addressed to the city supporting the effort.

Congressman Nadler did not even respond to my solicitation involving child safety as it pertained to Ukrainian Catholic children.

In any event, back to Trump's alleged antisemitism. During his speech, Trump invoked the name "Shylock" when referring to Democratic opponents of his Big Beautiful Bill. This was branded antisemitic, except that in this case it was not. It was a malapropism for which Trump is famous, unless Trump had Nadler on his mind. Trump clearly did not understand the term, as it simply has no application in this case. Trump clearly never read "The Merchant of Venice". This is so obvious from the context.

At the risk of sounding like an apologist for a man that I despise, Trump is not an antisemite. In fact, he defends Israel at every opportunity, even on war crimes. If anything, he is an anti-Palestinian, suggesting even ethnic cleansing in Gaza in order to build a 'Riviera.' His 'Shylock' trope merely shows that he is illiterate.

These two stories are both funny and sad in my view. It shows how far America has fallen. One man surrounded by sycophants has accomplished all this in less than six months. It also exposes politicians such as Congressman Jerry Nadler, who does not have an ethical bone in his body, and explains what our politics have become.

I suppose that's why I rooted for Mexico. Hola!

July 8, 2025

The Art of the Deal

Fifty-five-year-old Marco Rubio appears to be consistently duped by his elder counterpart, old Sergei Lavrov, who has been at Putin's side for over twenty years. Fealty is as important to Putin as it is to Trump. Repercussions are somewhat different so far, as there have been no reported cases of jumping from the fifth floor in America. Lavrov is known throughout the world as a psychotic liar, yet America's Secretary of State walks away from his meetings with Lavrov, lending credence to his counterpart's nonsense. Most recently, he described his Malaysian talks with Lavrov as substantive and constructive.

Simultaneously, Russia continued to bomb Ukrainian cities with more than five hundred drones and missiles on a nightly basis. Particularly hard hit has been the Ukrainian capital, Kyiv. Almost invariably, the targets are civilian sites.

Amidst this travesty and tragedies, finally, America's embarrassing President seems to have pivoted, but not to the extent of an epiphany. He discovered that American stockpiles are not as bare as previously announced and agreed to American munitions, including Patriot defensive missiles, to other NATO members. Several NATO member countries have stepped up with offers to buy American weapons and deliver them to Ukraine as aid. This is the most recent version of Trump's Art of the Deal, made very belatedly, but with profit, at the cost of many human lives.

I am not sure that this gets President Trump over the Nobel Peace Prize finishing line. In Trump's mind, this cannot hurt. Ukraine has been frustrated and perhaps even desperate, so following this 'deal,' President Zelensky may add his own name to the Netanyahu letter to the Nobel committee.

There is nothing inherently wrong with this picture or algorithm. Iran sold Shaheed drones and technology to Russia. At least American weapons will not be sold to Russia, under Donald Trump, that was a possibility.

There is a bill pending in the United States Senate that has been sitting there for some time. That is not unusual except for the fact that his bill has overwhelming support, 83 bipartisan cosponsors. The main Republican co-sponsor is Trump's pal and golf partner, Senator Lindsey Graham from South Carolina. No more duplicitous a cosponsor exists. The main Democrat is Senator Richard Blumenthal from Connecticut, a very strong, legitimate advocate for Ukraine. This bill, despite overwhelming support, is going nowhere unless it is endorsed by Donald Trump. The bill is not about direct aid to Ukraine, but rather about the imposition of sanctions (actually a 500% tariff) on those countries that are purchasing Russian oil and gas. Among those countries, aside from China, the most prominent is India. Those two countries represent 75% of the purchasing. While China is not considered a friend, India is, despite its record of collaboration with Russia and the less-than-stellar human rights record of its Prime Minister, Narendra Modi. Trump has promised to look into the bill and has stated that this bill is 'entirely my option,' so much for illusions of separate branches of government.

Recently, the United States imposed a 50% tariff on Brazil, one of America's largest trading partners, with which America actually has a trade surplus. The reason for the increased tariff is that Donald Trump sympathizes with a former president of Brazil, Jair Bolsonaro, who is being charged and prosecuted for attempting to carry out a coup d'etat in his country after he lost power. Trump is not hiding anything. He has stated very clearly that the tariff is being imposed because of Brazil's prosecution of Bolsonaro.

America is in trouble. Let's forget about America as a leader of the Free World. The issue is whether America still belongs to the Free World. Deals are the modus operandi of the Trump administration. Issues like ethics and morality are irrelevant inconveniences. The art of the deal has made America a conundrum and dangerous unto itself. Thank God that Europe is stepping up, and so global leadership is not entirely made up of Putin, Xi, Kim, the Ayatollah, and Trump. Ukraine is certainly doing its part to save the world for freedom and democracy.

American comedienne, actress, and talk show hostess Rosie O'Donnell, born in Commack, New York, moved to Ireland in January of this year, just before Trump took office. She has and continues to be critical of Trump. Most recently, Trump posted on social media that he is considering revoking her citizenship because she is a danger to America. It does not get any more ridiculous. Perhaps everyone who disagrees with America becoming an authoritarian regime should move as well. No, we will stay and work towards an America free of Trump and MAGA. This may be the time for a Second American Revolution. No Kings or Fools or Traitors!

July 12, 2025

Ruminations for the Curious

According to *The New York Times*, the current United States trade with the Russian Federation stands at 3 billion in imports and only 500 million in exports, thus a trade deficit of 2.5 billion. The imports are primarily metal, aluminum, steel, and uranium. These numbers, however, are significant in view of the sanctions imposed on Russia since 2014 by every president except the current Trump regime. In 2013, Russia exported close to 30 billion and imported close to 10 billion from the United States. In his second term, Trump has neither imposed nor lifted any sanctions dealing with Russia.

While 3 billion is not a large amount of money in terms of trade between the world's largest and relatively large economies, and furthermore, trade between the two has decreased dramatically since 2014, the fact that any trade continues is troubling. In addition, there must be a reason why Trump is imposing a huge tariff on Canadian metal while continuing to trade with Russian metal.

On this subject, other questions remain. Why is Lukoil still doing business in America? Since the initial imposition of sanctions on Russia, Lukoil's presence in America has remained pretty much stable throughout the 11 states where the franchises are located. But there was a reason. Russian gas was sent to a refinery in Sicily and from there distributed throughout the world.

That refinery in Sicily was apparently sanctioned by the European Union in December 2022. Now this conundrum is further explained, that the dealerships are private and owned by Americans, and Lukoil is no longer supplied by Russian gasoline but by American gasoline. Prices have come down accordingly.

Every time I see a Karoline Leavitt press conference or a Trump Cabinet meeting, I am reminded of George Orwell's *Animal Farm* and Napoleon the pig. Everyone refers to the Great Leader and offers praise. Ms. Levitt is never surpassed in this regard. She continues to refer to her boss as the leader of the Free World. In most instances, even when she does not have the faintest idea how to respond, she manages to do so through arrogance. Arrogance is often a weapon used by the uninformed.

Putin's Dimitri Peskov appears less arrogant or mendacious, but then he does not face any independent press. The American press mostly does its job and continues to irritate Ms. Levitt. She is thin-skinned and very programmed, but new at her job. She is only 28, but did run for Congress at 23. She lost. While her education and biography are not particularly impressive, they are replete with MAGA indoctrination. She does appear to be a rising MAGA star, and fealty should never become an issue with her. She needs to temper her manifestations of indignation. Her attitude has to be I am right, and you're wrong, but she cannot exhibit any human frailties. She has to be more robotic as per her indoctrination and less emotional. Transparency is considered a flaw within the MAGA circles. Karoline Leavitt does her best not to be transparent. The secret, however, for a press secretary is to appear to be telling the truth, and that is where Ms. Leavitt fails miserably, when she is obviously lying or fabricating. Perhaps this is not her fault since her boss is a very obvious liar. But everyone expects that from Donald Trump.

Thank you, Melania Trump. Apparently, it took some convincing, but Melania allegedly convinced Donald to sell defensive missiles to NATO members earmarked for Ukraine. The Russians had bombed a hospital in Ukraine. This touched America's first lady. At least this is the story being spread by the Trump White House. Frankly, no one knows what goes on in the mind of the stable genius, but the Melania story does offer a human side to not only a person but an entire family that, thus far, has manifested very little humanity.

Even Trump's humanity has its limitations. America is not giving Ukraine arms. It is selling them for profit through a middleman. 'Selling for profit' is the mantra of the Trump family. That's more like it. Philanthropy is unknown in the MAGA world. Perhaps Ms. Leavitt can spin that.

July 18, 2025

The Only Solution

This is an attempted analysis of the more than a decade-long war of Russian aggression in Ukraine, with the aim of finding a reasonable solution that would result in long-term peace. Of course, there are many factors here that cannot be addressed because of the inability to foresee unexpected circumstances, including force majeure. Nevertheless, this analysis is based on daily scrutiny of the events as they unfolded from the very first day following the fleeing of the Russian surrogate and Ukraine's president, Viktor Yanukovich, from Ukraine to Russia, finding refuge there, and the immediate attack by Russia and its surrogates in the Ukrainian peninsula of Crimea. The study utilizes primary, secondary, and even tertiary sources according to the weight they deserve. I travelled to Ukraine at least 2-3 times annually, met with soldiers and volunteers, read Western and Ukrainian press reports, as well as Russian misrepresentations made before the international community.

I do not pretend to be unbiased, as I am a Ukrainian born in America, well-versed in Ukrainian-Russian relations over 73 years of my life. I have also travelled to Russia several times during the early part of this century. I have never met the main antagonist here, but I have met several of his cohorts, including his foreign minister and his former permanent representative to the United Nations, whom I believe Putin sent to an early grave. My opinion of the Russians that I have met, as well as Russian culture and way of life, is very negative. This view I will not attempt to hide in my analysis. I submit that Russia is the aggressor here, guilty not only of starting this war but of conducting it without any regard for the lives of Ukrainian civilians, including children.

International law or norms do not sway Russian behavior, and over the course of the decade, Russia has become more brazen in this regard.

The easy solution is more often than not, not a solution at all. This adage is not particularly profound, but it does have many historical and contemporary significant and mundane applications. Winning and procuring an unconditional surrender, thereby dictating all terms, is the simplest result, but clearly the most difficult to achieve. Given the fact that Russia's war in Ukraine is well into its twelfth year, thus far, Russia has occupied at best only 20% of Ukrainian territory, an absolute victory beyond comprehension. Russia certainly possesses greater human resources and a larger supply of weapons, but that has been balanced out by Ukraine's ingenuity and assistance from its allies, the United States notwithstanding.

In any discussion of an absolute victory by Russia, intangibles have to be considered. To date, Russia has suffered much greater military losses than Ukraine. Concurrently, Ukraine has suffered civilian and infrastructural loss because the lion's share of the fighting has been on Ukrainian territory and because Russian aggression has been barbaric, with no regard for international law. Ukraine, on the other hand, even when invading Russian territory, has mainly targeted military and energy outposts. Perhaps the single most significant intangible is that the Ukrainian side of the war is existential, while Russia's is simply barbarian imperialism.

Russia fights because it is driven by a psychotic disposition to be an empire. This is a cultural psychosis. Russia does not need Ukraine, except that without Ukraine, Russia is not an empire of historic note. Ukraine's capital, Kyiv, was founded in the 5th century. Moscow was founded in the 12th century. The Kyivan state was in essence an empire by the standards that existed in the IX and X centuries, including a part of the Crimean Peninsula. Muscovy did not exist as an independent state until the XVI century and took both its Christianity and ultimate name from Kyivan Rus'. Muscovy was merely a village in swamp lands with no meaningful identity.

Ukrainians fight back because, without defending themselves, they would lose their land, their identity, and their existence as a nation. They are fighting on their own land. In many cases, they are protecting their elderly parents, spouse, children, future generations, and ensuring their future right to live on that land. Every Ukrainian grandmother is capable of concocting and using a Molotov cocktail. Russian clerics have provided the 'mens rea' and made it abundantly clear that the purpose of the 'special military operation' is to erase Ukrainians off the face of the earth.

Diplomacy is a simple solution, but not an effective one, because in order for diplomacy to succeed, there must be good faith on both sides. The term 'ceasefire' has been misused much too often. A ceasefire, while it may afford both sides an opportunity to regroup, is not an end to the hostilities. Regardless of the terms, a ceasefire would not prevent Russia from being a danger in the future, immediate or remote. It must be acknowledged that Russia's terms for a ceasefire are patently absurd. They are tantamount to a surrender by Ukraine. Certainly, any mediator cannot come from the United States because he/she would not be independent of the American president, who, aside from his past performance as a friend of the Russian president, is also entirely ignorant of the historical hostilities between the two nations. Frankly, Trump does not care if Ukraine exists. Even accepting his disingenuous saving lives concerns over his quest for a Nobel Peace Prize, Ukraine and Ukrainians have no future with someone who knows no history and has no moral underpinning.

Russian history and culture prove that the state and its people are hostile and inveterate imperialists. The Russian Federation today consists of eleven time zones. Only one legitimately belongs to Russia. The remainder are territories invaded and annexed by force. Some one hundred fifty nationalities reside within the Russian Federation. More than half are indigenous. What that means is that their lands do not legitimately belong to Russia. These indigenous peoples are persecuted in myriad ways. Often, they have been cannon fodder in Russian wars. Today, they are posted on the front lines. Their language and culture are suppressed. Despite the fact that the term autonomy is sprinkled throughout the Constitution of the RF, the term has no real application. Upon occasion, when there has been an uprising in any indigenous enclave, that manifestation has been quickly suppressed.

Putin did not make Russia. Russia made Putin. This is the most important fact that the West cannot comprehend. Even a marginal study of the history of the Russian empire would make this most abundantly clear. While Vladimir Putin is brutal, he follows a long list of Russian criminal leaders. Putin himself has patterned his rule and spoken out about his progenitors, Peter the Great and Catherine the Great. They were great only by the measure of Russian historians. Sure, they expanded the empire, but they did so with much blood being spilled.

From the Soviet era, Putin picked up the mantra of Josef Stalin. No greater killer has there been in the history of the world except perhaps for Mao. Even Hitler pales by comparison. Stalin managed to murder between 7 and 10 million Ukrainians in 1932-33 through an enforced famine, which included three million children. The weapon was not simply the lack of food, but the fact that food was confiscated and exported, and then the borders of Ukraine were shut so that the starving could not migrate in search of food. By Stalin's measure, Putin may seem benign. The history of Russia is a story of brutality, tyranny, blood, and millions of victims. That history has become the Russian culture, so that the Russian mother is complicit in the crime.

And so my solution is not the easiest because of its multitude of factors. The Russian Empire, perhaps can be defeated on the battlefield, but certainly not to the point of its absolute destruction or dismantling. A ceasefire is a temporary measure, if only to destroy the Russian economy in the interim. A XXI century economy is a complicated mechanism because it is composed of so many factors and variables. Precisely, because of this, the Russian economic conundrum has to be addressed. Russia is not so complicated. Its main export is oil and gas. Its main industry is the export of these commodities and some other natural resources. Its main industry is the manufacture of weapons, and Russia is not very good at it. War is good for Russia because it feeds the war industry. Sanctions are bad for Russia because they lower the price of its main commodity.

A representative of the Ukrainian community in Russia, Marika Semeneko, recently wrote a Master's thesis at the Central European University in Vienna, Austria, on the subject of what I consider to be Russia's weakest link or greatest frailty- its indigenous composition.

Here are her thoughts:

"The full-scale Russian invasion of Ukraine, launched in February 2022, catalyzed the emergence of new forms of activism among Indigenous peoples from Russia. Initially, activists organized anti-war initiatives to oppose the conscription of Indigenous peoples into a war justified under the pretense of "protecting Russians. As early as March 2022, Ukrainian mass media began circulating narratives about 'Putin's Buryats.' The Buryats, an Indigenous people living in the Republic of Buryatia in Eastern Siberia—approximately 7,000 kilometers from Ukraine— became a focal point of this discourse. In response, activists from the Free Buryatia Foundation, an anti-war movement, challenged the myth of 'Putin's Buryats,' arguing that 'the legacy of colonization and many years of Russification made the Buryats part of the Russian military machine.' In September 2022, following Putin's declaration of partial mobilization, Buryats were conscripted at a rate three times higher than in regions predominantly inhabited by ethnic Russians...Notably, at that time, many of these activists had not yet explicitly identified as Indigenous; instead, they were in the process of exploring an appropriate mode of self-identification. Their initial response was a reactive assertion of their ethnic 'non-Russianness.' For instance, in reaction to pro-war posters in the Republic of Kalmykia... that declared, 'I am Kalmyk, but today I am Russian,' the Kalmyk brand 4 Oirad produced T-shirts bearing the phrase 'Nerusskiy' (I am not Russian) in Russian. Consequently, members of the brand were forced to leave Kalmykia due to criminal prosecution related to the design. With the growth of anti-war activism, activists from various places, republics, and regions began identifying themselves as Indigenous. Putin's official justification for the full-scale invasion of Ukraine—framed through the discourse of 'denazification'—also provoked strong reactions from Indigenous activists, who began criticizing the government for its perceived cynicism. In response, Indigenous activists shared personal accounts of discrimination and systemic racism, arguing that Russia itself required 'denazification.' Highlighting the high levels of xenophobia toward ethnic non-Russians, many Indigenous voices were particularly outraged by a statement Putin made in 2022: 'I am a Russian man, but when I see examples of such heroism as the feat of a young man — Nurmagomed Gadzhimagomedov, a native of Dagestan, a Lak by nationality, our other soldiers, I want to say: I am a Lak, I am a Dagestani, I am a Chechen, Ingush, Russian, Tatar, Jew, Mordvin, Ossetian... I am proud that I am part of this world, part of the mighty, strong, and multinational people of Russia.' In response, Alexandra Garmagapova, head of the Free Buryatia Foundation, remarked: 'When the war needs soldiers, Russia suddenly becomes a multinational state. The essence of the empire is that Indigenous peoples are needed only to die for it. '...Beyond the Free Buryatia Foundation, a range of other Indigenous grassroots initiatives have emerged in resistance to the Russian imperial project. These include Indigenous of Russia, Beda Media, the Free Yakutia Foundation, the Free Kalmykia Foundation, New Tyva, From the Republics, Komi Daily, Republic Speaking, as well as independent activists. This emergent activism is marked by its pronounced heterogeneity and diversity, manifesting in a multiplicity of forms, expressive mediums, and political articulations. Rather than presenting a unified ideology, centralized vision, or singular demand, it is animated by a plurality of images for the present and future. The only shared declaration is encapsulated in a manifesto asserting that the fate of Indigenous peoples cannot be determined without their direct involvement. What binds these varied actors together is a common resistance to Russia's ongoing colonialism...'

By articulating Indigenous rights, autonomy, sovereignty, language, and culture as deeply interconnected claims rooted in colonial oppression—rather than as isolated demands—activists align themselves with a decolonizing insurgency. This insurgent perspective frames Indigenous activists as new political actors struggling not for segmented recognition, but for Indigenous well-being as a whole, without compartmentalization. My interviewees advocate for democratic, decolonized, and autonomous communities. This vision aligns with the concept of decolonizing democracy, which seeks to move beyond Western-centric models that frequently exclude those positioned outside dominant constructions of 'the people.' This concept offers a framework for understanding Indigenous activism in Russia as an eruption of memory—a resurgence of a once-suppressed, all-encompassing agency that periodically flares up and recedes, yet persists in collective memory. Given that decolonization does not produce universal knowledge but rather fosters a horizontal network of local epistemologies, the experience of Indigenous activism in Russia is particularly significant. It represents yet another 'home of thought' striving to dismantle power hierarchies and navigate overlapping colonial discourses—both Western and Russian—that compete with and exclude Indigenous peoples in Russia. Although this activism remains in its early stages and may wane at times, it is unlikely to be extinguished entirely; rather, it persists in memory, ready to re-surge. Perhaps their decolonization otherwise will ultimately find tangible expression. In my current research, I aimed to understand why Indigeneity has become so significant for activists at this particular moment. I conclude that they have found in it a path to emancipation, along with the language and arguments needed to resist imposed narratives and accusations of separatism or nationalism with negative connotations. Nevertheless, I believe the next crucial step is to critically interrogate how Indigeneity itself can operate as an exclusionary category, shaped by colonial frameworks. By reinforcing a binary between colonizers and Indigenous peoples, it imposes boundaries that, as several activists noted, can feel constraining. Many expressed that they often have to 'wear' these imposed identities in order to be heard - despite the fact that such labels do not fully align with their broader objective: dismantling colonial power hierarchies."

I am inclined to find the solution to Russian aggression, whether today's or in the future, through that prism. It certainly is not the easiest solution, but that is the point. It is a real solution. Dismantle the Russian empire.

The application here is not simply for the benefit of Ukraine. In a recent interview, the Prime Minister of Estonia, whose country has a border with Russia and spends more than NATO's goal of 5% of GDP on defence, stated that all of Europe has come to recognize the Russian menace and understand that kilometres will not protect them. That is something that President Zelensky had tried to explain to President Trump, that even an ocean is not an absolute solution to a Russian threat. Despite the fact that Russia has and continues to interfere in democratic processes in the United States, President Trump could not understand the point that President Zelensky was making.

Vladimir Putin is a temporary problem. Bereft of the ability to pay his protectors, his guards, and the police, Putin will succumb to his next rival. Are there rivals? Putin is very rich. There are many rivals who would like to be as rich. Under the circumstances, Putin may be next to leap from the 5th floor. And then there will be a period of chaos, providing an opportunity for the indigenous peoples to arise. Who will pay the military and the police to put down the uprising when there is no money to pay the enforcers?

And so the indigenous people will rise, and they will proclaim their independence, and Russia will draw back to some original borders. Eventually, a strongman should prevail in Moscow, and he/she will control the local unrest in the capital, but the genie will be out of the bottle, and the Federation (empire) will be out of Moscow's control. Having suffered monumental losses in the war and the civil insurrection, and with the economy depleted by a precipitous decline in the price of exported oil and gas, Moscow will be a bystander as independent states are proclaimed.

The countries of Europe, buoyed by this new development, should hasten to recognize the new states. The United States, with or without Trump, will delay recognition until the issue of the nuclear arsenal is addressed. In any event, weapon-grade uranium in the hands of several feckless governments is better than in the hands of one brutal regime. Clearly, the United Nations International Atomic Energy Agency will have to step in.

I am certain that long-term, this is a more realistic and lasting plan than a brief ceasefire, which could never result in a safer world. It certainly merits consideration and support for those indigenous peoples. At the very least, this strategy has more long-term possibilities. Besides, a brief ceasefire would undermine international institutions regarding such matters as arrest warrants, punishing war crimes, etc.

Can anyone imagine a legitimate ceasefire with Russian soldiers and tanks on Ukraine's (Finland's, Estonia's) border, and Ukraine deprived of NATO membership, and borders at best unclear? That's not much of a solution. And it would not get any better unless there is no Russian aggressor. That has to be the strategy – to make Russia non-aggressive. Even people sleeping in America would sleep better. That is the thrust of global peacemaking and security. Ultimately, history will record that in the XXI century, supporting Ukraine was about making the world a safer place by decolonizing and dismantling the Russian empire.

July 21, 2025

The People of Ukraine v. The President of Ukraine

The people of Ukraine are the best. I was about to say that Ukrainian democracy is the strongest in the world, but then someone may pounce and suggest that I am unreasonably biased because I am Ukrainian. I know, however, of no people who have manifested so often their will to live in freedom and democracy.

In 2004, the people of Ukraine voted for a new president. The election was clearly stolen. The people did not simply abide by the steal. They took to the streets overnight and staged a massive revolution referred to as the Orange Revolution. The revolution lasted approximately one month, and it accomplished its purpose. The sitting president of Ukraine, who had brought the stolen candidate onto the political scene initially as Prime Minister and was probably complicit in the attempted steal, had no choice but to relent and was compelled to call a second election. Now the people expressed their will a second time, and with the eyes of the entire world focused on Ukraine's election, this time the people prevailed, and their candidate was elected.

In 2013, the sitting president of Ukraine, unfortunately, a Russian puppet, announced to the world that Ukraine would not be joining the European Union. According to almost every major poll, this contravened the will of the people, and so the People arose once again. The president attempted to quell the uprising by force. People were physically hurt. That resulted in demands for the President's ouster. This Revolution of Dignity proceeded for three months, with at least 100 lives lost. Finally, the president was forced to flee the country. Where? To Russia. The People prevailed.

And now, more than eleven years into a war for the existence of Ukraine as a country, Ukrainians as a people and democracy as a way of life for God knows how many other countries and peoples, the

People of Ukraine manifested an undaunted will that could not be overcome. The President of Ukraine by all accounts, a good and just man, yet clearly stressed out by more than three years of a war on all fronts, and certainly, concerned with traitors and infiltrators within, took upon himself the unenviable duty to strengthen his control over the levers of government, lest the enemy get the upper hand within the government of Ukraine itself.

I believe that in good faith and aimed at protecting the branches of government and the state during wartime, he initiated and his party passed in the Parliament of Ukraine a law making all branches of government subject to the control of people whom he could trust. Except that Ukraine, as any truly democratic state, belongs not to the President, his people, or any branch of government, but to the People themselves.

A democracy is predicated on the will of the People, and the state exists solely for the purpose of serving the People. Any misuse of state power for personal enrichment by government personnel cannot be tolerated and must be prosecuted to the fullest extent of the law. Otherwise, there is no rule of law, equal treatment of People under the law, and no democracy, but an oligarchy. The president himself is not above the law.

Well, the President of Ukraine had to be reminded that a democracy is the rule of the People and that is what the People of Ukraine did. They took to the streets on their own. It was a spontaneous demonstration by the People of Ukraine that they would not stand for anything less than a democracy that is ruled by the will of the People. The President did not attempt to oppose the will of the people. Two days after the anti-democratic bill passed in the parliament and was signed into law by the President, that same President submitted to parliament a draft bill of a new law that would undo what the prior law was meant to do.

This was a tremendous victory not only for Ukraine and Democracy. It was a teaching moment for leaders of democratic states everywhere in the world, that they may be presidents, but not kings, and their duty is to serve the people who elected them and those who did not.

Congratulations to the People of Ukraine, as well as the President of Ukraine. As an American citizen, I can think of at least one President who can learn much from this experience. But in order to learn, you must understand democracy and be willing to serve.

July 25, 2025

Two Men Outside the Civilized World

America's President Donald Trump and Israeli Prime Minister Benjamin Netanyahu are eerily similar. Perhaps that's why they get along, and Netanyahu has actually nominated Trump for the Nobel Peace Prize. The Prime Minister recently stressed on television that there is no famine or starvation in Gaza. Surprisingly, Netanyahu's staunchest ally, Donald Trump, suggested that Netanyahu was lying. United Nations' humanitarian aid personnel have disputed that for months, and much of Israel's civil society, concerned with human rights, has been appalled by Mr. Netanyahu for a long time. What keeps him in power are the right-wing extremists.

Almost simultaneously, while in Scotland, Mr. Trump provided some fake news on a different topic. Sitting next to European Commission President Ursula von der Leyen, Trump extolled his own achievements in negotiating a deal with the EU, including a 15% tariff on EU products (half of what Trump initially threatened) and a 750-billion-dollar commitment by the EU to purchase American energy. What Trump did not say was that American consumers would be paying the 15% and that the $750 billion commitment was over three years and was non-binding on either party. The facts belie the magnitude of the commitment as well. EU countries only purchase about half of the $250 billion annually in energy, and American companies are able to export only a total of some $300 billion in energy annually all over the world. But let's not cloud the issues with facts.

Perhaps, more importantly, Trump changed his mind yet again on secondary sanctions on Russia from 50 days to 10-12 days from August 28, 2025. Russia responded later that night by bombing civilian targets, including a prisoner of war camp, a hospital, and a maternity ward, like never before. We will see what happens on August 9th.

The similarities between the two leaders are stark. Both lie and mislead. Both are hardly symbols of global leadership. One is a convicted felon. The other is under indictment with a trial pending. The distinction in this case, and perhaps only in this instance, is significant because of the human and moral element. One is a war criminal, the other not yet. At one point, President Trump did suggest ethnic cleansing as a solution to the Gaza problem. But he was not in a position to implement that solution. Of the two million people in Gaza, some 60,000 have died, many of them children. The remaining functional medical facilities are replete with children ailing from malnutrition. On the other side, the only people affected by Trump's misleading are stupid MAGA acolytes, since only they continue to believe Trump's nonsense. They also believe that climate change is not man-made, that immunization does not save lives, and that Donald Trump is an intelligent human being. He is certainly not intelligent. As to his humanity, I leave that up to the reader.

In any event, brazen disregard for the distinction between good and evil, as well as truth and lies, is a common characteristic of the two world leaders. Netanyahu falls into that category of global leadership because of Israel's position in the Middle East. While its geopolitical location is unenviable, at least some of its territory rightfully and historically belongs to the Jewish people. That fact in no way detracts from the rights of others, such as the Palestinians. Israel is the strongest and, in fact, the only nuclear power to date in the Middle East, and hopefully that remains because Israel is surrounded by unfriendly states. Still, that does not give someone like Netanyahu the right to disregard the rights of other people. A two-state solution with which Netanyahu cannot come to grips is the only solution.

Trump's problem is that he is neither morally nor intellectually equipped to be the leader of the democratic world. Still, he is the president of the United States, the wealthiest and arguably militarily strongest country in the world. The fact of the matter is that President Trump, more often than not, embarrasses America as the world leader. Other world leaders have long given him the benefit of a doubt, or rather, they have simply learned to pander to his moral and intellectual weaknesses and play him when the need arises.

In the short term, this type of play can work. By January 2027, the House of Representatives should become a representative check on Trump, notwithstanding Republican gerrymandering, and by 2029, Trump will be out of office. The next chapter still needs to be written.

July 30, 2025

Ukraine Acts Swiftly And Convincingly – The West Drags Its Feet

Ukraine's parliament has voted to restore the independence of two key anti-corruption agencies, moving to defuse the country's biggest political crisis since Russia's invasion. Politicians on July 31 voted 331 to 0 in favour of the bill, which President Volodymyr Zelenskyy submitted last week following pressure from thousands of protesters and top European officials.

The BBC reporter who provided this information stated that the President of Ukraine was embarrassed. I suspect that, subsequently, after being reprimanded by his more knowledgeable superiors, the reporter had a better understanding of how democracy works in Ukraine.

Even in wartime, when there are obvious exigent circumstances, the democratically elected President of Ukraine recognized that he is merely a tool of the people's will (Servant of the People, which is his political party's moniker). The giveaway should have been the vote count.

In wartime, enemy infiltration is a very powerful weapon. It can result in many lives lost. It can also influence military and political strategy. During World War 2, the Soviet Union infiltrated the American Executive Branch, State, and Treasury at least. President Franklin D. Roosevelt traveled to Yalta in February 1945 to discuss the end of the war with Soviet strongman Josef Stalin. His chief adviser was a Soviet agent, and FDR gave up all of Eastern Europe to Stalin. This resulted in a half-century Cold War.

President Zelensky's concern with Russian infiltration in the agencies of the Ukrainian government, not within Zelensky's control, should be understood. Nevertheless, Zelensky learned from his people that they would not accept anything less than an independent monitoring of state corruption. People were dying for Ukraine, and they would not stand for the ruling elite benefiting financially from the war. So Zelensky made a good-faith appraisal and a U-turn, ostensibly finding other ways to fight Russian infiltration. Zelensky's people submitted the new bill to Parliament, and Parliament, guided by the will of the people, endorsed it unanimously.

Democracy very rarely functions unanimously, but this was a manifestation of democracy and unity. I recall a similar, but less overwhelming manifestation of a united effort in Ukraine in May 2014. Russia had already invaded in February of that year. A presidential election was scheduled for May, with the winner needing a majority to be elected. There were more than twenty candidates, but there was also a need for unity to elect a president in the first round, because that would manifest to the world Ukraine's resolve to fight as one. Petro Poroshenko received more than 50% in the first round and was elected President.

Going back to the time of Ukraine's independence, when Soviet Ukraine proclaimed independence on August 24, 1991, Ukraine took a risk, which manifested its will unlike any other Soviet republic or satellite. Ukraine called for a referendum on independence, with many regions consisting of descendants of Russian colonizers. Despite the odds, over 90% of the entire country voted in favor of independence.

Between the anti-corruption bills, the European Union warned Ukraine that it was withholding some of the money earmarked for Ukraine's defense. This was done very hastily, as it took President Zelensky only two days to announce that he would introduce a new bill to essentially nullify the first. I do not know what the EU was thinking. Perhaps it was to put pressure on President Zelensky to do what he said he would. If the international community has learned anything, it has to believe that President Zelensky is neither Putin nor Trump. He is a straight shooter and true to his word.

Upon passage of the second bill, the EU leadership and leaders of EU member states welcomed the news. I trust that any diminution of aid is now moot.

Amidst all of this, it is important to note that Russia is bombing Ukrainian cities, mainly civilian targets, at an alarming rate. Military aid to Ukraine, unfortunately, largely remains in the promise stage. Not a single Patriot missile defense system has been delivered to Ukraine since Trump took office. President Zelensky has announced that Ukraine has secured three Patriots, meaning not that they are on Ukrainian territory, but that three have been promised to be purchased from the United States by European countries. At least seven more are needed. In fact, as for American weapons, to date, only President Biden's drawdown of weapons has reached Ukraine. Ukraine acts while the West talks. It's almost as if Ukraine alone is fighting for the entire 'democratic' world.

July 31, 2025

Putin Plays Trump Yet Again

Yesterday was August 8, 2025. Additional sanctions were to be imposed on Russia, and secondary tariffs on countries that continue to purchase Russian oil and gas. India, which purchases almost one-third of Russian energy exports, had a fifty percent tariff imposed on its imports into the United States. This is despite Prime Minister Modi and President Trump's close relationship as strongmen. The Prime Minister is a thug who kills Muslims in India and Kashmir. That fifty percent tariff, however, is still in the stage of merely a threat and not a reality.

In the interim from bloviating to reckoning, Trump apparently afforded Putin one last chance by sending his special envoy to Moscow, a political neophyte but adept at real estate. Certainly, more educated than the President. Putin, a murderer but not stupid, recognizing Trump's need for grandstanding, suggested a Summit between the two leaders. On the day of reckoning, Trump did nothing. There were no new sanctions. The Kremlin crowed: "We win again."

I am not sure about history, but in my lifetime, never has there been a more embarrassing American president. Perhaps America can withstand the farce currently displayed. The more serious problem is that because of America's wealth and prior leadership, the world, and in particular countries in need like Ukraine, which are actually physically protecting the democratic world, may not survive the vacuum in American leadership.

The Summit of two questionable presidents (yes, questionable because one was not elected democratically and the other has no competency or qualifications) will take place in Alaska. One Ukrainian friend suggested that Trump swap Alaska for peace. In any event, while the Summit is not meaningless because it will affect future American relations with Ukraine, it certainly is not a component of a peace formula. This is not a real estate deal. It is a fool's attempt to affect the lives of millions of people.

There is no point in analyzing the terms of any prospective ceasefire unless it is quite simply an unconditional one. In any event, the Summit will benefit Russia and Putin as they continue to bomb and murder Ukrainian women and children.

The press conference, if any, following the Summit may be as embarrassing as the Helsinki press conference in 2018. Trump is certainly capable of outdoing himself. If Trump is pleased with his achievements, even if they are to the great detriment of Ukraine and its people, he may renege on providing any support to Ukraine in the form of the sale of arms or sharing intelligence. Without a doubt, Ukraine has suffered more than ever during Trump's two hundred days in office.

It has been alleged that Russia insists on recognition of its annexation of four regions, Luhansk, Donetsk, Zaporizhzhia, and Kherson, as well as a lifting of American sanctions in return for a ceasefire. Should Trump agree to such terms, the Summit will go down as a sellout. Russia does control the four regions. There is an outstanding warrant for Putin's arrest by the International Criminal Court. The European Union and Ukraine will never agree to these concessions. America will be considered a rogue member of the United Nations for allowing a war criminal on its territory. America is already a rogue member of the global community for voting together with Russia and North Korea earlier this year against a UN General Assembly resolution condemning Russia's invasion of Ukraine. The triumvirate of Trump, Putin, and Kim will go down in history as three thugs.

Reality notwithstanding, the Summit will be hailed by both participants as productive at the very least. It may be followed by a second summit, which Trump has suggested to include President Zelensky of Ukraine. Zelensky has suggested representatives from European allies. Russia has not agreed to any second summit, and Putin has stalled on ever meeting with Zelensky. Ukraine's suggestion of European allies is warranted, certainly since a meeting of Trump, Putin, and Zelensky would be an ambush for Zelensky. Zelensky understands that very well, but dares not say it directly since he wants to maintain relations with America.

Ultimately, Ukraine's place is with Europe and America, as the antithesis to Russian imperialism is merely a camouflage. America has much grown up to do after Trump in order to reprise its role as an honest broker.

August 9, 2025

TRUMP AND PUTIN
IN ALASKA

A Bad Day for Ukraine - A Sad Day for America

I could not imagine a more substance-depleted and yet very revealing summit than Alaska 2025. The sycophancy was dramatic, and the stakes were monumental because hundreds of thousands of human lives were at stake.

A convicted felon, the leader of a country once at the very pinnacle of the Free World, was rehabilitating an international war criminal charged with indiscriminate murder of civilians and the kidnapping of children. Trump applauded Putin to commence the farce and concluded the travesty by pandering to his every word. He gave the mass murderer everything he wanted and needed for rehabilitation. Heretofore, he had been an isolated pariah. The democratic world received nothing. There was no ceasefire. Russia continued to bomb Ukraine overnight, Friday into Saturday.

Putin knew exactly what to say. He spoke of the root cause of the conflict, blaming the West, referred to Ukrainians as brothers with a shared history, once again preaching an alternative history, then commended Trump by repeating Trump's nonsense that the conflict would not have arisen had Trump been president, thereby once again impugning the West for starting the aggression. Trump ate it up and said nothing. This was a lead performance by Putin with Trump playing a supporting role.

Apparently, Ukraine's President Zelensky will meet at the White House with Trump this coming week, to be followed by a purported trilateral meeting somewhere in Europe, in a venue hospitable to the international war criminal. Hopefully, the White House meeting will not be another ambush like the Oval Office in February. The trilateral one will be one-sided since it will feature unequal numbers in favor of Russia. Ukraine will be unduly pressured. Trump will side with the enemy, except that now, Russia and Putin have become strange allies of Trump and America.

In an interview with his uneducated lackey, Sean Hannity, Trump stated that on a scale of one to ten, the Summit was a ten. He immediately added that this referred to the congeniality, thereby acknowledging that, as to substance, it was clearly a zero.

The Fox News sycophants initially seemed critical since they could not point to a single agreement reached. But then the word came down, and the spin ensued. Trump's former Secretary of State Mike Pompeo, in his interview on Fox, attempted analysis rather than spin. But he could not point to a single achievement, so at the end the word came down, and Pompeo lauded his ex-boss.

Why was this bad for Ukraine? Because Ukraine needs a ceasefire, and in the alternative, it needs the secondary sanctions on Russia promised by Trump three weeks ago, which are long overdue. A significantly sanctioned Russia on energy can become a bankrupt one without the ability to pay not only its soldiers but also its police who are keeping Putin in power.

Why was this sad for America? Because prior to the Summit, Trump held a long-distance meeting with European allies, including President Zelensky. The result of that meeting was an apparent assurance by Trump that a ceasefire was his mission in Alaska, and if Putin refused, the meeting would be cut short. No ceasefire was agreed to, but Trump did not walk out. Now he is saying that a long-term settlement is better than a short-term ceasefire, precisely what Putin had been saying all along, in order to bomb, destroy, and kill as much as he could and attempt to garner additional territory.

Trump also assured the Europeans that he would not discuss territorial swapping since that was entirely within the purview of Ukraine. Now he admits that territorial swapping was discussed and that Ukraine has to agree.

At the podium stood two endemically lying criminals essentially affable towards each other and looking forward to a productive relationship, moral considerations and the democratic world be damned. They did not take any questions because it's more difficult to maintain your lying composure when you are being cross-examined by the press.

True, Putin does not have this problem in Russia because there is no free press. Unfortunately, one of the speakers was the President of America, once a beacon of hope and a paragon for democratic principles, and one nation under God. God was entirely absent from that room.

President Zelensky has options, however. Without offending the evil lying clown in the White House, Ukraine must stay the course with Europe entirely on Ukraine's side. Every so often, something helpful may come from this White House, and long-term Ukraine and a real America could be natural allies once again. The next two events will be Zelensky's second ambush at the White House and a further ambush somewhere in Europe if the trilateral meeting actually develops. Don't hold your breath!

August 16, 2025

The Take Away from the Washington Summit

This summit is impossible to assess without a silver ball. Nothing is clear, and certainly nothing is written in stone. A trilateral meeting is anticipated. Trump seems to have agreed to America joining in security guarantees. Two factors have to be considered. One is that Trump changes his mind very often, and two, he lies at any opportunity, perhaps not even consciously. One thing is certain: the situation is no better than at the end of July when Trump amended his 50-day deadline for a ceasefire to 10-12 days and threatened Russia with crippling secondary sanctions. That was a more likely scenario than Russia agreeing to a ceasefire settlement with Western security guarantees like a NATO Article 5 provision.

President Trump stressed that Russia had agreed to Western security guarantees for Ukraine. The Russian Foreign Ministry publicly said no. Someone is lying, but who knows, since both Putin and Trump are endemic in that regard.

The overriding issue with these meetings is that while the Ukrainian and European side recognize that Putin is a criminal, intent on destroying Ukraine and anything else that stands in his way, Trump treats Putin as a respected member of the civilized world. Clearly, Putin plays Trump's vanity, and Trump is so psychotic that he genuinely does not recognize the play. And while to appease Trump's psychosis, allies pander to his flaws in the hope that America remains an ally, the attempts to bring an end to the war are going backwards.

Last Sunday, during an interview with ABC's This Week, National Security Adviser and Secretary of State Marco Rubio made a striking assertion that you cannot put pressure through sanctions on an adversary if you are trying to make a deal. Little Marco carries no weight in the White House despite the double position. Nevertheless, he does represent the level of political wherewithal among Trump's advisers. During Trump's first term, he did have some grown-ups in the room due to his own political uncertainty as a neophyte. Even Trump possessed a modicum of humility. Buoyed by arrogance, Trump chose sycophancy as the only criterion for service in the White House during his second term.

Pandering is a component of politics. For that very reason, five leaders of European states, as well as two leaders of very substantial international structures, travelled to America on short notice to be with Ukraine during its meeting with the American president. This certainly would not have been necessary under President Biden. But Trump is very tricky. There is always a danger that Trump can choose to align himself with the enemy. Long term, there is probably little danger, but at least until 2028, this could have a devastating effect not only on Ukraine but also on all of Europe. Not a single one of those leaders, including Zelensky and Putin, remotely likes or respects Trump. But they need him because he is the President of certainly the wealthiest and probably militarily the strongest country in the world.

The apparent purpose of these summits and, even more so, the anticipated trilateral one, is to keep Donald Trump and America on the side of the democratic world, and thus prospectively an ally of Ukraine. Ukraine cannot survive if Trump goes entirely rogue. People continue to die because Russia will not stop the killing. I suspect that there will not be a trilateral summit within the next two weeks or one with any results. That should make it apparent even to Trump that only a bankrupt Russia and a much more compliant one would be amenable to a ceasefire or settlement on rational terms.

So the immediate need is pressure, rendering Russia unable to fight. There is no need to withhold security guarantees or even NATO membership. Russia would understand a fait accompli better than weakness. Only then would a summit produce substantive results.

August 19, 2025

Very Difficult to Explain

Unfortunately, summit week has not been productive. In fact, it has been destructive like never before. Russia has bombed Ukraine with drones and missiles as if the summits offered an opportunity, and so it did. To a normal person in the White House, the message would be loud and clear: Russia does not want peace. But President Trump is not normal. There is no other way to explain his behavior.

Donald Trump has been president for four years and seven months. There was a four-year hiatus during which he had time to ruminate and defend himself in criminal and civil proceedings. Vladimir Putin has been the dictator of Russia throughout this period, including the hiatus. Trump has had ample opportunity to become familiar with Putin's form of negotiations, which are relatively transparent because the single overwhelming variable is lying. Certainly, the author of The Art of the Deal should be sufficiently sophisticated to recognize when his counterpart is playing him.

Clearly, the most bizarre demand put forth by Putin has been that Russia should be one of the countries included in security assurances or guarantees. I suspect that in history no aggressor has made such a demand. There is little possibility that Putin could have been misunderstood in Alaska. Simply from Putin's prepared speech at the press conference, it was clear that Putin was not about to agree that NATO countries would go onto Ukrainian territory without Russia's presence. Putin referred to the illusory root cause of the war.

While Trump is clearly not the deal master of his ghostwritten book, he is also not a complete idiot. He will never admit that the Alaska summit was a disaster worse than Helsinki of 2018. His mentor, Roy Cohn, advised him never to admit mistakes and never to apologize. So, Trump, internally recognizing his global embarrassment, referred to his often-used strategy: to smear his predecessor, President Joe Biden, for not equipping Ukraine with offensive weapons. The retort from the Biden camp is that ATACMS were delivered to Ukraine. There is silence about the time of delivery and the limitations imposed.

In Trump's first term, Ukraine was already at war with Russia. Late in that term, he supplied Ukraine with Javelins, also not an offensive weapon.

Joe Biden can be criticized for aiding Ukraine inadequately, only enough so that it would not lose the war, but certainly not win it. On the other hand, Donald Trump, aside from the noted Javelins, has provided Ukraine no munitions, has imposed no new sanctions on Russia, and held a summit with Russia's dictator in which he simply pandered to an international criminal, global pariah, and brutal aggressor.

The fact of the matter is that Trump's behavior cannot be explained. His surrogates or advisors are incompetent and often despicable. They deserve only a brief. Mention. Vice President Vance truly is "Just Dance Vance". He is a dancing puppet next to his boss, just biding his time until he can become president. Little Marco is an educated liar who has based his entire political career upon one lie that his parents fled Cuba to escape Fidel Castro. His anti-communism is his mendacious badge of honor. Then there is Steve Witcoff, a real estate billionaire with no political expertise. Finally, there is Pete Hegseth, with only a bachelor's degree and no expertise. And there is also Pam Bondi, having received her first big chance to rise. There are no grown-ups in the room.

That leaves Trump all alone. His bizarre behavior towards Putin and Russia cannot be explained. It can only be characterized as disastrous and bewildering. The longer Trump stays in office and deals with his close friend, by his own admission, Vladimir Putin, the more likely the 'kompromat' scenario is to bring grief.

God save Ukraine and America, two natural allies, inhabited by good people but torn apart perhaps by a former Soviet and now a Russian asset. The only other explanation is that he really is an evil clown trained by his master, Roy Cohn, with no consideration for morality, the truth, or anyone else other than himself.

Recently, conscious of his own mortality because he is 79 years old, Trump bemoaned that he might not get to heaven....

August 21, 2025

The Triumph of Statehood

My late father, Evhen Lozynskyj, belonged to that Greatest Generation of Ukrainians who grew up and struggled between the world wars of the last century, and who continued to fight for our statehood until the end of their lives. In 1961, he wrote about the mission of our diaspora to support the people of Ukraine:

"From ancient times, idealistic principles have been deeply rooted in the spirit of the Ukrainian people. They formed the foundation of an idealistic worldview, whose central idea was the idea of the nation, its independence, and the free development of its strength and values, and of its political and legal expression, the state.

Only the state can guarantee freedom and justice to every person within the framework of the common good of the nation, which is the fundamental and unshakable law of all social life.

The state is the collective good of the entire nation, of all its generations, living, dead, and yet unborn, bound together by common origin, language, history, culture, territory, and struggle.

Thus, in a condition of political enslavement, the foremost postulate for the Ukrainian nation is the achievement and creation of an Independent and Sovereign Ukrainian State. And it is the duty of every person of Ukrainian blood, wherever they live and whatever other homeland they may have, to serve the Ukrainian nation, especially when it is fighting for its very existence and freedom against the greatest enemy of humanity."

Today, we mark the thirty-fourth anniversary of our independence, the triumph of statehood. For a nation, there is no greater holiday, filled with joy and hope.

During these decades of renewed statehood, in Ukraine and abroad, our people have demonstrated extraordinary strength of will, respect for neighbors and minorities, diligence, understanding, and ingenuity. We remember the milestones of this determination:

1. The Declaration of Sovereignty in July 1990,
2. The Revolution on Granite in October 1990,
3. The Proclamation of Independence on August 24, 1991,
4. The Referendum of December 1, 1991,
5. The Orange Revolution of 2004,
6. The Revolution of Dignity of 2013–2014,
7. The Protest Against Corruption in August 2025.

These are the achievements of a mature democratic people, a people with a thousand-year history of expressing their will, from princely councils to the election of Kozak hetmans, and a long tradition of divine inspiration and Christian mercy.

The scars of long years of statelessness and the heroic struggles of past generations have raised new generations who set themselves the task of never again allowing Ukraine to be without a state, despite great hardship, overwhelming force, or betrayal by others and by their own. Our state is now here for eternity. No one can erase our people from the face of the earth, and no one can take away from us our most precious treasure, our hard-won statehood.

Such is the fate of Ukraine and the Ukrainians. Even in celebration, we must not forget the shadow of the enemy who still gazes hungrily at our land and our people, with eyes of hatred and weapons aimed.

Today we celebrate, and today again we must prepare to defend ourselves. In these past three and a half years, the world has watched us with awe. We have earned that awe with our blood and with our resolve.

The holiday of our statehood is the celebration of our people, joined by the support of true friends. Every Ukrainian has reason to be proud, but also to remain ready for the struggles that lie ahead.

Our great poet Ivan Franko wrote: "To struggle means to live." This is the credo of our existence and the mark of our unbroken spirit. We pray to the Almighty to grant us the strength, both spiritual and physical, to continue this struggle.

Glory to Ukraine!

Glory to its Heroes!

August 24, 2025

It's Getting Worse

On Monday morning, following Ukrainian Independence Day, I went to the Mountain Lakes, New Jersey, library as is my custom to read The New York Times and The Wall Street Journal. I walked up to the counter as the librarian was stamping the two publications. She commented on how it's always bad news. I replied that it's largely due to the cretin in the White House. He creates or exacerbates most of the problems. She said that she could not agree with me more, but she can't say it out loud in the library.

I then picked up the two newspapers and went to the armchair to read. Soon, I became infuriated as both newspapers reported that while Trump had not provided Ukraine with any American munitions to date, he did reimpose limitations on the use of ATACMS by Ukraine. They cannot be used to attack Russian territory. Ironically, Trump had recently criticized President Joe Biden for initially imposing limitations on the use of American arms in Russia as the reason why Ukrainians could not get the upper hand in the war. They could only defend. I exclaimed out loud, That SOB! The librarians looked at me and smiled.

I briefly wandered about, chose two books for check out, handed my library card to a second librarian, who, apparently recognizing my name as unusual, and since Ukraine has been so much in the news, asked whether I was Ukrainian. I answered emphatically, yes, very much so, and asked whether she was. She put her right hand on her heart and said No, but my heart is with Ukraine.

As I walked out, I thought out loud, Americans are good people, but I wish that Trump would simply die for the mercy of Ukraine and the entire world. But, then there is the jerk successor, I pondered - Just Dance Vance. He may be even worse. And then there's the Speaker. Johnson. He is a moron who hides behind his own version of the Bible. No one has done more to assist Putin's aggression than these three evil fools.

I decided that I have to pray. Political assassinations are more the purview of MAGA nuts such as the Proud Boys or, at the least, advocates for the misinterpretation of the Second Amendment, such as Thomas, Alito, and Kavanaugh. The Second Amendment is a deeply flawed anachronism. That provides two legal options: death by natural causes or impeachment. The latter is very unlikely as it would require a two-thirds vote in the Senate, where the Republicans currently hold a slim majority. The former is viable given Trump's age and morbid obesity. But Vance is relatively young and a hillbilly. Hillbillies tend to live a long time. Johnson should not be an issue after the 2026 elections. But Vance will go away only in 2029.

There is some hope. In any event, politics can be dynamic. Canada's Prime Minister Carney traveled to Kyiv for Independence Day and promised one billion Canadian dollars of munitions from Canada within six weeks. This was good news, given Canada's past performance as perhaps the lowest donor per GDP to the Ukrainian war effort. Hungary's Prime Minister had been bad at assisting Ukraine even when its deputy prime minister was of Ukrainian ethnicity.

Another bright spot was the plight of Hungary's Prime Minister Viktor Orban. Orban suffered two serious setbacks recently, one was a bombing by his Russian friends of the Transcarpathian region of Ukraine, where many Hungarians reside. The second was Ukraine's destruction of Russia's facility providing relatively cheap energy to Hungary and Slovakia. There will not be any Russian energy for Hungary and Slovakia anytime soon. Orban is a thug. So is Prime Minister Fico of Slovakia. Both understand only strength. This was a manifestation of strength.

It is true that America, with Trump at the helm, is getting worse. Still, more than 66% of Americans support Ukraine. But America is floundering as a democracy. Under Trump, it is becoming more and more an autocracy. Ukraine aside, the military with Trump and the miscreant alcoholic Secretary Hegseth is aiming to take control of

America's cities. Longtime federal employees are being fired at will, essentially in revenge. Trump's disloyal former advisers are under investigation. This is the revenge regime. Departments are being closed down. Some are undergoing a very telling name change. Trump today announced that the Department of Defense will be renamed the Department of War. That is very appropriate since Trump and his MAGA America are at war with everyone except Russia.

August 26, 2025

The President of America is a Russian Asset

"The top leader of the world's foremost superpower is, objectively, a Soviet or Russian asset," Portugal's President de Sousa said, according to the Portugal Pulse's report. "He operates as an asset."

Certainly, a strong and damning accusation. Portugal is not some outlier state. It is a founding member of the North Atlantic Treaty Organization (NATO). Certainly, this is a statement by a very high official.

I am certain that many high officials of NATO member states and others have shared this sentiment at the very least in their minds and, perhaps, in private conversation. Diplomacy requires a level of restraint, especially when dealing with a superpower upon whom you have and may need to rely in the future.

The statement itself carries a bifurcated message. One is that Donald Trump may actually be a Russian asset or, at the very least, he operates as such. In criminal law, the message is that while there may not be a 'smoking gun' or a document that specifically identifies Donald Trump as a member of some Russian secret service, there is certainly ample circumstantial evidence of this fact. Most criminal cases are decided on circumstantial evidence.

Consider two instances of joint appearances at a press conference by Donald Trump as President of the United States of America and Vladimir Putin as Strongman of the Russian Federation, two seemingly adversarial countries with very different forms of government.

The first was in July 2018 in Helsinki, Finland, a particularly interesting venue since Finland has a long border with Russia and a sad history. Donald Trump was faced with an apparent dilemma: accepting the findings of American intelligence or the words of

Vladimir Putin. He chose Putin. On a global stage, this was much more than disgraceful. It was a betrayal of American intelligence and thus treasonous.

The second instance took place very recently in August of this year in Anchorage, Alaska, also a very interesting venue given its history of belonging to both countries at different times. It was not simply a working meeting. Trump rolled out the red carpet and applauded Putin upon his arrival. Immediately prior to the summit, Trump had reached a consensus by his own admission with his European allies, including Ukraine, that if Putin did not agree to an immediate ceasefire, Trump would walk. Putin did not agree. Trump did not walk. He betrayed his agreement and his European allies. Russia brutally bombed Ukraine the day before the meeting and the day after. Nothing else really mattered except that allegedly promises were made and not kept, and the bottom line is that Putin has had a free hand ever since.

The first example was a case of treason. The second was betrayal. Two very significant and related acts that point directly, albeit circumstantially, to Trump's acts as a Russian asset. Treason is the betrayal of one's country. Betrayal goes beyond the country itself and extends to others.

There is so much more, however. Trump's actions in undermining American democracy during the January 6, 2021, attack upon the Capitol, as well as many of his Executive Orders undermining Congress during his second term, and contempt for judicial rulings are all significant factors in establishing his treasonous behavior as President.

No one outside the Kremlin has done more to support Russia, its aggression in Ukraine, and undermine American democracy than Donald J. Trump.

A case for impeachment certainly can be made, but not with this House. A trial in the Senate would be fruitless. Consider such objective paragons of morality and democracy as Senator Lindsey Graham of South Carolina, who would constitute the jury.

What should be done is to make a clear case for America and the world that Donald J. Trump is a Russian asset. There is no other reasonable explanation for Trump. This is no longer a Ukrainian or American issue. It is a concern for all people who believe that Russia is a global scourge and that the best weapon against authoritarianism is democracy. Otherwise, we may not only lose Ukraine, but also America as a bulwark of democracy. The Founding Fathers and Mothers would never forgive us.

August 30, 2025

Is Trump a Russian Agent or an Asset?
Is His Behavior Intentional?

Further to my recent piece on this subject, following some comments from my readers, I believe that some clarification is needed.

All agents are assets, but not all assets are agents. However, the lack of a smoking gun or a document does not preclude agency. There is simply no direct evidence. Consider two of Trump's three marriages as opportunities for secret services affiliated with Moscow to influence Trump.

Ivana Trump, born in Czechoslovakia, brought Trump into the view of the Czech secret police. Files later revealed that her father, Miloš Zelníček, was a documented member and informant. He provided reports on his daughter and son-in-law. The StB (the Secret police of Communist Czechoslovakia) monitored Trump's visits to Czechoslovakia, ensuring that information about the rising New York businessman was regularly passed on to Moscow.

Melania Trump, born in Slovenia, came from a household monitored by the Yugoslav state security. Her father, Viktor Knavs, had a file in the

UDBA (Directorate for State Security) archives. While there is no proof of active collaboration, the existence of a file confirms that the Yugoslav secret police considered the family worth tracking. Mainstream profiles confirm Knavs' Communist Party membership and state-sector employment, a background that would have kept him on the radar of security services.

Nonetheless, this is inconclusive by legal standards.

Russia, from czarist times, has always been a police state. In the last two centuries, the Cheka, NKVD, KGB, and its successor agencies, the FSB and SVR, have spent decades cultivating businessmen, politicians, journalists, and public figures in the West. Not all have been willing participants. The measure for Russia has not been intent but utility.

Consider Donald Trump from his first Moscow trip in 1987 to his conduct as president and, perhaps, beyond. There is a consistent pattern. He has been vulnerable to manipulation, financially entangled with Russian-linked networks, and politically aligned with Kremlin objectives.

American investigators have documented this, and European intelligence services quietly acknowledged it years before it was spoken aloud by the Portuguese president recently.

The issue of Trump's intent is a whole separate matter. I would submit that the criminal element of intent is present. It has evolved over the years. Trump is essentially a simple man. Initially, Trump was consumed with himself alone, his persona, and his wealth. The Machiavellian principle of the ends justifying the means was and is deeply embedded within Trump. The dishonorable Roy Cohn had been his mentor, and the Russians were helpful. There was a callous indifference to morality, principles, and ramifications.

Russia further cultivated Trump. It saw a potential asset. Trump acquiesced but sought more. He wanted to develop his properties in Russia. Financial largesse and fame were the motives. A Trump Tower in the center of Moscow became the symbol of his aspirations, money, and fame.

When Trump decided to run for President, initially, few in the United States gave him much of a chance. Russia saw an opportunity and proceeded to help. Russia became very much involved in Trump's initial election bid. The Muller findings could not attest to the efficacy of the Russian effort, but did determine that the effort was there. Trump recognized that Russia worked on his behalf, but

250

as per his upbringing by Roy Cohn, he denied it and called it a hoax. Still, he wanted to continue this symbiotic relationship. Thus, his performance in Helsinki in July 2018 clearly manifested his intent as a Russian asset.

With the war in Ukraine in full force, Trump has intentionally taken the Russian side. I do not believe that Trump is under any pressure or a "kompromat." He simply sees his and his family's future as more beneficial with Russia rather than Ukraine. The equation is simple. Russia is stronger and larger. Trump is well aware of Putin's intentions. The specter of a Trump Tower extends to Kyiv as well in the event of a Russian victory.

In conclusion, there is no direct evidence of Trump being a Russian agent. However, he is certainly a Russian asset. He is not pressured into this position. He has chosen to be an asset so that he may benefit. In the case of Ukraine, which since day one of its independence has sought to be an American ally, Trump has betrayed Ukraine. He has also perpetrated treason against the United States because he has betrayed the American Constitution and everything that America has stood for almost 250 years. In fact, he is molding America into a police state, not unlike Russia.

September 3, 2025

The Fecklessness of the United Nations

Clearly, Russian aggression in Ukraine, beginning with the invasion in February 2014, contravenes the basic principles of the United Nations Charter. Add to that the brutality and war crimes, crimes against humanity, and genocide, and Russia has been an egregious transgressor of international law and the UN Charter. And its covenants and conventions. On more than one occasion, Russia has replied that it does not care, it will do what it wants.

The UN has, unfortunately, been largely ineffective, despite several General Assembly resolutions condemning Russia and an arrest warrant issued against Russia's leader by the UN International Criminal Court. The lack of efficacy of the UN in stopping conflicts has been explored widely. Frankly, there is no easy solution.

Antonio Guterres, the ninth Secretary-General of the United Nations, took office on 1st January 2017. He has been praised for his activity and criticized for his lack of efficacy, like most leaders. In view of the fact that the main purpose of the UN is to stop global conflict, and the largest conflict since World War 2 is before our eyes every day, I feel that a critical assessment of Secretary General Guterres is warranted.

In October 2024, Secretary General Gutteres attended and spoke at the BRICS conference in Kazan, Russia. Regarding the war in Ukraine and Russian aggression, he said only the following:

"We need peace in Ukraine. A just peace in line with the UN Charter, international law, and General Assembly resolutions."

In August 2025, in Shanghai at the SCO (Shanghai Cooperation Organization), he said even less:

"In Ukraine, it is past time for a ceasefire leading to a just, comprehensive and sustainable peace, in line with the UN Charter, international law and UN resolutions."

That was all. By any measure, the UN Secretary General said very little. The leader of the main international structure meant to ensure peace and security attended two conferences organized or attended by the main aggressor, with comparable thugs in attendance, and said less than 50 words about the aggression itself. Is it not surprising that international law does not work and remains a conundrum?

There had been numerous conventions, covenants, and treaties well before the formation of the United Nations in 1945. Just prior to that, there was an attempt to form the UN's predecessor, the League of Nations. Although the idea came from President Woodrow Wilson, it was killed by the United States. President Franklin Delano Roosevelt sold his soul to the devil and Eastern Europe to Josef Stalin to make the UN a reality. It was essential because, in international law, there were no institutions. The formation of the Security Council with veto power allotted to the greatest danger, the Soviet Union, was a major mistake. But this was done so that the main institution could be formed.

In retrospect, the reason why international law is a fiction even today is that the UN is ineffective, not only because of its structure. People like Antonio Gutteres have added much to the inefficiency. There is no logical reason why Secretary General Antonio Gutteres traveled at least ten thousand miles to Kazan and Shanghai to disgrace himself and the institution he represents. The UN Charter offers much clarification, even if the Security Council, with its composition, undermines the very Charter. The Preamble reads:

"WE THE PEOPLES OF THE UNITED NATIONS DETERMINED to save succeeding generations from the scourge of war, which twice in our lifetime has brought untold sorrow to mankind, and to reaffirm faith in fundamental human rights, in the dignity and worth of the human person, in the equal rights of men and women and of nations large and small, and to establish conditions under which justice and respect for the obligations arising from treaties and other sources of international law can be maintained, and to promote social progress and better standards of life in larger freedom..."

The question then is: how did Secretary General Guterres, while attending the conferences in Kazan and Shanghai, promote these principles? The answer is obvious. He did not. The efficacy of international law without appropriate institutions and additional methods of implementation is a major problem. The UN is a deeply flawed organization, both organizationally and structurally. Yet it is the only such structure with a purpose of securing global peace, and more importantly, the only one existing. Amending the organizational documents would be too much since at least two permanent members of the UN Security Council are essentially outliers of a peaceful world, authoritarian, and predisposed to the most heinous acts, such as genocide. Russia has acknowledged on numerous occasions that its purpose is to wipe Ukrainians off the face of the earth. China, without declaration, is working towards that end with Islamic constituents, Tibetans, etc.

UN personnel, however, have to be held accountable, except that no one is. Gutteres is merely one example. He is serving his second term. I recall at least one Permanent Representative of Ukraine to the United Nations assuring me that Guterres is a good man. He may be, but he is certainly not suited to be effective when the world consists of such thugs as Putin, Xi, Kim, Erdogan, Modi, and others. All of them are killers. Guterres is merely a lamb. He does not stand a chance among wolves.

September 7, 2025

Where Is NATO?
In Memoriam Charlie Kirk

Poland, through its Prime Minister and Foreign Minister, has announced that it would ask the United Nations Security Council to look into the recent Russian drone invasion of Polish territory. This announcement was ironically very symbolic, because it denoted an element of exasperation by the Poles since nothing that comes before the UNSC accusing Russia of wrongdoing ever succeeds. Russia owns a nefarious veto power, and certainly, no one expects a brutal abuser like Russia to abstain or recuse itself from the final vote. There is no solution or remedy at the UNSC.

Additionally, and unfortunately, this action by Poland also manifests its disappointment with its NATO member states. NATO bemoaned that the attack exposed to a large extent NATO's unpreparedness, and after Article 4 of the NATO Charter was invoked by Poland, NATO Europe stressed that it was looking to the United States for answers and action. But, recently, under Trump, the United States has often played the role of an ally of Russia. America's history under Trump in this regard has been disgraceful. And once again, Trump disappointed. He lifted sanctions off Belarus, a Russian ally, from whose territory the drones were activated.

We live in a strange world. Charlie Kirk, a notorious right-wing extremist, Neo-Nazi, and white supremacist, was killed by an assassin. Any loss of life is tragic, and so we mourn this death and pray for the repose of his soul.

However, there is much about Mr. Kirk that cannot be left unsaid. I recall my own brief interlude with Mr. Kirk in January 2024. Mr. Kirk was on a rant about Harvard University President Claudine Gay for somehow supporting the Palestinian cause against Israel by allowing Palestinian students to protest and thereby being branded an anti-Semite. I hate that often misused term. Opposing

Netanyahu's policies is not anti-Semitic. I wrote to him, and he wrote back. Here is the extent of our dialogue:

"Dear Mr. Kirk:

I wasted five minutes listening to your disparagement of Claudine Gay. She attended Princeton, Stanford, and finally, where she earned her Ph.D. You do not even have a bachelor's. Does the lack of an education provide Chutzpah? Why should any educated person watch your program and listen to your rant? Go back to school!

Askold S. Lozynskyj"

Mr. Kirk replied:

"Lol! Going to school makes you smart?"

I was reminded that during his 2016 campaign, Donald Trump often played down the importance of education. He stressed that he loved the poorly educated.

Like Trump, so was Kirk, his unhinged disciple.

My condolences go out to the Kirk family. It is a personal loss. But America will not miss him much. His insensitivity was often irrationally offensive. Much of his arrogance stemmed from being ill-informed. Perhaps a college education would have done him some good. Ironically, he was murdered at a college, an institution that he disparaged, and by a gun-wielding madman. Still, Trump's America has not learned the lesson of gun possession and violence. Trump lambasted the liberals for their rhetoric of hatred.

Kirk could not have been killed by that rhetoric without a gun capable of targeting a victim at a two-hundred-meter distance.

About Ukraine's President Volodymyr Zelensky, Mr. Kirk called him a CIA puppet who marched his people to slaughter. Following President Trump's ambush of President Zelensky in the Oval Office in February 2025, Kirk blamed President Zelensky for 1 million deaths.

Charlie Kirk also once said, "I can't stand the word empathy, actually. I think empathy is a made-up, new age term that does a lot of damage."

I have to refer to Jesus on the Cross, who spoke to his Father, asking him to "forgive them for they know not what they do". Kirk's ignorance cannot be forgotten. However, his rudeness and aggression can be forgiven because, hopefully, most Americans are better than Mr. Kirk. Charlie Kirk, may he rest in peace, will be remembered, but mostly for the wrong reasons. He will not be deemed a martyr for a cause because his cause was not for the sake of humanity.

Today marks the 24th anniversary of one of America's major tragedies. The reason why we pay special attention to the events of September 11, 2001, is that innocent Americans died through no fault of their own. People continue to die all over the world from causes other than natural causes, innocent people who have not done anything to deserve their tragic fate. There are such people disproportionately so in Ukraine, there were in Israel on October 7, 2023, and there continue to be such people in Gaza who had nothing to do with the killings in Israel. There are other places as well. America has to become once again a force for humanity. Unfortunately, we have lost our way. The only way back and forward is through education, sensitivity, humanity, and empathy. Yes, empathy!

September 11, 2025

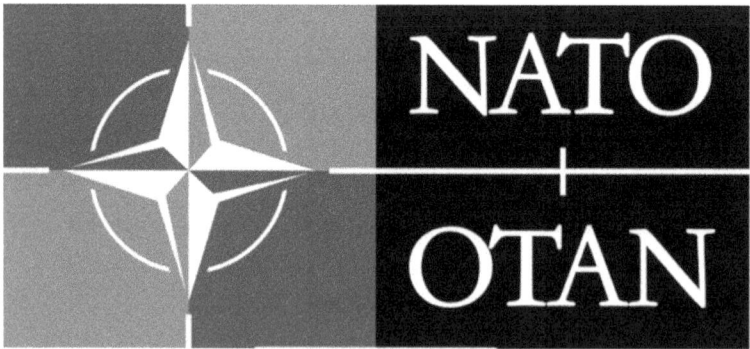

Education in War-torn Ukraine

Much has been commented about Ukraine's seemingly late military service threshold, i.e., by a two-faced friend of Ukraine, such as Trump stooge Republican Senator Lindsey Graham of South Carolina. In Ukraine, mandatory military service begins at the age of 25. Graham often travels to Ukraine, offering advice on the war, yet fails to aid Ukraine in any way on the floor of the U.S. Senate. He actually voted against aid and most recently cosponsored a bill on sanctions against Russia, which went nowhere with no explanations except that sanctions are the prerogative of his infamous boss, Donald J. Trump.

There is more than one cogent explanation for the delayed military conscription, which has been provided by the President of Ukraine. Essentially, there are two reasons: the need for procreation and education.

Ukraine has suffered from wartime casualties by death and migration. Ukraine was, at one time, when it proclaimed independence in 1991, a country of 52 million. While a census has not been taken recently, the current population is estimated at 30 million, which represents a 40% drop.

The need for young people in Ukraine to marry and start families is almost critical. Equally important is the need for education. Higher education begins normally at the age of 18. For that reason, the 18-24-year window has been established.

Ukrainian land has been considered for a long time as the breadbasket of Europe, particularly due to its rich soil. It has been said that if one simply spits on the ground in Ukraine's most fertile regions, a tree or bush will blossom and grow. Throughout history, Ukrainians were mostly involved in working their land.

Since the mid-19th century, with the abolition of serfdom, there has been much migration from villages to cities. Children from villages have been enrolled in higher education institutions. This had commenced well before Ukraine's declaration of independence in 1991. Even under occupation by Russia, Soviet Russia, Austria, and Poland. Romania and Hungary's education was accorded a high priority. Liberal arts were the focus initially, but under the Soviets, natural sciences became a very significant option, particularly because scientists had to be exact and could not praise the system. Poets and artists, including attorneys, all of whom essentially worked for the government, were entrusted with that propaganda. The level of education in each case, however, was very high.

I would like to share a personal experience with my late paternal uncle. He was a jurist, an attorney, and a judge, educated and practicing during the Polish occupation of Western Ukraine during the two World Wars. A requirement in his studies at that time was learning Latin, the language, its history, and literature. When I attended secondary and higher education at Jesuit institutions in New York, I studied both Latin and Greek, classical languages. In fact, my bachelor's degree was in Latin and Greek. I often joked around and competed with my uncle as to our prowess in Latin. I recall when I visited him in his hospital room in 1997, when he was close to death and 90 years old. He was seventy years removed from his college education. My own study of Latin was less than twenty-five years removed. With due humility, I had to admit that his knowledge was superior to mine. He actually composed sentences/ My recollection was relegated to reciting verse that I had memorised.

In the course of the last 20 years I have often traveled to Ukraine even in wartime and lectured on legal topics such as ethics, international law, the rule of law before students at Ukrainian universities in such cities as Luhansk, Donetsk, Kharkiv, Kyiv< Lviv, Ternopil, Ivano-Frankivsk and Chernivtsi I have almost always come away with a feeling that these students are superior to myself and my fellow students when I was in college or law school.

My uncle, before he died, stressed to me the importance of education in Ukraine. He had some money earned as a merchant, which he was leaving to his sister, two nephews, and one niece. He suggested that we follow his wishes and assist in the education of poor students in Ukraine, particularly those coming from villages. Upon his death, we established a private foundation, and from that point on, over the last twenty-five years, the foundation has supported the education of students who fall below the government threshold for free education. This year alone, we have to date paid out one hundred scholarships to students at universities from Ivano Frankivsk in the west to Kharkiv in the east. Because of the war, the focus has been on children of soldiers, orphans, and those who have been dislocated.

I would submit that this type of assistance is as important as helping the Ukrainian soldiers themselves. The future of Ukraine depends on those young men and women in Ukraine between 18 and 24 who are currently enrolled at the University graduate and postgraduate levels.

September 13, 2025

Global Issues that Matter

Banal sayings such as "politics makes strange bedfellows" and "politics is the art of the possible" still predominate in the world we live in. The evidence of this lack of morality seems to be everywhere in spite of the fact that we are at the end of the first quarter of the XXI century, eighty years removed from a war which almost caused a global conflagration and the formation of an organization of member states. (193 to date) That was supposed to foster global security, sustainability, and bring peace. Perhaps it is ironic that the Second World War ended with American war crimes, the atomic bombs leveling Hiroshima and Nagasaki with close to two hundred thousand civilian victims, but then who's counting.

There is little peace anywhere. Eastern Europe is in turmoil. Russian strongman Vladimir Putin continues to flex his muscles with impunity, sending each day more than 500 instruments of death, drones, and missiles against civilian targets in Ukraine, and apparently, now Poland. The Middle East, likewise with the Israeli Prime Minister Benjamin Netanyahu flexing his muscles, staging a famine, and refusing any rights to Palestinians for existence, is shielded by an age-old canard that if you criticize his policies, you are an anti-Semite. That has as little effect as calling Ukrainians neo-Nazis when Ukraine's president is Jewish. Africa is replete with conflicts between tribes and religions, and the Far East is always on the verge of at least sporadic fighting and internal ost genocide perpetrated by China and India, the two most populous global oppressors of its minorities.

UN officials themselves stand for very little and fail to respect the very principles and decisions of their institution. Secretary Gutteres visits Putin in Kazan and Party Secretary Xi in Shanghai. With no opprobrium towards the killers or accountability for the Secretary. Business as usual is the message, and that message resonates loud and clear.

Consider last Friday's UN General Assembly endorsement of a two-state solution between Israel and Palestine. It seems such an obvious solution. The vote was overwhelming, 142 in favor, only 10 against, and 12 abstentions. The problem, not surprisingly, in the Trumpian world we live in is that America voted against. The UN Security Council could take up this matter for a more meaningful expression, except for the portended American veto. No other UNSC member voted against the endorsement at the GA, only Trumpian America.

Yes, the United States of America under Trump is among the rogue states that voted against. In prior years, America simply abstained. The UNGA endorsement is essentially meaningless but symbolic of what is right and moral and how out of step America is. It is also symbolic of the global community's ineffectiveness.

This is the Trump America that had earlier suggested ethnic cleansing of Palestinians in Gaza and turning it into a Riviera. It should be understood that this is a very different America than the one envisioned by the Founding Fathers. Trump is a convicted felon. More than that, more than half of his personal wealth is from cryptocurrency acquired and enhanced by legislation that he provided to his sycophantic Congress during this brief period of eight months during his second term. During his first term, he made a private fortune as well; his daughter received five licenses from China, his son-in-law Jared acquired a billion dollars in loans from the Saudi's. Jared's father, Charles Kushner, is also a felon who served almost two years in prison and was recently confirmed as America's Ambassador to France. You really cannot make this up.

This is the same Trump who incited an attempted coup d'etat in America, which failed. In corrupt Brazil, former President Bolsonaro was sentenced to 27 years for similar activity. Trump was never indicted for his attempted coup, and now, Trump, with his comrade in treason, has imposed a 50% tariff on Brazil for prosecuting Bolsonaro.

I leave the most absurd for last. Trump's most obsequious advocates are his cronies at Fox News. During a recent discussion of the mentally ill homeless population, a Fox News luminary, Brian Kilmeade, said that if the mentally ill homeless refuse to accept medical assistance, "Give them an involuntary lethal injection or just kill them."

September 14, 2025

The Outrageous – Let's Talk Turkey and Other NATO Rogues, i.e., The United States of America

During America's Secretary of State Marco Rubio's recent trip to Israel, the Prime Minister of Israel, in essence a thug under criminal prosecution in his own country, Benjamin Netanyahu, heaped praise upon American President Donald J. Trump, especially for his 'moral clarity.' 'Lightning did not strike Netanyahu, surprisingly. Considering the source, I suppose that is not much of a compliment either, but Trump will take it. Yet, he still needs the Nobel Peace Prize, which Netanyahu has initiated as well. Trump, as I have often noted, is a convicted felon. Netanyahu is also under an arrest warrant from the International Criminal Court for war crimes- peas in a pod. But Netanyahu is clever. He knows that the way to Trump's heart is through his ego.

There is at least one other notable leader of a relatively respected country that makes both Trump and Netanyahu seem respectable and even benign. That is Turkish strongman and President Recep Erdogan.

Turkey has a history of bad behavior, culminating in 1915 with a genocide perpetrated by the Turks against their neighbors, the Armenians. The numbers vary from five hundred thousand victims to three times that amount, depending on the source. However, the fact that it was a genocide is beyond dispute and recognized by much of the world, including the United Nations.

Turkey's aggression both in the past and today was and is largely induced by religion, militant and sectarian Islam. There was a fifteen-year period of time, a hiatus if you will, between 1923 and 1938, when the Republic of Turkey was founded and ruled by Mustafa Kemal Atatürk, when the Republic was normal and largely secular. That relative normality lasted under Ataturk's successors. And then came Recep Erdogan.

Erdogan's Turkey is somewhere between clerical and secular. Today's Turkey still exercises its aggression, particularly against its ethnic Kurdish population, and includes Turks opposed to Erdogan. Its democracy is sketchy at best, although elections are held.

One of the ironies of Turkish politics is that Turkey is a long-standing member of NATO and probably its strongest but most unreliable member n Europe. NATO was founded by ten members in 1949. Turkey joined in 1952 as the twelfth member, and it was probably a necessary mistake.

Turkey currently allegedly strives to become a member of the European Union, but its behavior and global alliances serve as very significant obstacles. In the last year alone, Erdogan participated both in the BRICS Summit in Kazan, Russia, and the SCO in Shanghai. China, neither of which can be considered friendly to NATO. But Erdogan is a brazen rogue because of the size of Turkey's military. He is a member of NATO but very friendly with Vladimir Putin, much like Donald J. Trump.

Further, while EU countries have substantially decreased their oil imports from Russia since Russia's full-scale invasion of Ukraine in 2022, Turkey has actually picked up the slack. Some 20% of Turkey's energy imports come from Russia. Turkey has a refinery strictly for Russian oil.

On the other hand, Turkey has also sold Ukraine many of its very effective Bayraktar drones, which were very important to Ukraine at the beginning of the war. Now Ukraine produces 60% of the weaponry it uses.

Suffice it to say, it is difficult to determine whose favor Erdogan cuddles. Unfortunately, some may say that the same ambiguity surrounds Donald Trump. At least Trump did not travel to Kazan or Shanghai. But Erdogan did open the Black Sea to Ukrainian grain for export. The balance sheet remains too close to call. That's politics devoid of humanity or morality, and a perfect example of Darwinian survival of the fittest.

And now the intimidation came. Russia recently sent 19 drones into Poland. All were shot down except that the debris caused some damage on the ground. A few days later, Russia sent drones into Romania, which were shot down. Yesterday, Russia and Belarus staged military exercises in Belarus (Zapad-West). Reuters reported:

"U.S. military officers observed joint war games between Russia and Belarus on Monday for the first time since Moscow used Belarus as a launchpad to enter Ukraine, as U.S. President Donald Trump deepens ties with Moscow's closest ally."

Orban's Hungary and Erdogan's Turkey (both NATO members) participated.

September 16, 2025

Keir Starmer's Experiment With Donald J. Trump

There is no other way to explain Trump's second official state visit to the United Kingdom at the personal invitation of King Charles III. Two of Trump's major flaws, aside from ignorance, are arrogance and narcissism. The Prime Minister of the UK felt that a state visit would play to both those flaws.

The UK, frankly, the entire Western democratic world needs the power and wealth of the United States, which today, by virtue of Trump's autocratic rule and the sycophancy of his subordinates, belongs to Donald J. Trump, a man as suited to be in the White House as President as he is suited to be at the Kennedy Center as Chairman.

As to meetings with the king and other royalty, the initial feeling was that it was important that Trump and his entourage did not embarrass the United States of America. There were no substantive risks as royalty in the UK is not even symbolic of power, but a showcase for tourism.

The UK has a number of ridiculous showcases, beginning with the royals and including such aberrations as the Church of England, a remnant of the royals. This is the Church of England, predicated on the rule by the King of England, who in the 16th century wanted to divorce his wife, but the Catholic Church would not concede, so he killed his wife, which was probably more outrageous than simple divorce, and then instituted his own church, which amazingly exists to date. I recall my visit to the UK in 2008, meeting with representatives of the Church and maintaining silence, when I really wanted to say: How do you justify your existence.

England's royalty and its church are more embarrassing than the fact that England, the inventor of football (soccer), has not won the World Cup since the 1960s. It's a good thing that the English generally have a wonderful sense of humor, sometimes lost on their immediate neighbors, the Scots, Welsh, and Irish, or even those whom they ruled once as an empire.

On the other hand, and on a more serious note, the English people are a model for free discourse, which includes protests. Even the debates in Parliament are an example of free speech and expression. America's revolution was a manifestation of that free speech and protest.

Trump was not able to circumvent those protests even though Starmer's people did everything possible to shield the American president. Trump and America have behaved very badly during Trump's tenure, and the English people had to respond. Even the Epstein embarrassment was fuel for the fire.

This state visit was a very expensive undertaking for both sides, but in particular for the Brits. However, it has been said by many that the reason why the UK retains the semblance of meaningless royalty and explains it on a balance sheet is that it is income-producing. People do go to the circus. So the cost of the pomp and circumstance could be disregarded, in particular if the Prime Minister gets what he is after in the long term.

So the question is whether anything was accomplished by the experiment. There is, of course, a caveat of wait and see. Nothing is ever achieved with Donald J. Trump; all agreements are meaningless, whether or not they are signed, until action is actually taken by Trump. Trump's idea of a good deal is where he wins and the other side loses. But there are good deals for both sides.

Unfortunately, the press has reported nothing of consequence. On the subject of Ukraine, the biggest global conflict since World War 2, the BBC reported:

"An area where the pair were seemingly united was in condemning Russia over its full-scale invasion of Ukraine, after Trump said earlier this week he could impose tougher sanctions on Russia if Nato allies meet certain conditions.

Starmer condemned recent Russian missile attacks that saw damage to the British Council building in Kyiv, and said the recent actions of Russian President Vladimir Putin were not those of someone who wants peace.

The US president said Putin had 'really let me down', admitting he thought solving the Russia-Ukraine war would be one of the easier conflicts to deal with.

He added, however, that he did not regret holding the peace summit in Alaska with Putin a few months ago, and he felt an "obligation" to help find an end to the war due to the enormous loss of life in the conflict."

In the history of the world, how many world leaders have lamented that they were 'really let down' by their obvious enemy, one who is responsible for the killing of millions? Nevertheless, Trump will remember this state visit and meeting with the king. He will refer to that as yet another triumph in his long biography of accomplishments, and the fact that no other American president has had two visits. That may work when Prime Minister Starmer seeks real support for issues that matter, like the war in Ukraine.

Donald J. Trump is a Neanderthal, but the American people elected him. That is the sad reality, but the facts must be addressed. Good job, Keir!

September 19, 2025

Update on Russian Aggression and American Duplicity Since Donald J. Trump Bid Farewell to King Charles III,

Russia has continued its brutality in Ukraine with more than 600 drones and missiles in one night. Nevertheless, Ukraine has managed to move some 50 miles east in the Donetsk Region, and Russia has invaded the Estonian airspace. The European Union has imposed new sanctions on Russia.

America under Trump has done the opposite. Trump has announced no further sales of Patriot missile systems and disingenuously promised additional sanctions against Russia if Europe stops purchasing Russian gas and oil. At this point, EU members account for the purchase of only 10% of their gas and 1% of their oil from Russia. With the destruction by Ukraine of the Druzhba pipeline, the gas percentage will decrease further as Orban's Hungary and Fico's Slovakia have been gravely affected. True, Erdogan's Turkey, not an EU but a Nato member, purchases 20% of its oil from Russia.

Trump has not imposed any new sanctions on Russia nor delivered any aid or sold weapons directly or through a Nato intermediary to Ukraine. Naturally, these facts belie everything that Trump has said or will say. As always, actions speak louder than words, and so at almost every opportunity, Trump is saying things that he has no intention of doing.

Domestic issues in America are equally troubling. The unfortunate assassination of a conservative and Christian voice, Charlie Kirk, has been magnified to an unreal level. Even the head of the Roman Catholic Church in New York, Cardinal Dolan, has joined. (The Cardinal has been remiss in his pastoral duties and has manifestly supported Trump on Day One.)

The fallout over the Kirk assassination has been very negative. For the sake of transparency, I need to state that I was never a disciple of Charlie Kirk and his obsession with St. Paul. In fact, I felt that Kirk was disingenuous with his attacks on education and citing scripture while blatantly lying about the Russia-Ukraine war.

Charlie Kirk, in death, should be remembered for his good deeds, but his flaws and failings should not be ignored. Furthermore, anyone who criticizes Kirk should not be condemned or punished. Cardinal Dolan of the Roman Catholic Church should not nominate him for sainthood.

The biggest problem, of course, is Donald Trump, who is attempting to control all branches of government as well as the rights and freedoms under America's Bill of Rights. Hate speech is a concept that cannot be defined. Unfortunately, as human beings, we are capable of both love and hate. The problem, however, is violence and calls to violence, as well as the deeply flawed and misunderstood right to bear arms.

President Trump is the poster boy for that, as he, with his words and perhaps even with conspiratorial deeds, brought about the violence at the Capitol on January 6, 2021. This resulted not only in property damage but also in human death. Trump should have been criminally prosecuted for that behavior. A partisan vote in the Senate does not qualify as a trial by one's peers. While he was President, he was not acting or performing his presidential duties. He was a candidate for office and should have been subject to the same scrutiny as any other candidate.

A significant problem is that the judicial system of a quasi democracy, but nevertheless a banana republic, Brazil got it more right in its prosecution, conviction, and sentencing of a former president for leading an attempted coup d'etat. The events of January 6, 2021, were precisely that, an attempted coup. It is important to note how our American Constitution, or rather its interpretation, failed in that regard.

Ukraine finds itself at a crossroads. It has managed to do quite a remarkable job in defending itself against arguably the world's second-largest military power. Additionally, its talented people have managed to defend themselves for almost four years, fending off much larger forces. There are estimates that some seven hundred thousand Russian soldiers are fighting in Ukraine. Furthermore, the people of Ukraine have managed to fill the vacuum of a lack of military equipment brought about by the failures of the West, which have resulted from European unpreparedness and American duplicity. Today, Ukraine produces sixty percent of its weaponry.

That duplicity did not begin with Donald Trump, but it has been severely exacerbated by his willingness to be a Russian asset. Even under President Biden and more so under President Obama, America was lacking in its genuine support for Ukraine. In both cases, the assistance provided was invariably inadequate so that Ukraine would not lose, but it also could not win.

Certainly, not to his credit, but practically speaking, Trump provided an element of clarity. Still, President Zelensky pursues American assistance as only he can by pandering (yes) and diplomacy.

I firmly believe that Volodymyr Zelenska's election in 2019 was a Godsend. He is not only committed, but he is also very astute. The intangible factor here, which supersedes all others, is that Ukraine and Ukrainians are defending their lives, their existence.

America finds itself at a crossroads as well. This is certainly not the America of George Washington, Abraham Lincoln, even Jimmy Carter or Ronald Reagan. However, solutions abound in the elections of 2026 and 2028. The Russian asset Donald Trump is term-limited. According to some polls, 51% of Republicans currently disapprove of his presidency. The New York Times recently carried a story of a Russian who did not agree with Russian brutality and refused to serve. He escaped Russia, went to Indonesia, established residency, and then came to the United States seeking asylum. His request was denied by a Federal Trump judge, and he was repatriated, not to Indonesia but to Russia. Why didn't America simply deport him to Indonesia? The answer is obvious. Trump is a Russian asset.

We live in very turbulent times. Politics has never been about good and evil. However, the evil today is being legitimized by what was once considered the greatest country on earth. If you think that Trump has not been effective, you need to consider the facts. Despite his lack of education and his primitiveness, he has managed to do more harm than any person in American history.

Ukraine will prevail and endure because of its righteous cause and its undaunted people. So the outlook is positive.

September 20, 2025.

United Nations – Endemic Problems With Little or No Solutions

President Trump's speech at the opening of the United Nations' General Assembly this year was symptomatic of his psychosis. He was critical of the UN but not helpful. He was, as usual, full of himself, touting his alleged accomplishments and denigrating before the entire world his American predecessor. He was disgraceful.

Nevertheless, FOX News labeled him a 'Truth sayer'. That statement was symptomatic of FOX News and its self-awarded mantra of being 'fair, balanced and unafraid', the last characterization being anywhere near the only correct one.

FOX is indeed unafraid and shameless in simulating the Russian press. Its support of Trump and right-wing extremists in general is unparalleled in the history of free journalism in democracies. Additionally, many of its hosts exceed limits of bias to the point where they simply become cheerleaders for their cause, which is often blatantly uninformed. They are clearly propagandists, not journalists.

Trump spoke for almost one hour, egregiously abusing the fifteen-minute regulation and the patience of world leaders and their diplomats. Adding insult to injury, or in reverse, his teleprompter went dead at one point, so that there was ample opportunity for him to make a fool of himself extemporaneously. At one point, he actually unabashedly stated that he is always right, then went on to say that global warming is a hoax. The world scientific community must have been in an uproar, but probably only laughed, considering the source. Every American who saw this spectacle should have been embarrassed. I am sure that the MAGA were proud of their unhinged leader.

Trump has spoken now five times at the opening of the UN GA, and each time he has been more unhinged. America needs not apologize anymore. One diplomat said, "The man is stark, raving mad." I would submit that that diplomat was the real truth-sayer, and I am certain that there were many others.

However, Trump's deficiencies should not be the focus of the traditional opening of the annual work of the United Nations. Aside from clogging New York's transit arteries in the fourth week of September each year, the 193 nations within the UN should at least try to make a point in this new session to consider the UN's efficacy or the lack thereof. The point of the opening session is to offer something new to make a difference. After all, the UN is eighty years old with frankly little to show.

The UN was formed in 1945 after World War 2 to stop war. President Franklin Delano Roosevelt was the main architect, although he did not live to see its formation. Roosevelt gave away all of Eastern Europe to the Soviet Union so that they would join. They not only joined but have taken advantage of Roosevelt's naivete, or some would say complicity, ever since. Given today's events, certainly, the problem is intractable. It lies within the institution itself or its affiliates themselves and, perhaps, its leadership. The leadership is hopelessly feckless and not about to get any better.

For example, some three-fourths of the UN membership have or will recognize Palestine as a state, yet Palestine will continue to retain only observer status. Ultimately, it is up to the Security Council, and any decision can be simply blocked by such international pariahs with veto power as Russia and Trump's America. Under President Trump, the US and Russia have become almost allies. At least Russia was correct on the two-state solution for the Middle East. America has been wrong on the Middle East and Ukraine.

There are currently so many conflicts throughout the world because of the inefficiency of the UNSC. The purpose of the UN is to prevent conflicts. It says so in the preamble to the Charter. There are so many war crimes being perpetrated in connection with these conflicts and even attempted genocides because other UN institutions, such as the International Criminal Court and the International Court of Justice, both in the Hague, have no teeth. Once again, Russia and America are to blame.

Further blame may be accorded to non-charismatic and weak individuals, such as the ostensible leader of the UN, Secretary General Antonio Guterres, a simple Portuguese functionary, accommodating, amiable, well spoken at times, but essentially a weak leader who often speaks of principles but never even attempts to implement them. A rotating system of countries, many of whom carry no substance, chairing the SC does not lend the SC any strength, and the permanent members' veto power renders the SC meaningless in addressing real conflicts. The SC is owned once again by Russia and America. What Russia or America opposes has no chance.

International law is a bundle of conventions, covenants, and institutions. However, if it lacks any means of implementation, it is rendered almost useless. Dialogue is good, but only when some sovereignty is relinquished for the common good and the rule of international law, and only when law means justice. There are such things as stupid laws.

The biggest irony here is that in his speech, America's President Trump criticized the UN for its inefficacy, and people like him who lead America have been among the worst offenders and, perhaps, most responsible for this failure. Interestingly enough this is not a Republican or Democratic issue because President Delano Roosevelt a Democrat and the single most persuasive and instrumental founding father of the UN as mentioned was a Soviet stooge because of Soviet agents throughout his administration and President Donald J. Trump, a Republican is a Russian asset, never failing to appease his longtime friend by his own admission, a war criminal Vladimir Putin. That's why nothing gets done, and so for eighty years, Russia has been a global threat and remains so. Trump has done nothing for four years and eight months to diminish that threat.

A suggestion for efficacy would be a moderate revision or amendment to the UN Charter where global security remains within the purview of its Security Council, but even its permanent members cannot be recused from voting on matters involving their own bad behavior. Thus, bad behavior continues with impunity. Perhaps a bad actor wielding veto power can be neutralized through the unanimity of the other members or a three-fourths vote of the General Assembly.

Such an amendment would, at the very least, provide a light at the end of the tunnel, a vision for the future, and perhaps persuade member states to improve their behavior or at least the appearance thereof. Russia would certainly take notice. Taking notice and then lying to refute is one thing, but behaving is quite another. Russian functionaries are trained quite expertly.

Yes, it may result in a walkout by Russia, but then Russia would become manifestly a pariah, which it is. I suspect that only very few would walk out with Russia. China would not be China's main concern is not military but economic domination. In any event, it would be a step towards a quasi-rule of international law. Now we have organized chaos. In any event, it is certainly time to move on from UN business as usual.

September 24, 2025

FOX News – Is it State Television?

Federal Communications Commission (FCC) chair Brendan Carr, a Trump appointee, threatened the American Broadcasting Company (ABC) and its parent Disney with licensing issues over Comedian Jimmy Kimmel's comments regarding the killer of Charlie Kirk. Kimmel had suggested merely that the killer may have been a MAGA acolyte. ABC suspended Kimmel. There was an uproar about the First Amendment and freedom of speech. There ensued much discussion. Apparently, it was decided that even hate speech was protected. But inciting violence was not. Trump suggested that the FCC go after other programs and individuals like 'The View' and Jimmy Fallon at NBC.

Clearly, FCC chair Carr had overstepped both his authority and the Constitution. Even Vice President Vance said that Carr was joking. In any event, Jimmy Kimmel was not inciting violence, and so he was reinstated. Donald Trump was not pleased. Nevertheless, this was essentially a happy ending.

Not quite! While threatening ABC and its parent Disney, Mr. Carr has shown no inclination towards threatening FOX News with licensing issues. No one is more guilty of inciting violence than FOX. Of course, I am ignoring the Proud Boys and the like. White Supremacists in MAGA have a case for inciting violence as well.

In the last week alone, FOX commentator Brian Kilmeade, who, aside from commenting on many programs, also has his own show, called for the execution of the mentally deficient homeless if they refuse to accept medication. He did later apologize. Another and perhaps more prominent FOX luminary commentator, Jesse Watters, who also has his own show and often chairs a circus entitled 'The Five,' called for bombing (and/or gassing) the United Nations. Watters has not offered any apology. Brian Kilmeade and Jesse Watters are considered perfectly normal commentators at FOX.

It should be pointed out that in both instances, Kilmeade and Watters were not simply spouting hatred, which would be protected under the First Amendment. They were inciting violence against the mentally deficient homeless and UN personnel who had been accused by Watters of deliberately staging a malfunction of the escalator at the UN when it was being used by the Trump entourage at the time of his entry into the UN for his GA appearance. President Trump made the same accusation.

FOX News is replete with such characters as Kilmeade and Watters. Amazingly, President Trump is not particularly pleased, however, with FOX and its owner Rupert Murdoch. The reason, according to Trump, is that FOX does not go far enough. There appear to be other networks, such as Newsmax, which have picked up the slack, but FOX remains the most popular.

FOX does carry the news, but in most instances, it is adulterated. Its mantra is 'fair, balanced and unafraid,' which is repeated quite often even by such relatively innocuous real journalists at FOX as Bret Baier. Some of the other players are Greg Gutfeld, Dana Perino, Laura Ingraham, John Roberts, Martha MacCallum, Harris Faulkner, and others. FOX used to have Pete Hegseth and Jeanine Pirro, but President Trump gave them jobs in his administration and its departments.

There is a round table discussion program entitled 'The Five,' which consists of four conservatives of little gravitas and one token liberal. The liberal is mostly not too prominent since he/she must take abuse, and are simply shouted over by the other four. FOX insists that the program is balanced. In fact, it's a circus.

The media in America is invariably accused by Trump and others like him of being liberal and biased against him. Some of the so-called liberal media, such as CNN and MSNBC, as well as CBS and ABC, have taken steps to appear objective yet remain faithful to the fourth estate paradigm of seeking the truth. At his press conferences, Trump, on the other hand, often levels ad hominem attacks on those members of the media who do not spout his nonsense and pose legitimate questions. I suppose the difference between Trump and Putin is that in Trump's case, he simply personally attacks the opposition, while Putin pushes them off the fifth floor and arranges for a suicide note.

The same is true of 'The New York Times' The Wall Street Journal, and The Washington Post. However, in order to appear unbiased and, I suspect, to ensure success at his money-making operation, Amazon, Jeff Bezos, and The Washington Post abstained from endorsing a candidate in the last presidential election. Some applauded that decision. I found it to be irresponsible. The Wall Street Journal, owned by the Murdoch family, retains a right-wing inclination which is very evident in its opinion page if not its editorials, but the news is presented relatively objectively. As long as I have read or heard Peggy Noonan, a former Reagan speech writer and now a columnist at The Wall Street Journal, I have rarely agreed with her, mostly on a personal level, because she is so full of herself. The New York Times is the best as far as I am concerned, but I read it only for its news coverage. I never read the editorials or opinions because they are meant to be biased. I would rather make up my own mind based strictly on the facts and my own biases.

That brings me back to FOX News. I have been exposed to state-run news during Soviet times as well as when I traveled throughout Russia (I mean throughout, not only Moscow, St. Petersburg, but southern Siberia as well) in the early 2000s. The Soviets were, and the Russians are, experts in brainwashing.

The press is merely one of the government's tools. Russia Today and Tass remain notorious weapons. Governmental control goes beyond the press. It organizes and controls NGO's. In fact, Russia has a nongovernmental structure on human rights, which is also a part of the government. That governmental non-governmental organization actually appeared at the UN and offered a program about respect for human rights in the Russian Federation. There was an audience because people have a predisposition to listen to authority. Only in a genuine democracy is government recognized as the problem and not a solution. Where people are manipulated, freedom cannot exist.

FOX News today is that type of network. Certainly, it is a network for news, but invariably, the news is presented with a slant, or it is ignored. Frankly, I do not fully understand the predilection except that its purpose is to make President Trump look good.

Laura Ingram is a FOX commentator. She is an attorney by education, if not by profession, and a conservative writer whom I once enjoyed reading before she joined FOX and before Trump. She has become a disturbing case in point. She has a program on FOX entitled The Ingram Angle. After Trump completed his speech at this year's opening of the UN General Assembly, she opened her program with a banner celebrating Trump as the Truth Sayer. Her obeisance to Trump was frankly disgraceful since I listened to Trump's speech, and I was sickened. Aside from 'louting the rules, he went off on such ridiculous rants as "I have always been right' and 'Global warming is a hoax'. There was much more bordering on insanity. I changed the channel with the words, 'Laura Ingram has lost her mind.' I did not say that Donald Trump has lost his mind because that happened a long time ago.

State television in a democracy is an aberration, and worse, it's an attempt at forging something very disturbing – an authoritarian state. Think about it!

September 25, 2025

Quo Vadis?

The initial question and perhaps the most salient one is, without any American support, how does Ukraine finance the war effort? Since Trump took over, America has been entirely missing in action in the Russian war against Ukraine, except for Trump's blabbering and posing about ending the war. Yet the war continues unabated and even more aggressively. Russia certainly does not appear poised for peace. In fact, since Trump has become involved in bringing peace, Russia has fired substantially more missiles and released more drones than at any previous time. It's almost as if Russia and Putin are laughing at Trump and America.

In fact, Trump has no strategy for peace, yet he insists that he does. And why not? In his previous life, he dealt with real estate. Now he is dealing with human lives, and he is confused at best. Ukraine has not gained from Trump's bravado, but President Zelensky, although recognizing that Trump is an evil clown, acknowledges that Trump is the President of the United States, once a superpower, wielding great influence in the global community. The individual clown matters so much only because of the power and wealth at his disposal, but he has to be charmed.

Realistically, that is no longer so. There have been two recent examples of voting in the United Nations' General Assembly where America, in a shameless minority, voted against condemning Russian aggression and a two-state solution in the Middle East. America under Trump has become an embarrassing rogue state. But still an embarrassment that has to be entertained. The question is, do you entertain or move on? Perhaps you can and should do both.

The Financial Times recently carried a piece by German Chancellor Friedrich Merz in which he proposed giving Ukraine a one hundred sixty-billion-dollar loan, interest-free, backed by frozen Russian assets. The money would be used strictly for military equipment with European Union guarantees until 2028 and would be coordinated with the G7.

The column by Merz was a dramatic change from Germany's previous position, which refused to address the issue of using Russian frozen assets as being legally inappropriate. The money referred to is located in Brussels. There is other money located elsewhere, some in the United Kingdom and elsewhere. The use of this money, even as simply collateral, would enable Ukraine to continue the defense of its territory and beyond. The money would be earmarked for reparations, and if Russia refused to pay, Ukraine would be forgiven this loan.

Perhaps, this might bring Putin to the negotiating table, where, among other matters, Ukraine's reconstruction damages would be an item on the agenda. In the interim, Europe and Ukraine would provide weapons for defense.

Merz's proposal would answer some crucial questions as to how Ukraine could continue to finance the war. The money would be used for the manufacture of weapons in Ukraine and the purchase of European weapons. European Commission President Ursula von der Leyen had suggested the use of the Russian assets several weeks back. Other EU countries had made similar suggestions way back. Ukraine is currently benefiting from the income generated by these assets.

A meeting of the European Commission is to take place to firm up this proposal, which partially serves as a strategy for the continuation of the war, as Russia seems to be nowhere near agreeable to a ceasefire, and frankly speaking, Trump and America have been useless.

On Saturday, September 27, Russia's Foreign Minister Sergei Lavrov was particularly belligerent and arrogant at this year's UNGA opening. He did speak before an empty auditorium. Clearly, he was voicing the position of his boss. Nothing close to reasonable or accommodating has come from Russia since the start of the war, and, if anything, the rhetoric has become more bellicose.

On another topic, there is a critical question of justice in America. Quo Vadis American jurisprudence? The Supreme Court of the United States has become emblematic of a judicial system in the hands of an authoritarian ruler. In an emergency session, the Supreme Court recently ruled in a bizarre fashion that the President had the power to cancel some four billion dollars appropriated by Congress for foreign aid. The vote was now a traditional six to three, with a caveat that this was a temporary ruling and not based on the merits. As an attorney of almost fifty years, I do not know what that means.

It's important to note that this Supreme Court, in this term, has been shameless and quite arrogant in abusing its powers by acting as a political rubber stamp for the excesses of the President and completely dismissive of the Constitution's checks and balances and the separation of powers. The notorious Clarence Thomas and Samuel Alito have been the most shameless. At least Trump cannot be blamed for those two. Trump's contribution is Neil Gorsuch, Brett Kavanaugh, and Amy Conan Barrett, severely indoctrinated right-wing ideologues.

Perhaps more importantly. Some of the Justices have been severely compromised by accepting blatant favors from supporters or people looking to influence. In addition, at least two justices have been less than models of restraint in political activism. The Court has been widely criticized for not having a code of ethics. The Court then drew one up but asserted that the Code would not be binding. The Supreme Court has been as arrogant as the President.

I hesitate to conclude that America's judicial system looks very much like that of a banana republic. The president provides a list of his political enemies. The system is focused on retribution. The Department of Justice, which currently serves the president and certainly not the country, prosecutes the cases presented by the President. In a criminal matter, lower courts can dismiss or find the defendant not guilty. A verdict in favor of the defendant cannot be appealed. However, if any case reaches the Supreme Court legitimately, it becomes a done deal. The court routinely rules by a six-to-three majority. Sometimes Chief Justice Roberts finds a conscience. The others are zealots.

President Trump, during his first term, managed to set up a judicial body to his liking. The fact is that the system lends itself to political manipulation since federal judgeship is strictly partisan. Essentially, what transpired is that no one or very few expected an authoritarian to take the reins of nominations and manipulate the system for his own benefit. I suspect that many of Trump's senior advisers during that first term were under the misguided impression that they were serving a president rather than facilitating a tyrant. The soon-to-be-indicted John Bolton fits that profile.

In a genuine democracy, justice is blind. Under Trump, justice is entirely under the control of one man. Whether Republicans admit it or not, America today is an authoritarian regime where twisted justice is meted out by the person in charge. Whether America can survive is very unclear.

Trump is term-limited, but it's a long way to 2029. And even so, what will the 2028 election look like? A hillbilly certainly has a chance in this lawless environment. America is unrecognizable today. What will it look like in 2028? I shudder to predict because any rational forecast can be undermined by the powers that be. God Save America!

September 28, 2025

Patriots and Tomahawks or an Epilogue

The Times of Israel reported:

"Israel has delivered a Patriot air-defense system to Ukraine, which has been operational for a month. President Volodymyr Zelensky confirmed that the system has been installed and is currently in use. The Ukrainian President announced that Ukraine will receive two more Patriot systems in the fall. The Israeli Air Force has stated that it is decommissioning the Patriot systems, which will be replaced with more advanced air defenses. The US has also been involved in the transfer process, sending Patriot missiles from Israel storage sites to Poland for eventual delivery to Ukraine. The transfer of these systems marks a significant shift in Israel's role in military assistance to Ukraine, especially following the cooling relationship with Russia."

Ukraine's President Volodymyr Zelensky acknowledged receipt of the one Patriot defense missile system from the State of Israel. He did not comment on the other systems to be delivered from Israel via Poland. There are rumors that several more are on route from European allies, specifically from Norway and the Netherlands. Germany has promised to deliver two more in 2026.

This news about the Patriots is particularly important because there are no substitutes for Patriots within the Ukrainian or European arsenal, and America has announced that it will not be selling any in the near future.

Ukraine has asked the United States for Tomahawk missiles with a range of more than one thousand miles to help with Ukraine's effort to bring the war into Russian territory. Reuters reported that on September 28, 2025, Washington confirmed it is examining the possibility of providing Ukraine with U.S.-origin Tomahawk cruise missiles, a move that would mark a significant shift with far-reaching operational and political consequences. The request, driven by Kyiv's need to pressure Russian logistics and air power far beyond the front, would extend Ukraine's ability to hold distant targets at risk and complicate Russia's air-defense posture. Vice President JD Vance said President Donald Trump would make the final determination, underscoring the decision's sensitivity and escalation stakes. So far, Trump remains silent.

On the other hand, the record shows that since Donald Trump took office on January 20, 2025, Ukraine has not received any weapons directly from the United States.

As much as Trump's peace efforts regarding Russian aggression towards Ukraine have been disastrous, America under Trump has signaled an epilogue as to constructive Ukraine-America relations. Sure, dialogue will continue, but words will not help Ukraine prevail against Russia. Until Trump, the US was Ukraine's biggest aid and weapons supplier.

This opens a new era for Ukraine, albeit not by choice. That may change in a few years, but for the moment, Europe is Ukraine's closest ally. The war has shown that Ukraine is certainly the strongest military power on the European continent, Turkey notwithstanding, since the bulk of Turkey's military of some three hundred thousand is for internal use, to shore up the Recep Erdogan authoritarian and corrupt regime. That is what authoritarians do. Frankly, this is what is now happening in the United States. Internal use of the military is contrary to the very concept of a democracy.

There is a symbiotic relationship between Europe and Ukraine, as well as mutual respect and reliance. Leaders such as Starmer, Macron, Meloni, Merz, Tusk, and even Stubb of small Finland have been very eager and accepting of Ukraine. Poland currently has a chauvinistic President, but he will have to come around for the sake of Poland's security. Outliers such as Orban of Hungary and Fico of Slovakia will come around because of pressure. The Czech Republic is currently in a bit of a quandary. In any event, the United Kingdom, France, and Germany carry the military might of Europe, and these countries' leaders and people are favorably disposed towards Ukraine for many reasons and perhaps, most significantly, their own benefit. Europe is being assisted by Ukraine in preparing for drones coming from Russia. That is a crucial component – mutual defense.

No matter who delivers the Patriot defensive missile systems, they are still American-made, and they will not be sold or delivered to Ukraine by America. Whether America sells Tomahawk or Barracuda missiles to Ukraine remains very much in question, and the answer may be negative or, at the very best, dilatory. America has expanded intelligence sharing with Ukraine to cover energy spots on Russian territory, but has restricted the use of ATACMs.

In conclusion, taking into account that Ukraine has not received any aid in any form or fashion from America since Trump took office, the relationship between America under Trump and Ukraine can only be characterized as BETRAYAL.

That's really a harsh characterization and hopefully, one that will not survive. Ukraine remains hopeful. This is a country and a people that were supposed to disappear in a week's time. It's now almost four years later. Ukraine endures. God Bless Ukraine! God Bless America! But an America without Trump would be preferred. There has been a substantial change in the Vatican. America needs a change in Washington! So does Ukraine!

Until then, BETRAYAL is the only way to characterize American-Ukrainian relations.

September 30, 2025

Postscript to the World in Which We Live

Politics is a dynamic exercise. Positions and alliances may change even on a dime. That should not happen, but it does and has very often in the past. Consider some current questionable NATO members, beginning with Hungary. In World War 2, Hungary sided unabashedly with Nazi Germany. So did Italy, Romania, and Bulgaria, for that matter, all current NATO members. The United States and the United Kingdom were allies with the Union of Soviet Socialist Republics, otherwise known as Communist Russia.

In constructing a paradigm for world order and security, meaning essentially preventing war, since the latter half of the 19th century, internal covenants and conventions have taken place and been concluded, particularly, the treatment of soldiers, prisoners, and civilians. The XX century went further and saw the creation of institutions for the sole purpose of preventing wars.

Religions have also been dynamic forces in civilizing mankind, forming societies and structures, some good but some bad. Essentially, religion has attempted to bring in an element of morality to an otherwise amoral world. Unfortunately, political activism has often overridden religious dogma. Islam is perhaps the most notorious religion in this regard, much too involved in the political spectrum as a tool of proselytizing. The Catholic Church has been at fault as well, albeit not nearly as much, since its missionary work has been restrained.

I would submit that in the modern era, the late Pope Francis was an aberration, and so may he rest in peace! Putin himself has been a mendacious representative of Russian Orthodoxy. His primate Patriarch Kirill, while somewhat respected in global Christianity, has no relationship with any Church of Christ. He is a product of Russia's police state. Yet the veneer of his religious leadership somehow persists. In the Middle East, right-wing clerics influence the policies of Israel as Prime Minister Benjamin Netanyahu, perhaps well-meaning as a Zionist, is compulsive in his dealings with the Palestinians, refusing to give them what is rightfully theirs, an existence. Thus, Israel behaves as a terrorist state, incorporating elements of war crimes, ethnic cleansing, and genocide. According to the International Criminal Court, Netanyahu is a war criminal.

This is the world in which we live. It's easy to suggest that in the XXI century we should be much more advanced. I write with much hope, only to see that hope diminished by a cruel reality.

I am often concerned by possibilities even worse than reality. George Orwell and his dystopian society are on my mind, and frankly, he is very relevant today. The fact remains that one of today's major killers was entertained by the President of the United States with a red-carpet treatment and general warm acclaim. As far as I am concerned, that is dystopian.

There have been other bizarre events and proclamations such as by the Holy Father of the Catholic Church praising one of history's most notorious tyrants Tsar Peter I of Russia and the removal from the White House of the President of a victim nation that has suffered for centuries at the hands of its brutal oppressor represented by that vicious tsar so acclaimed by the world's preeminent spiritual leader.

In conclusion, we need to recognize that we as a civilization have made very little progress. The global community is not so much removed from what it was before the introduction of such concepts as international law, justice, and human rights. That is very unfortunate, but very true. Until we recognize that fact, we will continue to be unable to distinguish right from wrong, the truth from lies, and the victim from the aggressor. And that should be the entire point of our journey as human beings.

October 4, 2025

INDEX

France, 27, 87, 117, 160, 263, 288

Free Buryatia Foundation, 214

Free Kalmykia, 215

Free Yakutia, 215

G20, 38

Garmagapova, 215

genocide, 7, 13, 61, 65, 86, 99, 138, 139, 140, 157, 161, 171, 252, 254, 262, 265, 291

George H. W., 101

Georgia, 9, 23, 25, 67

Germany, 24, 26, 27, 47, 87, 135, 154, 160, 284, 287, 288, 290

Golash, 21, 22, 23

Gorbachev, 68, 90, 179

Guterres, 10, 11, 59, 252, 254, 277

Harris, 19, 20, 22, 23, 28, 30, 71, 280

Helsinki, 15, 121, 149, 182, 229, 237, 246, 251

Holodomor, 40, 41, 42, 138, 139, 140, 179

Houthis, 12, 13

Hungary, 24, 25, 29, 36, 59, 87, 110, 155, 160, 174, 180, 244, 260, 267, 271, 288, 290

Hungary and Slovakia, 25, 59, 244

ICC, 37, 38, 137, 161

Indigenous activism, 216

international law, 58, 64, 137, 161, 165, 169, 178, 211, 252, 253, 254, 260, 277, 278, 291

Iran, 109, 112, 137, 184, 185, 186, 188, 191, 192, 204

Iraq, 185

Istanbul, 4, 160

Italy, 87, 290

Jackson, 49, 51, 70, 110, 161, 201

Japan, 180, 192

John, 34, 35, 40, 41, 101, 105, 173, 280, 286

Kalmykia, 214

Kamala, 20, 22, 71

Kazan, 9, 10, 37, 54, 59, 60, 61, 62, 63, 65, 66, 127, 171, 252, 253, 254, 262, 266

Kharkiv, 32, 53, 163, 193, 260, 261

Kherson, 32, 53, 83, 134, 193, 229

Kirill, 1, 43, 44, 290

Kremlin, 1, 2, 4, 55, 56, 65, 76, 90, 112, 134, 136, 137, 138, 157, 160, 170, 228, 247, 250

Krushelnytska, 89

Poland, 18, 74, 77, 92, 93, 94, 95, 98, 138, 160, 162, 163, 173, 174, 176, 177, 179, 180, 255, 260, 262, 267, 287, 288

Politico, 24, 25

Pope Francis, 1, 2, 3, 4, 43, 153, 290

populism, 49, 59, 160

Potemkin summit, 60

Putin, 1, 4, 7, 9, 10, 11, 12, 13, 15, 16, 19, 20, 25, 28, 29, 32, 35, 36, 37, 38, 43, 45, 56, 58, 59, 60, 65, 72, 76, 104, 110, 113, 117, 118, 120, 121, 124, 125, 126, 133, 134, 138, 143, 149, 156, 157, 158, 160, 170, 171, 181, 182, 183, 185, 186, 194, 204, 206, 208, 210, 213, 214, 217, 226, 228, 229, 232, 233, 234, 235, 236, 237, 238, 243, 246, 247, 251, 254, 262, 266, 270, 277, 281, 283, 284, 290

relations with Putin, 128

religious leadership, 290

Requiem, 40, 41

Roman, 21, 22, 23, 92, 154, 173, 271, 272

Romania, 155, 160, 260, 267, 290

Rome, 43

Russia, 9, 10, 12, 15, 16, 18, 19, 20, 25, 26, 28, 32, 34, 35, 37, 38, 43, 44, 55, 56, 60, 61, 62, 64, 65, 66, 67, 73, 74, 78, 79, 84, 88, 90, 99, 102, 108, 109, 110, 112, 113, 115, 116, 117, 118, 121, 127, 128, 133, 134, 136, 137, 138, 139, 140, 143, 144, 145, 146, 148, 149, 150, 151, 152, 155, 157, 158, 162, 163, 164, 170, 171, 180, 181, 182, 183, 185, 186, 191, 192, 194, 204, 205, 207, 210, 211, 212, 213, 214, 216, 217, 218, 219, 222, 225, 226, 227, 228, 229, 232, 233, 235, 236, 237, 238, 243, 244, 245, 246, 247, 248, 250, 251, 252, 254, 255, 259, 260, 266, 267, 269, 270, 271, 272, 274, 276, 277, 278, 281, 283, 284, 287, 288, 289, 290, 291

Russian atrocities, 180

Russian Federation, 10, 43, 60, 62, 63, 64, 65, 72, 99, 109, 143, 148, 149, 166, 170, 171, 207, 212, 246, 281

Russian Orthodox Church, 6, 43, 45, 136

sanctions, 10, 16, 24, 25, 35, 36, 88, 109, 110, 117, 128, 158, 161, 183, 194, 205, 207, 222, 228, 229, 235, 238, 255, 259, 269, 271

Saudi Arabia, 13, 159

Scholz, 37

www.ingramcontent.com/pod-product-compliance
Lightning Source LLC
Chambersburg PA
CBHW052109030426
42335CB00025B/2902